THE
QUEST

*From the Hollywood Hills to the Amazon
Jungle, One Woman's Search for Enough*

A MEMOIR

EMILY PEREIRA

ISBN: 978-19-5-036744-3

LIFESTYLE
ENTREPRENEURS
P R E S S

Published by

If you are interested in publishing through Lifestyle Entrepreneurs Press, write to: *Publishing@LifestyleEntrepreneursPress.com*

Publications or foreign rights acquisition of our catalog books. Learn More: *www.LifestyleEntrepreneursPress.com*

Printed in the USA

For Mousy + Jack

Author's Note:

This book is a memoir. To write it I relied on my own personal memories. All recollections are subjective and affected by time. Like many memoirists, I have chosen to change names and characteristics, compressed or omitted some events and re-created dialogue.

Acknowledgements:

Deepest gratitude, Mom and Dad, for this beautiful life, and all the love and lessons you've gifted me along the way. Your unyielding support and generosity knows no bounds. Mom, you've known for years... since the old lady with wrinkly tears. Dad, thank you for showing me there's no rules when it comes to art.

Merci Mané for co-creating this magical jungle life with me and for trusting my wild intuit! Je t'aime mon chéri. Saïa Moon and Teotihuacán, you are and always will be my why.

Molly, through thick and thin sister, I love you. Nina, I'm so grateful for decades of truth, love, and support. Jesse for always being a force of love, generosity and kindness. Andrea, I'm so suuuuure. Your beautiful influence has touched me deeply. Ma Petite Georgina, merci. 'Tu m'as montré la force de ta douceur, Avel. Je ressens ton amour doux mon ange. Englis, nada sería posible sin ti. Gracias mi amiga.

Jody, thank you for your healing gifts and loving mentorship. Suzanne, I'm beyond grateful for your otherworldly genius, and showing me what true sisterhood and divine feminine leadership is all about. Elly, I'm forever thankful for all your insights, guidance and encouragement.

Peter, thank you for believing in me and all the beautiful "tings"—big and small. To Yael, Stevie and Forrest thank you for always being the most loving, supportive, home-away-from-home I could ever ask for. Thank you, Peter Gorman, for leading me on the adventure of a lifetime, and muchas gracias to all of the beautiful spirits that welcomed me so warmly in Peru. Deep gratitude, Samantha, for showing up on my doorstep with that guitar with a red ribbon around it in the pouring rain. Your vote of confidence was and is everything. Also for reading the very lengthy first draft, laughing and crying with me and mostly, encouraging me to continue. To my beautiful sisters, you know who you are... I cherish each of you and am grateful and honored to fly beside you in this lifetime. Thank you for believing in me and holding the vision for this book in your hearts all these years.

Huge thanks to everyone who helped birth this book: my favorite counterpart, evvvva, Henry Gilmore, for always having my back while I was writing this. Lee Constantine for helping me think outside of the box. Jesse Krieger for the opportunity—you are the publisher I was waiting for all along. Wylie O'Sullivan and Zora Nauf for your edits and encouragement. Tracey Ashby for your patience and kindness. Michele Santo, thank you for always being so amazing. Liz Favani for your gentle spirit and beautiful aesthetic.

To Jamison, for holding space for me to heal and discover my creative depths, I'm forever grateful. Pamela, for more shenanigans, love and learnings than I could ever possibly count. Litu_l, our sunny days are etched fondly in my heart. To the OG crew: Abby, Aber, Chris and Davy, for the grand times and haaaard times. I'm deeply grateful for it all.

And... for Jamesy, a thousand thank yous for seeing beauty in me when all signs pointed otherwise. All the words in the known and unknown universes wouldn't be enough to express my gratitude for all the love, laughter, art and gifts you've bestowed upon me.

Foreword

Though I must have known Emily Pereira for lifetimes, we found each other when "not enough" was in its heyday. The Great Recession of 2008 had sent the world into heaving collapse, and banking, housing, and finance had finally struggled to their feet. In the wake of that economic destruction, the internet gold rush came galloping in, the badass girl boss movement was exploding, and Emily Pereira danced into my life, riding the cusp of a brand new, glorious wave: the rise of the divine feminine. A surfer at heart, she is always inside any new wave, leveraging the power within it.

Of course, I loved Emily immediately. To know Emily is to fall in love with her. She carries with her an infectious laugh, insatiable curiosity, a vast penchant for amusement, and the antidote to that horrible feeling that often plagues the human condition: *not enough*.

"My agent ran away," she told me the first day she called. "After she read the manuscript, she quit publishing, left NY, and she's living on a beach somewhere, painting and sailing... I guess she's following her *own* Quest."

As a writer and editor, I could understand why. *The Quest* is a page-turning, laugh-out-loud literary journey that leads the reader on a tailspin of fantastic self-discovery. Its pages offer the reader a surprising blueprint for how to step beyond what we've been spoon fed and fly into a creative horizon of limitless liberation. I was fairly sure it would sell immediately.

But as we worked our way through the publishing networks in LA and New York, *The Quest* twirled in and out of agents' hands and created its own unique and mystifying timeline (as Quests tend to). We did not know then that the book was simply waiting for the world to break open. And in 2016, it would.

On the global stage we watched the collapse of our version of Rome. The divine feminine was breaking away from the toxic masculine. On public online forums and in the world's highest-profile media outlets, women were raising their voices in defense of the feminine. Christine Blasey Ford was naming her rapist before the Senate Judiciary Committee, over 40 high-profile Hollywood females spoke their truth about Harvey Weinstein's sexual perversions and abuse, Chanel Miller's seed story for the memoir *Know My Name* was read on the floor of congress, and over 4 million people protested worldwide during the 2017 Women's March. Outrage was "in." Tarana Burke's #metoo movement became the banner women lifted up everywhere. It would be the hashtag of our generation.

The energy of Kali swept through the country. Artemis was at the helm.

Meanwhile *The Quest* was abiding the storm, waiting for the moment to burst onto the scene. Emily was using this time to shed the last tendrils of conventional holds: quitting corporate, moving to the jungles of Costa Rica, starting a family and founding online and in-person sanctuaries where women could retreat and transform their lives.

And then, *The Quest* chose its perfect publisher, one who knew how to color outside the lines of conformity and would gift the memoir to the world just when we were needing it most.

As women are emerging, exhausted from the dense wilderness of fighting the patriarchy, the memoir is assuring us we do not have to put on the armor again. We do not have to beat our fists against the walls of what we thought was the only world. *The Quest* gives us the trapdoor out of the paradigm of struggle and gives us back what some had begun to feel was a lost commodity: an infinite capacity for joy.

The book's core architecture is the heroine's journey, a sensual clarion call outlined in Victoria Lynn Schmidtt's Heroine's Journey Project and manifested in Emily's arc — from a woman being held hostage by the culture's insistence on perfection, to one who is harnessing her singular creative fire, that, once saddled and ridden, can take you absolutely anywhere. Before our eyes, we watch the narrator transform into: guide, jester, fortune teller, and, finally, cartographer, creating maps to the rich treasure chest of possibility within.

This story is catalytic to how we create real revolution. This is not just one woman's truth, but who, at her essence, every woman has the power to be. When we unravel the binds of conditioning, we find within us the epicurean, music-player, sensualist, writer, dancer, adventurer, the one who contains an astounding force that can bust through the binds of "not enough," and live out the most extraordinary lives.

The Quest is not just an "I can" but a "you can, too."

If you are holding this book in your hand, you can expect to have one of the grandest, most exhilarating journeys of your life. Just know that when you turn this page, you will never be the same again, in the very best possible way.

Suzanne Kingsbury

Bestselling Author of *The Gospel According to Gracey* and *The Summer Fletcher Greel Loved Me* and the Founder of Gateless Writing, Inc.

PART I:

CRAZY

GODDESS

1.

"Who will save your soul
If you won't save your own?"
—Jewel

"So what have you been creeeeaating?" James singsongs into the phone.

My mind goes blank. *Creating?* I know he's an artist, and that I'm definitely not. *Maybe this is artist lingo?*

I wouldn't call selling pharmaceuticals a creation. I evade his question.

"Ummmmm... I'm living in LA with my boyfriend of five and a half years, I work in sales, and uhh..." My lower lip begins to quiver; I bite down on it. Every secret I've shoved deep inside is threatening to reveal itself.

"I've, uh, kind of been having a hard time lately. I'll be up in San Francisco next week and was wondering if there is a chance that maybe I could see you?" I squeak nervously.

"I think that would be a *very* good idea."

When we hang up, I exhale suddenly and realize I haven't been breathing. I angrily slap the back of my hand against my wet cheeks, flop back into a stack of goose feather pillows, and reach around inside the drawer of my bedside table for one of those little white pills that will make everything better. At least for tonight.

～

"Congraaaaaaaaatulaaaaaaations on breaking through," James greets me as I open the door to my sister's apartment, my home for the week. His coffee-colored eyes are framed with more creases than I remember, and his beard has turned grey, but his gentle vibration is unmistakable. I nestle my head into his armpit for a few moments longer than is appropriate, drinking in the scent of Old Spice and wondering why it took me so long to call.

"Let's have a seat," he suggests.

In the living room, he drags two chairs together so they face each other and sits across from me. Holding my hands in his, he presses his thumbs firmly into my palms.

"Are you aware that your lips are purple?"

"Yeah, they do that sometimes," I answer despondently. "I mean, when I'm cold. And, actually, I can't ever remember being so cold in my entire life. Right now, I'm wearing tights beneath my pants, two pairs of socks, plus Ugg boots and four layers on top, plus this beanie I found in my sister's closet."

He cups both his hands over my right hand. "Do you feel that?" I feel nothing.

～

It's worlds away from the first and last time I saw him, nearly six years ago at a hotel in Mill Valley. Back then, his hands didn't touch mine but hovered and bounced about an inch above them, which instantly made them tingle. I remember being unable to pull them away, as if magnetic strings were gently guiding them in a synchronized rhythm. It felt like electrical currents were shooting through my palms. I began to cry, suddenly aware of the pain, fear, regret, and shame I had been carrying with me.

James never physically touched me, but his hand gently grazed about an inch above each energy center, the vibration humming to life in each one. As he moved up from my stomach, my heart felt all big and red, like it was bursting out of my chest, like a cartoon, but before I could catch it in my hands, it snapped back inside by some invisible grounding force.

James was "reading me." He asked me questions that revealed parts of myself I didn't want to see, or things I'd never thought about before. Things like: "Do you ever find yourself driving and suddenly you become aware that you're driving and have been on the road for some time, but you were somewhere else in your mind, not paying a bit of attention to the road at all? And you don't even remember where it was that your mind drifted off to?"

Guilty.

"Have you ever wondered who's driving the car?"

"Not really. I think by the time I realize I haven't been paying attention, I'm just relieved I haven't crashed."

"This is called being out of body. Which means the spirit that is you has literally left your body, and a being—or spirit without a body—is operating yours."

I had never heard the term "out of body" before. I asked some questions and got some answers, but all of that is a little blurry now. I do know that first session took two and a half hours but felt like twenty minutes. When I went into the bathroom to splash some water on my face, I caught a glimpse of myself in the mirror.

Holy shit! was my first thought. *What is happening?* I'd never looked so beautiful. My eyes, normally brown, were honey gold, flecked with green. My skin was dewy, and I looked more innocent somehow. Brighter, untarnished, like a piece of silver that's finally been polished after years of neglect. I also felt physically lighter, but the lightness was emanating from inside. I was bursting with hope and happiness. Even though I had never heard of most of the things he talked about, for the first time, everything seemed like it was exactly how it was supposed to be. I wanted to dance a jig and sing a song at the top of my lungs. It felt better than any drug I had ever tried, any "A" I had ever made, any goal I'd ever scored. As James walked me down to the lobby of the hotel, my body felt buoyant.

"Thank you so much, James. That was amaaaazing..." I said dreamily. "Oh, I almost forgot..." I rested my purse on the reception counter as I dug around for my checkbook.

I practically skipped out the door, completely missing the horrified look on the face of the lady at the front desk. Much amused, James told me about it later: Our interaction must have looked like a young girl paying a middle-aged man for sex.

~

"OK, come on back," James calls softly. I snap out of my memory.

"It's really good to see you," he says, looking at me carefully. I squirm a little, knowing that he is seeing far more than my bloodshot eyes and protruding cheekbones. Even in my marshmallow get-up, it's impossible to hide the fact that I've gotten very skinny. I'm not talking model-on-the-cover-of-a-magazine thin. I'm talking bluish, translucent, *not-hot*, no-curves-what-so-ever boney.

Over the past four months, I've tried telling myself it's OK; I've always been on the small side. But the day a pair of my pants, still buttoned, slid off my hips and down to my ankles, I couldn't pretend any longer. I started taking a bodybuilder supplement and had the tailor take my pants in.

While I've had to shrug off co-workers' concerns, my shrinking form has been easier to hide from my family, who are pre-occupied with their own lives. Mom's been traveling in Europe, Dad's been consumed by his separation from my stepmother, Arah, and my sister, Sophie, has been consumed by worrying about my dad.

In many ways, Dad and Arah's break-up has been more dramatic than my own parents'. My Mom and Dad had only been together for four years of my life, while Arah and my Dad were together for almost twenty. Though I'd grown to love Arah over the years, at first I was elated to have my Dad's undivided attention back after having shared him for so long. Suddenly he, my sister, and I were doing things we hadn't done together in twenty years, especially our regular weekend trips to Tahoe. Dad even started referring to us as "three bugs in a rug" again.

My sister and I joined forces in an attempt to prop him up—calling him daily, visiting him monthly—doing anything we could to shoulder his pain so he'd be happy once again. I didn't see it for a long time, but my sadness over my own break-up hid nicely inside my Dad's grief, providing camouflage for the fact that my heart was just as heavy as his.

I even brought Dad as my guest to Switzerland for the global award trip I won last summer, and for two weeks it was if we'd traveled back in time to the carefree days when I was his Ol' Em the Pem. The moniker has no meaning in itself, but the affectionate way he said it conjured up images of wonderful things from days past—girls serving vanilla cokes on roller skates at the drive-in; fresh milk and ice cream delivered to your door. I don't know if Sophie's and my efforts have made anything better, but our crusade has brought us three closer than we've been in years.

It wasn't until about a month ago, the night before Thanksgiving, that Sophie mentioned my weight. We were at Dad's beach house in Bodega Bay, where he'd been camping out for the past eight months.

"You're *soooooo* skinny," she said, trying to disguise her disgust as concern.

I hooked a quick turn into the kitchen, pretending I cared about a turkey centerpiece I'd never looked twice at in my life, but there was no avoiding her. She followed me and repeated more loudly, so my father could hear, "You're *so* skinny, Emily."

My jaw clenched, and my face flushed. I wanted to punch her. True, I looked like an eleven-year-old boy, and she could be a 1940's pin-up girl. Couldn't she see this was not my choice, but the non-stop anxious chatter in my head was melting the calories right off?

I darted back to the dining room and busied myself with the table. She came up behind me and tugged on the excess fabric that my butt used to fill.

"Too skinny." This time in a baby voice. Maybe she knew she was crossing into dangerous territory and hoped saying it in a baby voice would protect her.

I lost it, grabbing her arm and shoving my face in hers. "You tell me how good you'd look if you just found out that your boyfriend of five and a half years cheated on you? With a girl he met in a cell phone store?"

The apples of her pink cheeks flushed white. She was beginning to sense that maybe I wasn't stable.

"You tell me how hot your body would be if you hadn't gotten a good night's sleep in months, and that the person that you basically have built your entire life around has turned out to be the complete asshole you convinced yourself he wasn't?" I screamed, shaking her by the shoulders. I was beginning to hyperventilate.

"I'm sorry," she stammered quietly. "You just look so skinny... I'm worried about you."

My dad, who normally steers clear of our squabbles, came into the room and said sternly, "Sophie, BACK OFF. I'm SERIOUS. BACK OFF!"

"And, she has a kid," I said flatly.

My last sentence hung in the room like a volatile gas. Nobody spoke for what seemed like a very long time, for fear that if they did, everything would blow.

This was the first anyone in my family had heard of trouble in my relationship with Aidan, and from the look in my sister's eyes and the weird twisty thing she was doing with her mouth, I could see she was majorly confused. I'd always been hesitant to share bad news with my family, whereas it was in Sophie's DNA to broadcast any remotely negative thing. One summer, when we were home from college, I was having dinner with my dad, Arah, and a friend when Sophie burst in and announced, "I HAVE AIDS!"

Translation: I just had my annual gynecology appointment and they did an HIV test.

The test came back two weeks later, negative.

So to Sophie's mind, keeping something so colossal to myself made no sense.

∾

"Is it OK if I touch you here?" James motions to my left forearm, gently pulling me back to present time once again, his voice filled with concern.

"I'm just monitoring your pain levels. You're out of body right now, which is why you're like a human popsicle, and just in a *little* bit of survival." When he says "little," I know he means quite the opposite.

I nod, but I don't really understand what he's doing.

"You are grieving," he continues. "Are you aware of this?"

Of course, I'm grieving, I am mourning the death of my life as I know it. I'm probably going to have to move to the east side of town and live in a shithole apartment and find all new friends.

I nod again.

"When we experience emotional pain, it becomes stored in the body. When we release that energy, we are grieving."

"Oh. I see," I say sheepishly.

"I want you to do something for me. Hold your hands together, an inch apart, and repeat after me." I do as I'm told and use all of my concentration to try to still my shaking hands. "I, say your name," he directs me, "am a beginner of life, giving myself permission to heal and to release and to recognize myself in my highest affinity."

I take a deep breath and, with great purpose, slowly repeat

what he said.

"Now, keep holding your hands an inch apart, and let's put a color in that space, a nice emerald green, and the element we are using today is healing. Now pull all of that right into your heart. See it travel all throughout your body, filling you up with that healing emerald green."

I slowly pull my hands up to my heart, gingerly cradling the energy for fear that even the slightest nudge will spoil whatever magic is supposed to be going on between my palms. I envision the color like a bucket of green water dumped over inside me, running down my arms and legs, slowly seeping into all the pores and crevices.

"So what we want is for you to give yourself a little permission to release. Your permission levels have been very low in this lifetime. Oh, and there you went."

Before I have a chance to ask, "Where'd I go?" he continues, "You hide a lot; are you aware of this?"

I nod meekly, feeling extremely exposed.

"And, you are deep in WE-ME mode."

"WE-ME mode? What's that?"

"It means that your basis of affinity for yourself is in a couple mode, versus, 'This is me, Emily, and I am senior for me.'"

I must look confused because he explains, "Essentially, you don't feel whole without a man in your life."

Sirens blare outside, and for a delusional second, I think I've been found out, and they're coming to take me away to the place they take people who pretend to be confident and have their shit together, but who are actually just "big hat and no goat" as my grandfather used to mix up that saying in his thick Portuguese accent.

"It's not bad or wrong," James says with no judgment. "The majority of women on the planet feel this way. There is *programming* on the planet to feel this way."

The sirens fade, and I realize that I am safe. For the time being anyway.

"When you say programming..." I prompt him, my naïveté waving like knickers in the wind.

"Just remember, there's nobody greater than you for you," he says with such calm, powerful certainty that I almost believe him. *Almost.*

My mind wanders back over all the times I've put what I wanted aside because Aidan wanted to do something else, eat something else, watch something else. If he needed something that would take me clear across town, away from work, I took care of it, even if it was just a few blocks from his office. Because, he reminded me, it was *his* job that was going to take care of us, in the end. And guess who stupidly believed every last word?

"Why do I do this?" I moan. Then, desperately, "Is it too late to change?"

"Well, you're here, aren't you? It took immense courage for you to meet with me today. So I really want to congratulate you again."

I give him a dubious look, but thank him.

"WE-ME," he continues, "means that your only vision of self exists in a couple—as in, 'We is me.' And when this is the case, a male is greater than you. If a male is greater than you, you have to perform a lot because you believe that you're not good enough just being yourself. When you're in performance, you're out of affinity because you aren't being authentic. And affinity connections are what you *so* desire, but it's impossible to love yourself if you are constantly trying to prove yourself to someone else. Do you have thoughts that you aren't good enough and that you have to do better to make him happy?"

I nod, increasingly depressed about how weak I've become. I've always prided myself on being strong and independent. Don't I get any credit for going to boarding school at fourteen? Charging off to Spain as a foreign exchange student when I could barely conjugate an irregular verb? Traipsing through Costa Rica and Panama for months with just a surfboard and pack on my back?

Apparently not.

"The reality is, if you're always trying to be perfect, you can never be yourself, and performance is stressful and exhausting. Then, when there's a break-up, the woman ends up thinking that there is something wrong with *her*, that she's done something bad, and this sits in her space."

"I *am* exhausted. To the core." All those sleepless nights trying to figure out how to make it right again, how to make him love me still. Instead I'd always end up aiming a gigantic magnifying glass over all my own mistakes.

He starts gently pulling the skin away from my shoulders and working his way down my arms. Suddenly, he pauses, an odd look flashing across his face.

"What?"

"It's something unusual," he stalls, laying his palm on my forearm. "Hmmm..."

"What is it? *Tell me.*"

"It's just that I'm seeing a very unique green energy. It's really covered over by lots of other energies, so I almost missed it."

I try to place the look on his face. *Is that shock? Awe?*

Very slowly and seriously he says, "In the twenty-five years I've been working with folks, I've never recognized this energy in anyone else besides myself."

"So this is a good thing?"

"It's a green energy that has a frequency of healing."

"It's interesting that you say green because I've always loved everything green." So much so that I've never been a fan of the desert.

He shakes his head again, almost in disbelief. "Do you understand what I mean when I say frequency?"

"Yeah. I mean, sort of... well, I think so. Actually, I don't know."

He smiles. "Well, essentially, you're made up of independent frequencies that consist of strands of color, sound, and information. These frequencies combine to form resonances. And these resonances intertwine to create one vibration that is you. Your vibration is different than every single other person on the planet depending on the information you've gathered in this lifetime and past lifetimes. This is called your epic path. This frequency of green is part of your epic path from many lifetimes ago. Is this making sense?"

I nod, though if I were quizzed on it, I'm not sure I'd pass.

Satisfied, he returns to my immediate situation. "The belief that a guy will make you happy, provide for you, and protect you is a tall order because now you have to *perform* to match those requirements. You're nothing more than a rodent running on a wheel if you think that someone else is going to make you happy. This codependency breeds resentments. And then there you are, a fabulous woman, living her life in pain. You *are* fabulous, you know that?"

I raise an eyebrow and smile ruefully. I don't feel faintly

fabulous. Not even .000000000000000000000000000001 fabulous.

"I know it doesn't feel like it right now, but you are," he says matter-of-factly. "The spirit that is *truly* you is very special and powerful."

How can he be so sure?

～

I really don't know *that* much about James. I met him while working at an art gallery, during a time when he was one of its more celebrated artists. He'd been close with the owner, Chloe, for years.

That summer, Chloe needed someone to fill in for her front office person, and I, needing money for my trip to Central America, jumped at the chance. Chloe was a savvy business-woman and an artist, too. She was a friend of my parents, and I'd always adored her. When she told me that she'd been working with a spiritual teacher—an energy healer and clairvoyant—for thirteen years, I didn't fully grasp what she was talking about, but my curiosity wanted to know. I was always told a clairvoyant was some kind of charlatan burning incense and looking into a crystal ball, exploiting people's despair for an easy buck. And I'd never heard of an energy healer. Coming from a long line of medicine enthusiasts, I grew up going straight to the doctor if I had so much as a splinter in my finger or a blister on my toe. I didn't know what I'd find in James, but certainly not a UC Davis and Stanford-educated teacher, writer, and artist who has shown his work internationally.

～

"If you're wondering why I'm so sure of this," James says, his eyes twinkling, "it's because I recognize you as spirit; the essence of who you really are underneath all of these illusions you subscribe to. The first thing I want to get across to you today is that there are *no mistakes*. Harmful choices? Sure. But absolutely no mistakes."

"I want to change," I whisper, determined.

"You *must* change," James agrees. "You have spent nearly six years with a very competitive male, in agreement to being treated like a punching bag."

"He never touched me."

"You don't need to be hit over the head with a baseball bat to be harmed. You've been ridiculed, manipulated, rejected, and isolated... is this true? You've had to numb out so much just to survive. Which is why you no longer feel vibrations like you did the first time. And if you hold this pain and resentment in your physical body, you will begin to create something you really don't want."

"What do you mean, exactly, when you say *create*?"

"Well, everything that happens in your life, whether you view it as desirable or undesirable, you are responsible for."

Oh, brother.

I consider it for a moment. "Kind of like the law of attraction?"

"Very good! Like attracts like, so if you are carrying around a certain energy vibration, you will attract more energy of that same resonance, which then compounds with the energy you already have. A person's external world and physical condition are reflections of what's happening on the inside."

"But sometimes don't bad things happen to good people? I've known really kind people who've gotten serious illnesses and even died from cancer."

He's quiet for a few moments, then explains, "A person may be a kind person, but if they've attracted something that is negatively impacting their physical body, like a serious illness, they're holding densities inside them. This doesn't make them bad or wrong. It may be that their internal thoughts are negative; they feel badly about things that they may or may not have created. It could be as simple as feeling terrible about a bad grade in school, holding a grudge, marrying someone they perceive to be the wrong person. It can also be an energized picture they are still carrying from another lifetime affecting their vibration. All sorts of things are inside people that they have no awareness of because they are unconscious of the swirling energy of the universe. This negative thinking starts to form a block and a density that in turn attracts dense frequencies into their body. *Dis-ease* is the resonance of pain in the physical body."

I think about my excessive, and fruitless, trips to the doctor over the past year for recurrent health issues.

James says very seriously, "Right now you have deep resentments and very negative thoughts about you. If you hold this pain in your physical body, you will begin to create a serious illness."

"A serious illness?" I whisper, "Like cancer?"

"Cancer is one of the options," he confirms gently.

"Why do I want to be with someone who treats me this way?"

"An important understanding is, even though Aidan may have punished you, *you* are responsible for everything that happens in your relationship because you are here to learn about one person only—yourself. No matter how many relationships you have, your life is about *you*, and how much you truly wish to learn and grow. Right now, your fear levels are off the charts and you have little belief in yourself."

Great.

"I don't want to overwhelm you too much for one day, so we are going to end here, but first I'm going to teach you a few tools to help you eliminate some of this resentment and rejection that sits in your universe, and then you are going to get something to eat. Because *you* are starving..."

As if on cue, my stomach lets out a little rumble.

"OK, the first thing you *must* do is, call your energy back! You're like a high-voltage battery pack powering Aidan because you're directing so much of your vital life force through him."

"I didn't even know I was doing that," I say, embarrassed. "How do I get it back?"

"Give your energy a color and fill up an image of him with that color. Now imagine pulling that out of him and putting it back inside you. You can visualize a vacuum if that helps. You've been happily handing over your life force. In addition to powering his creations, when your energy is in Aidan's space, he'll be irritable with you because it's essentially like you're sitting on his head. And more importantly, you have very little energy left for you to create anything for you, and you are immensely creative; are you aware of this?"

I shrug. "I've never really thought of myself as creative."

"I see that you have a high aptitude for writing," he says, looking just to the right of me, "and that it would bring you great fulfillment." My heart tingles.

"It's your competitive programming that's freezing you out of your creativity. But we can talk about that later. Right now, are you ready to learn how to transmute?"

James' precision and temperament is a cross between a third-grade art teacher explaining the fundamentals of paper-maché and a high school cheerleader rooting for her team.

"OK, close your eyes and visualize a balloon right in the middle of your forehead. Now, let all of the punishment go out of your body and into the balloon until it's totally black. Any non-validation and ridicule—see it go into that balloon."

I try to follow his instructions, but the memories and emotions squirm away like minnows sensing an approaching net.

"You're doing a great job! OK, now take all of Aidan's punishments that are in you, any negative thoughts, and anything at all causing you pain, put it inside the balloon, and pop it!"

I squeeze my eyes shut and start at the bottom—pulling up from my feet all the rejection: all the times he turned his back to me in bed, refusing to cuddle or kiss me, not looking me in the eyes when we had sex. I drag them up past my knees, collecting more as I go. The times I reached for his hand and he yanked it away. I gather the lying, cheating, and manipulation. As I get up to my heart, I feel a sharp pain, as if someone shot an arrow right through the center. And there, I gather all of the promises he's made, accepting now, for the first time, that he had no intention of keeping them. When I get up to my head, I stuff all of them into the balloon so they can't escape; its belly swells. And then I envision pulling that arrow out of my heart and stabbing it right into the middle of the balloon, releasing it all out of my universe.

"Wooooooooow..." James says softly. "That was really amazing. How do you feel?"

I take a deep breath. "I guess I feel a little clearer. Actually, even just breathing has been a struggle over the past few months."

The tightness that had become a permanent fixture in my chest is gone. I wipe a few stray tears with my sleeve. James hands me a tissue.

"You may not feel all of the benefits right away, but if you continue to use your tools, they will help you immensely."

"They will?" I ask doubtfully.

"When you imagine destroying the balloon—you can visualize a plate of glass with people's faces on it, or words like 'resent-ment' or 'competition,' if that's easier—you are changing the molecular make-up of this energy form, which in turn affects surrounding energies. It is a very powerful healing tool that can help you release unwanted energies that are in your space. In doing this you radically change your thoughts, emotions, and ultimately, your entire life path."

I try to grasp the physics of what he just said.

"You know, Emily," he says, looking at me intently, "you don't have the slightest clue about who you really are."

2.

*"I'd rather laugh with the sinners
than cry with the saints
The sinners are much more fun..."*
—Billy Joel

I wasn't easily seduced by Aidan, in the beginning. The night we met, we didn't even talk much. My best friend, Courtney, invited me to go with her up to Los Angeles for the weekend to stay with Charlie, her new love interest, and his roommates, George and Aidan. She and I had been renting a little place in San Diego for the summer, fresh off post-graduation adventures—Central America for me, Australia for her—and welcomed any distraction that kept us from thinking about getting real jobs.

We arrived at their place in Brentwood to discover that they had the night all planned out for us. We started at a local sushi joint, with a constant stream of sake bombs. After two months of pestering fog, a period Southern Californians refer to as May-gray and June-gloom, the warm Santa Ana winds had finally blown in. Maybe it was the summer weather, or the excitement of instantly clicking with new people, but there was a distinct feeling in the air that anything could happen.

Courtney and I, both from Northern California, had the usual notions of LA as a smog pit full of superficial people. But one evening of bouncing around to the guys' favorite bars overturned our biases. At last call, Courtney knocked her drink into mine and joked, "LA... who knew?"

"Um... apparently, a lot of people. But the secret sure is alive and well in Northern California!"

Night gave way to morning, but nobody was willing to turn off the party. Fueled by vodka sodas and cocaine, we decided to go swimming—and continue drinking—at the Bel Air Bay Club, where George's family had a membership. As we curved down to the Pacific Coast Highway, the air was clear, and the Malibu Mountains offered a dramatic backdrop for the glistening ocean.

Sitting on the beach at the base of the Palisades, the Bel Air Bay Club has unobstructed views of Malibu and the Santa Monica Bay. According to the club's official history, it was founded in 1927 for the burgeoning Los Angeles leisure class, and that was *exactly* our attitude that day. With the entitlement of people too young to understand the time and effort required to afford such luxuries, we rolled in like a circus troop cavorting through a Sunday sermon. We played paddleball, took full advantage of the buffet, and let the cool surf pummel us into the shore.

It wasn't until George was walking from the bar to our cabana, balancing eight Bloody Marys on two makeshift Frisbee trays, that we went from mildly to exceptionally obnoxious. He'd almost made it all the way when he went down hard. The drinks sailed through the air, spraying chunky tomato juice on innocent, ummm... much more mature, bystanders.

"FUCK. That's fucking bullshit. These piece of shit trays..." he muttered, peeling himself up off the sand. Our neighbors didn't find this scene as hysterically funny as we did. And that was apparently the last straw.

"Sir, this is a family establishment!" bellowed a small man in uniform. "That kind of language *will not* be tolerated here. I am going to have to ask you to leave."

"That's fine; we'll just go to our *other* beach club!" he retorted with such conviction that the rest of us could barely hide our laughter as we marched out indignantly behind him.

At that point, we should have all gone home, but apparently nobody had an off switch. Plus, George wasn't kidding, there was *another* beach club. Blasting "Celebration" out of the open windows, we sped down the PCH to the Jonathon Club, where Charlie's family had a membership.

When we eventually got back to their Brentwood apartment, I drunkenly looked for a place to lie down, stumbling through a wasteland of half-empty beer cans, cigarette butts, and an indolent chicken gizzard that had been on the counter for at least a few days. Unexpectedly, I found a room with an empty bed, neatly made with what appeared to be clean white sheets and huge down pillows. Potted plants were placed carefully around the room, in stark contrast to the rest of the apartment, which seemed inhospitable to all life forms. I lay down immediately.

Many hours later, I woke up to someone in the bed with me. I rolled over to find Aidan looking at me with a big comfortable smile on his face, like we'd been sharing a bed for years.

"Hi?" I said uncertainly, quickly patting my crotch underneath the covers to see if my bathing suit was still on.

Phew.

"How's it goin'?"

"Oh, you know..." I trailed off and started to laugh, thinking about our shenanigans over the past 24 hours. "How's it goin' with you?" I noticed for the first time that his eyes were the color of baked clay.

"Pretty sweet. I could use a little food, but other than that, I would have to say pretty sweet."

"I think I saw some chicken out in the kitchen."

"Yeah... uh, that's George's." He laughed again. "He likes to cook." He had a very slight lisp.

Immediately, I was completely at ease. I tried to think back to the night before—had we made a special connection? I was almost positive we hadn't. As I looked around the dark room, I saw the plants and quickly remembered how I got there.

"I like your plants."

"Thanks. They like you too." His eyes twinkled.

Over the next seven hours, we put three movies into the DVD player but never watched them. We sat eating pizza and talking about everything from our childhood memories to our future plans to breaking the sound barrier. I learned that this guy was a small-town, touchdown-scoring computer genius with an infectious laugh. The internet start-up that had recruited him had quickly blown through its funding, so he was currently jobless, but I didn't worry for him for a second; he had big ideas and was full of confidence.

Because of a resistance I didn't quite understand, I initially put him in the friend zone. But our friendship quickly turned flirty, and he soon won me over with daily phone calls, flowers, and packages, which usually included books on subjects in which I'd expressed an interest. A few months later when we officially started dating, I fell hard.

In our first year together, Aidan started his first internet company, I moved up to LA and secured my first job in pharmaceuticals, and we began dreaming of our future together. For a while, it seemed like we were really, really lucky. We had promising careers, beautiful and hilarious friends, and our whole lives ahead of us. We went on adventurous and extravagant vacations, lived a goalie kick from the beach, and when we were all together, I felt happier, safer, and more accepted than I ever had before.

With degrees in both math and physics and a minor in economics, Aidan had a firm understanding of everything from the elegant nuances of quantum physics to the molecular make up of a fart. If you knew him from work, you might think he was a quirky computer nerd; if you saw him play sports on the beach, you'd see a gifted, lightning-quick athlete; if you happened to be one of George's girlfriend's prim and proper Vanderbilt friends who was crouched down, ready to scream surprise at George's birthday party, and witnessed Aidan speed by, take a corner too fast, and slam George's car into the side of a building, then scamper drunk out of the backseat in a blonde mullet wig, George trailing behind in a Rasta wig, before dialing 911 and fleeing the scene, you might think he was a total delinquent.

Then again, if you were around the following day when the police issued *him* an apology for arriving late at the scene of the accident, you'd know what I knew at that moment: He was one lucky punk.

He loved recounting how the police asked him why he'd left the scene of the accident before they arrived. He'd say, with a shit-eating grin, "I told them I had someplace to be."

I found this combination of mind-blowing brilliance, alpha-male ingenuity, and an outlaw state of mind as intoxicating as a tequila sunrise with a light lunch. He represented freedom and safety in equal, heaping measures. Aidan always told me that we were special, and that rules didn't apply to us. Don't ask me why a small-town boy from the Pacific Northwest was convinced we were so exceptional, but he was. And while I was with him, I believed we were too.

3.

"If you want to scare away the vampires,
You've got to guide them into the light"
—Michael Franti

After James leaves my sister's apartment, I sit on the couch in a patch of sunlight, my mind trying to make sense of everything my spirit has just revealed. It feels like James ran an MRI on my soul, and the prognosis is extremely grim. Oddly enough, after making many painful recognitions, the anxiety that's been marching tirelessly through my body for the past four months has slowed to an easy stroll.

My stomach rumbles again, and suddenly I'm ravenous. I envision a bowl of pesto the size of my head, a crusty sourdough baguette, cheesy enchiladas smothered in mole sauce. Unfortunately, my sister's cupboard doesn't deliver, and I'm forced to settle for fat-free buttered popcorn, a cup of Ovaltine, and a questionable banana. Unsatisfied, I head to the deli. Outside, the dark clouds that have filled the sky for days are blowing west over the Golden Gate Bridge. The wind rustles through eucalyptus trees, through my hair and my pores as if I'm made of gauzy cotton. I breathe the ocean breeze and notice a glimmer of hope deep inside me, a faint pulsating glow like an avalanche rescue light buried beneath layers of snow. I do a little skip. It feels so good I skip all the way to the deli. My breath presses against my lungs as my feet pummel the pavement. Beads of sweat gather above my small smile.

Back in my sister's kitchen, I devour my tuna sandwich. Then, on my way to the couch, I glimpse myself in the mirror. Remembering how beautiful I looked after our first meeting six years ago, I'm hoping some of that magic transpired today. I gasp.

What? The? Hell?!

I look different all right, thanks to the big knot forming in the middle of my forehead. I gingerly touch it with my ring finger; it's extremely sensitive. Moreover, my eyes have swollen into narrow slits. Perplexed, I replay the morning. I remember James touching my arm, but never my face. I take a deep breath and try to remain calm, but panic has already descended. Suddenly ridiculously hot, I rip off my layers of clothing and grab the phone.

"Hello?" James answers on the third ring.

"We've got a problem," I say, trying to remain calm. "There is a huge knot in the middle of my forehead, and it seems like it's getting bigger."

"When did this start?" The concern in his voice makes me more frightened.

"I have no idea." I don't remember receiving any funny looks at the deli.

"There's no reason to panic. I will be back in thirty minutes. And don't worry; it's just a release. Everything is going to be OK."

"Promise I'm not going to look like this forever?"

"I promise."

When he arrives twenty minutes later, the bump is twice as big as when I first noticed it. He grazes it with his index finger. "Hmmmm. I had a feeling this was the case."

"What is it? What's happening to me?" I cry out like a woman menaced by an oversized reptile in a 1950's sci-fi thriller.

"Well, I don't want to overwhelm you with too much information all at once, but it looks like you are trying to *bump* it out of me," he jokes.

I just look at him.

"Well, I thought that was funny." He chuckles to himself.

I give a courtesy smile but continue to stare.

"Well, you're definitely in a release."

"Um, yeeeeeeaaaah... What does that *mean*?"

"Well," he begins slowly, "there are actually a couple things going on here. You are releasing a lot of the pain you've been swallowing for the past five and a half years in order to uphold the image that you have this perfect life. As you've just learned, when we're in pain, emotionally, we harbor it in our physical bodies as a very dense energy. You also have deep rejection and resentment in your heart from years of not being recognized in your relationship with Aidan, especially after you worked hard to be so perfect. We just did a mini-healing, and you are beginning to physically *let go* of some of that dense energy. This is why your eyes are swelling."

I have a zillion questions, but my mouth suddenly feels trapped in a Moroccan sandstorm.

"Because you've started to do this work with me, you've been hit on the head with some energy. Right in your third eye, so you will not see the truth."

Although I only have a partial understanding what he is saying, I have no choice but to believe him.

But... energy from where?

"There are many energies that you can't see, but they're even more powerful than the ones you can see. And your entourage is pretty shaken about you seeing me, so they threw a little energy at you not to see."

"Entourage?"

"Yep, your entourage; everyone has one."

"So, what do you mean, *exactly*, when you say entourage?"

"Essentially it's made up of energies coming from individuals in your life with whom you've made spiritual agreements. Some may have a body and are directing energy toward you, and some may not have a body, but they can still impact you pretty good."

"I see," I say hesitantly.

"Are you aware of some people who might be pretty strong in your entourage right now?"

"Aidan?"

"Good! Anyone else?"

I'm not totally sure how this works. "My mom?"

"Yes!"

"My dad?"

"Very good!

"My sister?"

"Your sister is very strong."

Well, I am in her apartment.

"Is there anyone else?" I'm fascinated.

His gaze shifts, so it seems like he is looking above me. There is someone coming in really strong, a female..." he pauses. "Do you know a blonde girl whose name starts with the letter C?"

"Courtney?"

"That's it. *Yeesh!* Who is she?"

"She's my best friend. Well, supposed to be," I add quietly.

"Are you aware that the energy she is directing towards you is anything but friendly?"

I nod, tears welling up in my eyes, thinking about how our interactions have become more strained every time we see each other, and how she's the last person I feel I could go to for support right now.

"There are a couple others in there as well, but they aren't very strong right now."

"So, what are they doing?"

"It's as if they are huddled around you like a campfire, directing energy towards you. That energy can dramatically impact how you're feeling, even the things you do and say."

"Is it all bad?" I feel a little creeped out.

"No, it isn't always all bad. Your entourage is constantly shifting and changing; whether you're attracting more positive or negative beings into your entourage depends on you and what vibration you're running. On a good day, you could have what people refer to as 'spirit guides' assisting you, but right now your vibration is very dense and most of your entourage is pretty stirred up that you are seeing me."

"Why? Don't they love me?"

"They may love you, but that doesn't mean they want you to change and grow." He stares at me like he's looking right through me. "Do you have any idea why they wouldn't want you to change and grow?"

I pause for a second. "Because if I change, then they will have to look at their own lives?"

"Very, *very* good!" He seems surprised. "But keep in mind that you are personally responsible for everyone in your entourage. Does your sister have some washcloths we can use?"

"Check in the closet to the right of the bathroom."

Something tells me I wouldn't be in this situation if I hadn't waited nearly six years to call him again.

It wasn't that I'd forgotten what I'd experienced during our first meeting. For months I thought about how I couldn't pull my hands away, and the sensation of my heart lurching out of my chest. I'd planned on seeing James again the next time I came home for vacation. Then I shared it with Aidan, and he dismissed it as if I was a child talking about an adventure with an imaginary friend. When I brought it up again, he insisted what I was saying just didn't make sense, which made me doubt the validity of my own experience. I run two fingers softly over the swollen mound on my head.

Maybe it doesn't make sense, but this bump is very real, and James is very real, and what he's said—as painful as it is—rings very true somewhere deep inside me.

James comes back with a stack of steaming washcloths.

"With your permission, I'd like to put this over your eyes?" he asks with an endearing professionalism.

"Whatever you think will help..."

"The heat from these washcloths is helping to accelerate the process. It is literally steaming the energy out of you."

It sounds a little hokey, but I really don't have any other options, and the warm washcloth feels nice. As I lie there, I can't help but think about Aidan. Tears flood my itchy eyes and roll onto my shoulders.

"How we *doooo-ing*?" James asks as if he doesn't know I'm

having an elaborate pity party underneath the washcloth.

"I'm OK," I choke out.

"You're going to let me know when that gets cold, OKAY?"

"It's cold."

Like an attentive nurse handling the bandages of an intensive care patient, James spends the next three hours carefully removing one washcloth and gently securing the next, "pulling energy" off of me with his hands, and attempting to make me laugh with his corny jokes. I have little awareness of the seeds of truth he's planting in my mind; I only know that his presence is very comforting.

After he leaves, I look in the mirror for the hundredth time. The bump is showing little sign of retreat. I crawl into my sister's bed and pull the covers over my head.

That night, I have a very clear dream that I'm walking down a barren road when I come to a fork stretched out before me like a wishbone. Aidan is walking one step ahead, and he won't look at me or respond when I call out to him. Meanwhile, the heads of our many friends bob up and down beside us, lighting our way with washed-out pastel colors. I try not to show them how sad I really am.

Then, instantly, I'm back at the wishbone intersection and have the chance to go down the second path. It's dark and unfamiliar, with tree branches curling high overhead and down toward the ground; I can't decipher the shapes and shadows. Terrified, I turn around, poised to run back, when suddenly a red-tailed hawk lit up like a firefly swoops down in front of me, spraying gold dust in its wake.

I glance at the entrance to the other path, and a cold chill ripples through my body. I turn back again and see that the hawk has illuminated the dark path. Those shadowy branches, so terrifying a moment ago, are now just tree limbs covered in bright green moss with yellow flowers. Relief floods over me in a warm wave, and my eyes fling open.

I lay in bed for a while, reflecting on how real the dream was, until I remember the bump and immediately run a finger lightly over my forehead. It's still there. I go to the mirror, and then resign myself to hiding inside for another day. I don't feel like doing anything anyway. I feel like one of those antidepressant commercials, and it makes me more depressed. Then anger sets in.

How could Aidan do this to me? I loved him when he had no job, nothing, stuck by him during terribly stressful times, and now he makes it big and casts me aside.

The phone vibrates on the bedside table, and for a split-second, I hope it's him, calling to say he misses me desperately and can't live without me. No such luck; it's James.

"Hi," I answer.

"How we dooo-ing?"

I can't help but smile at how James emphasizes certain syllables for far longer than necessary.

"Oh, you know... bump is still large and in charge, and the squinty eye thing seems to have minimal improvement," I say, sounding far more blasé than I feel.

"OK, I want you to say something. Don't analyze it; just say it," he says firmly.

"Uh, OK."

"Say: I'm not in agreement to any pain or harm. And I want to see the truth."

I enunciate it so clearly that even my English-teacher grandmother would approve.

I do want to see the truth... don't I?

"James?" I ask shyly. "Can I ask you something?"

"What would you like to know?"

"When did you... well, how did you know that you were..."

"Capable?"

"That's what I was trying to say."

He hesitates before saying, "Well, when I was about three, I was walking my tricycle along the sidewalk by my house and felt something above me, so I looked up at the sky. I now know that presence was a being. Do you remember what a being is?"

"A spirit without a body?"

"That's right."

"Then, as I was looking at the insects flying around my mother's pretty flowers, I felt a pressure on my forehead. Suddenly, everything began pixilating into transparent visions of bright colors and shapes streaming away and towards me in ever-expanding spirals and waves. Bits and pieces of color appeared and disappeared everywhere, until the walls of the house itself disappeared into a pixilated transparency of streaming color. Simultaneously, I could hear my mother and her friend talking inside as though I were standing next to them, as well as the lady in the house next door and many other voices, when by normal standards, this would be impossible."

"Whoa." I'm fascinated. It sounds an awful lot like the visions I've seen on LSD.

"I felt this pressure on my forehead, which is now very familiar, and simultaneously noticed little brown spots on the cement. I remember thinking, *What are these spots?* I studied them for a moment but was more interested in the voices I was hearing from inside the houses. So I kept walking along, continuing to move in and out of this altered state very quickly, until I became puzzled when I looked down to see the brown spots forming into a pool of liquid, but none further up the path. This is all very funny now," he reflects. "I finally understood that I was squirting blood out of the center of my forehead. Of course, I was interested in this occurrence but, strangely, I wasn't scared by it and actually enjoyed watching it fly through the air."

He pauses to see how I'm digesting everything.

"Go on."

"So, I finally went inside thinking maybe this was something I should ask my mother about, but when she saw me, all pandemonium broke loose because naturally she was startled with this vision of a little boy with blood squirting out of his forehead. She was convinced that I'd fallen and wouldn't listen to a thing I was saying. But I knew something very special had just happened. The altered state continued for some time as I lay on my bed, watching the brightness appear where there were walls or objects, until I finally fell asleep."

"Blood was just spurting out of your forehead?" I ask in disbelief, rubbing a finger over the lump on my own forehead.

"Yup, and that was just the beginning. At around four or five, I discovered the ability to take pain out of the adults around me, although the way I was doing it was very detrimental to me, as I literally would just fill my body with their pain. I thought the black coming up my arms and into my body was black ink, and I would watch it grow and grow inside of me until my little body was filled with it, and it felt so awful that I had to go out of body to avoid the pain my body felt. Eventually, I would find my way to the bathroom and lock myself in. Lying down in a fetal position on my mother's tiny round pink carpet, I would moan into the floor, trying to release the illness out of me by grounding it into the planet. I would sing a little song that would carry all the blackness far, far away from me."

My mind flickers to something I read as a part of training for selling in the oncology market. A Greek physician named Galen, way back in the days of Hippocrates, believed that cancer was a result of an internal overdose of black bile, and tumors were an outcropping of this dysfunction. He alleged that there was no cure in cutting the tumors out, as the black bile just seeped right into the treated area. For centuries people believed cancer was a systemic disease. Then, in the 1500's, a physician named Vesalius began doing autopsies in search of this black bile, but found none, and changed the way we've thought of cancer forever.

Was Galen seeing the same black inky energy that James is talking about? Is that why the people who came after him couldn't see it?

"And now, when you do your healings, you take pain out of other people?"

"I do. Unfortunately, many people illusion heal unconsciously, which accounts for many illnesses all over the planet."

"Illusion heal?"

"On a simplistic level, illusion healing is when you attempt to fix things that are external to you."

"Wait, I'm confused. Isn't that what you're doing?"

"No, it's not what I do *anymore*, but unfortunately, I did this for quite some time. I would try to fix the raging in my family and would take in enormous amounts of pain, before I understood that the real key to healing is neutrality."

"Can you give me an example?" I ask, totally confused now.

"Let's say someone is crying and raging in pain and you sympathize or empathize with her. This is illusion healing."

"But I thought empathizing or sympathizing is just understanding what someone is going through. You know, being there for them."

"*Empathizing*, you physically feel how the person feels and you start to cry and rage. *Sympathizing*, you don't actually cry, but you *feel* badly for the person. So with empathizing, you *attach* to someone's pain, and sympathizing you *judge* someone's pain that is external to yourself. This opens us up energetically to absorbing the other person's pain, which eventually manifests into illness."

"Okaaaaaaay," I say, wondering if Sophie's and my attempts to save our dad are illusion healing.

"This is in stark contrast with *compassion*, when we acknowledge that someone's in pain, but we understand we do not have to fix, judge, or attach to that pain. We have conscious choice to be in acceptance of that person's pain, and we can choose to give her communication about what's happening in her space or direct her to assistance."

~

I chew the corner of my lip. The idea of absorbing others' emotional pain and thereby making oneself sick is so far away from anything I've been taught to believe.

I make a living selling pharmaceuticals, for crying out loud!

"Is this something people, like... know about?" I sputter, remembering something I read about humans only using 18 percent of our brains.

If we used more, would it be commonplace to heal our own bodies?

"Some people are awake, yes, but I don't think the pharmaceutical companies want this type of information getting out— people being able to heal their own bodies?" He laughs at the absurdity of it. My stomach does an uneasy somersault thinking about my job.

"Can you take the pain out of *me*?" I ask skeptically.

"I can, and I've already begun to, but energy behaves very similarly to smoke, and if you don't make some changes, not long after I remove it, you'll fill your body with pain and toxic energy once again."

Shit. That's what Galen saw too.

I close my eyes and sit for a long time without speaking, and James doesn't interrupt me. My head is spinning—spiritual entourages, emotional pain becoming physical illness, healing our own bodies? For as out there as it sounds, it also somehow makes sense. I have a feeling he's trying not to overwhelm me, and that there's a lot more to it.

Finally, he asks, "Are you there?"

"I'm here. Kinda confused, but here."

"All that confusion you have, it's an illusion. Truth is easy; illusions make things complicated."

"I just don't know what I'm supposed to do about Aidan," I say, exhausted.

"Have you looked?"

"Of course, I have I looked!" I exclaim. "I have examined every angle of every scenario one hundred times over."

"I asked if you've looked, not if you have analyzed."

"Oh."

"OK, take a deep breath and close your eyes. Then pull your hands over the back of your head to clear away the energy that isn't you and ask yourself the question, 'Which way do I want to go?'"

I do as he says, but all I see is blackness.

As if on cue, he says, "If all you see is blackness, pop a couple balloons."

Oh, this fun thing again...

I pop one big black balloon after the next, in the forefront of my mind, for what feels like quite a while.

Finally, I say, disappointed, "All I see is black."

"That's OK; you are just seeing everything at once. If you keep popping balloons, you will eventually expand the energy enough to see."

Suddenly, I remember my dream. I tell James about it.

"I mean, is that symbolic of what's going on with me or what?"

"Well, there is nothing symbolic about it. The different paths you were going down were different dimensions on the astral plane. What people call sleep—which for most people means putting your head on the pillow, blackness, and waking up to a shining sun—is the time when you, as a spirit, literally go out of your physical body to the dimension that lines the planetary construct. And within the dimension that is the astral exists an infinite number of dimensions."

I've always been a vivid dreamer, filling up journals with my dreams in high school and trying to interpret them with various dream books. I had never come across this information.

"In these places, you interact with many different spirits and gain a great deal of connection and information that you then use on the physical plane as you go through your day. Where you go on the astral plane and whom you connect to can either assist or prevent you from changing and growing. You must understand all astral creations are realities. All of this dream symbology stuff really isn't worth the paper it's printed on.

"The astral plane is a lighter dimension than our dense planet. On the astral, there is no time or space. We can fly, walk on water, pass through walls, and create things instantly that the analytic mind is unable to comprehend. That death energy you experienced on the astral was you peeking into your future life with Aidan."

I let out a long, exaggerated sigh. It doesn't matter how badly I want to go back and try to fix it or change myself; I somehow know now that it's impossible. The corners of my mouth quiver slightly. With quiet certainty I say, "It's over."

"It's been over for a long time," James confirms evenly.

4.

"Ain't life grand?"
—Widespread Panic

After Aidan and I had been dating for a few months, we rented a big beachfront house in Puerto Vallarta with Courtney, Charlie, George, and George's girlfriend, Sadie, who he'd been dating on and off since they studied at Harvard. What happened there became a story Aiden and I loved to tell, and while I still think it's funny, I also find it telling in a way I didn't see at the time.

Things started out ordinarily enough. The boys ripped off their shirts and did cannon balls into the pool, and Courtney and I changed into Brazilian bikinis I'd bought us for the trip—mine cherry red, hers bubblegum pink.

When we came outside, the boys were lining up shots of tequila. Courtney hated tequila, due to an incident freshman year of high school, but she bravely downed the shot, and then let out a little shriek. I could tell she was trying not to gag as she did a running leap into the pool.

A few hours later, Aidan and I anchored ourselves by the edge of the pool, watching the bright orange sun sink into the horizon. Pink and purple clouds were scattered across the sky. With margaritas melting in our hands and our toes intertwined underwater, I couldn't have been happier. And from the look on his face, I knew for certain he felt the same way.

We were talking about what to name our future pet. "Steve," he said seriously, "for a dog." His lisp grew more pronounced when he drank. Contrasted with his physical strength and the fact that he rarely showed vulnerability, it was the most endearing thing I'd ever heard. "Steve or Mustache. I just like saying the word, muuuuuustaaaache."

"I like hotdog for a dog and—"

"Oooh and Gene for a cat!" he cut me off excitedly. "Hello, have you met my cat, Geeeeene?" Looking at his tan, chiseled jaw and full red lips, I was baffled at how I wasn't interested in him in the beginning. As he kissed me on the lips, shivers ran down my legs.

"Where's George?" Charlie interrupted. "They were just here a second ago. Or maybe that was an hour ago..."

Suddenly we heard the hum of a diesel engine and painfully loud Mexican radio blaring from the driveway. In walked George, cigarette hanging from his lopsided grin, beer bottles shoved in both sides of his cargo shorts. His Hawaiian-style shirt was off just a button, and a mane of wild, dark chest hair sprouted out the top. A big white plastic shopping bag hung from his arm. Sadie trailed awkwardly behind him.

"Hey, bro, where'd you go?" Charlie asked.

"I had to go... you know... pick up some odds and ends."

"Odds and ends, huh?"

George laid out his purchases: three cans of chew, one packet of carne seca (half eaten), a mini carton of chicle (watermelon flavor), four packs of smokes, a lighter shaped like a pelican wearing sunglasses, one tube of Zinka (yellow), a book of crossword puzzles (en Español), two Mexican nudie mags.

"That's quite a collection of odd and ends, George," I said, stealing a glance at Sadie, who seemed completely oblivious to, well, just about everything. He was sporting a new pair of mirrored shades with the price tag still hanging from the bridge.

"Those are the ends," he mumbled, "these are the odds," and pulled a small white bag from his pocket.

"Me gusta la farm-meeee-seeeecia!" Aidan sang as he did a perfect back flip into the pool. Inside the bag was a smorgasbord of pharmaceuticals. There were white ones in a blister pack, pink ones in a bottle, and a handful of blue ones rattling around loose.

"Vhat to ve have here..." Charlie leaned in.

"The white ones are Xanax, the pink, Somas, and the blue, well, just trust me with the blue ones." And that we did. With an illusion of invincibility born of youth or stupidity, we each popped a blue pill into our mouths. Courtney put "Mexico" on the radio, and we all sang along.

It was dark when I suggested we go skinny-dipping in the ocean. The idea was not greeted enthusiastically. Courtney and Charlie looked extremely cozy in the hammock as they chatted with Sean, Aidan's friend from Seattle, who coincidently was staying down the road. George and Sadie floated in the pool, deep in conversation.

"Let's go in a little while," Aidan said with a wan smile.

∾

Drunk, high, and determined, I skipped off toward some rocks I'd seen earlier. They jutted out to a point, creating a sort of lagoon where the water appeared to stand perfectly still, like a big basin of black paint. The moon hung low, casting an inviting light.

I slid my clothes off and dove in. The water was cooler than I anticipated, and it sobered me up a bit. I did a few butterfly strokes to warm up, then pressed my legs together, shimmying like a mermaid through the dense water. I heard a loud splash; Aidan had joined me.

"I knew you'd come to your senses!" I grinned triumphantly.

He swam over and spouted water in my face.

"Hi, Nerd!" he teased playfully.

I wrapped my legs around his waist. He treaded water, holding me up for a few moments, before I propped myself up on his thighs and attempted a back flip, but only managed a back flop. We played around for a while, and then floated on our backs looking up at the peaceful sky.

Suddenly, a rogue wave nearly four feet high crashed on top of us, driving us into the rocks.

"What the hell?" Aidan exclaimed. "These rocks are fucking sharp!" As I tried to grab hold of them, I realized they had spiky, jagged edges.

Aidan was making some headway at the tip of the point, so I doggie paddled over.

"Ow! These aren't rocks; they're sea urchins!" Aidan shouted as he fell backwards into the ocean.

He extended his hand to look at it in the moonlight. Five needle-like spines stuck three to four inches out of it. Treading water, he grabbed one of them and yanked it out.

"Oh, shit. This is not good. They're pronged."

"What does that mean?"

"It means they break off inside your hand when you try and pull them out."

Before I could respond, another wave slammed us up against the rocks. I could now see all of the black spiny sea urchins standing at attention, their slumber interrupted by the waves.

"OK, we are just going to have to suck it up and go for it," he said. "I'll go first and then help you up." His face was twisted in intense concentration as he pulled himself up. I treaded water silently.

"Are you OK?" I called when he reached the top.

"Yeah, but it's even worse up here. They are everywhere! C'mon, hurry!" he said, dancing back and forth, trying not to put too much weight on one foot. Another wave slammed me into the wall of rocks.

"Help!" I tried to protect my face from making contact. My entire right side was stinging. I realized I might get seriously hurt. Aidan hobbled over.

"Grab my arm, up high, by the crease!" he ordered.

Exhausted from treading water and from partying for so long, I mustered all of my strength to reach as high as I could. He clasped his hand around my wrist and hoisted me out of the water.

We had no choice but to cross the carpet of urchins back to the casa. Our friends' jaws dropped when they caught sight of our bloody, shivering bodies punctured by urchin spindles.

"Omigod," Courtney cried, "what happened?"

My teeth were chattering loudly, and every part of my body stung. I could only nod.

"Urchins," Aidan explained.

Someone brought us towels, and everyone started talking at once. Courtney ushered me into our casita and gingerly laid me down on the bed.

I had at least twenty spines in each hand, mostly the plump palm area, but in my fingers too. There was even one under my middle fingernail. No part of my body was spared. We counted sixty, then stopped counting.

Courtney fussed over me. We decided Xanax would help dull the stinging pain. Courtney went to work with a pair of tweezers, but she soon learned about the prongs. Aidan waddled in, stepping delicately with urchin-laden feet, and announced that he and George were heading to the farmacia to get help. I laid my head back and closed my eyes as Courtney tried digging them out with a safety pin.

I must've drifted off because the next thing I knew, Aidan awoke me saying there was no antidote. We'd have to go to the hospital.

"Seriously?" I sat up, immediately realized it was way too painful, and flopped back down.

"Litul." Courtney was using our shared nickname from high school, when we were the smallest girls in our class.

Heavily drugged, I tried to open my eyes.

"We need to get you dressed for the hospital. You've been sleeping for a couple hours."

"Really? What's Aidan doing?"

"He's been doing blow and taking tequila shots for the last hour to... uh, to dull the pain," she said with a half-smile.

"Will you help me get ready, Litul? I need to take a shower and wash this blood off. It's kinda freaking me out." The blood mixed with the sea salt had made rusty brown, vein-like pathways down my body. I tried to stand up, but the pain was piercing, and I crumbled to the floor like a puppet that had lost its puppeteer.

Courtney propped me up and helped me into the shower. I was fading in an out of consciousness, and the last thing I remember saying was, "Litul, promise me you will dress me in something nice for the hospital?"

"I promise, Litul."

~

I awoke to excruciating pain. I looked down to the end of the operating table to see three people speaking in hurried Spanish and stabbing the bottoms of my feet with what must've been miniature knives.

"Agggghhhhhh!!! Dolor, dolor," I moaned, trying to remember the Spanish words for, "Stop that right now!" Tears streamed down my face. I went to wipe them away, and my hand hit plastic.

Courtney had put sunglasses on me. And a bright orange visor. And a bikini and a tank top and a jean skirt. In spite of the pain, somewhere in my head I heard my mom saying, "Always wear nice underwear just in case you have to go to the hospital." Why I was more embarrassed by my get-up than by our drunken and drugged-out states still remains a mystery.

A woman came in with a long skinny needle, rolled me over, and inserted it into my butt, all business. A warm sensation slowly spread through my body until finally the stabbing in my feet began to dull. Then panic set in.

Uh... so that needle was sterilized, right?

All of a sudden, I remembered Aidan.

"Mi novio, mi novio… donde esta mi novio?" I asked with alarm.

A few minutes later, somebody rolled Aidan in on a wheelchair. He was passed out, a wide piece of gauze wrapped around his head, which slumped to the side. His hands and feet were covered in gauze, too.

"Aidan!" I shouted, ripping off my glasses.

He tried to lift his head, but managed only to open one googly eye and looked at me like he'd never seen me before and had no interest in knowing me. I demanded to know what kind of painkillers they'd given him. They told me they hadn't given either one of us painkillers when we showed up, because we were "feelin' no pain."

I wanted to leave, urgently. I sat up and used my arms to help swing my legs off the table, saying, "Necesitamos salir pronto," motioning to a non-existent watch on my wrist. They objected; I insisted. They wrapped my feet in gauze before I padded down the long hallway, pushing Aidan in his wheelchair. A nurse ran after me and stuffed my flip-flops in the pouch on the side of the chair.

"Gracias," I mumbled. We didn't make it very far before I stopped, overheated and trailing a long strand of gauze. Aidan had a pool of drool at the corner of his mouth.

A guy with a thin black mustache, a pristine white one-piece and matching cap, and a .45 caliber in a holster approached us. I had him pegged as something between a nurse and a security guard. He motioned us into a room, "a descansar." Utterly exhausted, I rationalized that we could rest here for a while.

The room had two single beds. I positioned Aidan's wheelchair between them so we could be near each other and laid down.

After about thirty minutes, the door was flung open, and Sean burst in, a la Kramer from Seinfeld.

"How did you know we were here?" I asked.

"I was the only one sober enough to get you guys here last night," he said breathlessly.

"Thanks," I said with a sheepish smile.

"We have to get you out of here. You're getting charged two-hundred and fifty dollars an hour for this room!"

Two-hundred and fifty dollars an hour was *not* in the budget. I sprang into action.

"Wake up!" I shouted, shaking Aidan. "We have to go!"

He was completely out, so I did something I'd seen in cartoons: I threw a glass of cold water in his face. He lurched awake, confused and angry, then closed his eyes again.

Sean pushed his wheelchair into the bathroom and positioned the showerhead directly over him, which worked immediately. We hobbled to the front desk, where we were handed a bill for two thousand five hundred dollars.

"I thought we didn't even get any pain medication?" I protested in Spanish.

"Forget it. Let's get the hell out of here." Aidan threw his credit card down on the desk. A few minutes later, gauze trailing behind us, we walked outside into the blistering afternoon sun.

5.

"Sometimes, sometimes
You just have to walk away—
Walk away... and head for the door"
                                    —Ben Harper

Back in Los Angeles, a couple of weeks after seeing James, I wake with a start and push my sleeping mask up onto my forehead to see the clock—6:58 a.m. Four hours... not bad, considering my average has been around three for the past few months.

I get up and grab an inside-out tee shirt from the mounting pile of clothes on the chair. As I turn it right side out, I see it's one that Aidan gave me during our first year together.

～

On the Venice boardwalk we'd come upon two girls, probably nine or ten, having a yard sale. They actually had some pretty good stuff: the original *Light Bright* set, a *Pretty-Cut-and-Grow* doll, and a *Hungry Hippo Game*. I saw one of those bouncy balls from a machine at the supermarket. It was in a Ziploc baggy with a bendy straw, a key, a pickle flavored scratch and sniff sticker, a feather, and a barrette. When we asked to buy the bouncy ball, they looked at the baggie, then at each other, and then at us. The one handling the cash box flicked one of her long brown braids behind her back and said matter-of-factly, "You can't break up the kit."

"But we don't want all the other stuff, and someone else might really want, no wait, *need,* a pickle scratch-and-sniff sticker and a key that goes to nothing," I angled.

She sighed and repeated, "I can't break up the kit." Aidan and I exchanged amused glances: Why were these little girls refusing to break up the "kit?"

Did they have some amazing business plan that ensured a big pay day if they kept the kit together?

We offered them three dollars, the price of the whole baggie, for the ball alone; they stood firm. In the end, we bought the entire kit. They handled the transaction with no emotion, like steely entrepreneurs hardened from years of doing business. We bounced that little ball down the boardwalk, laughing our heads off.

A few days later, I received a FedEx package containing a large Ziploc bag filled with the following things:

> *A glow-in-the-dark pencil sharpener*
> *A token to a public bathroom*
> *A calling card with 1,000 prepaid minutes on it*
> *A tee shirt that said "Balloonists Do It Better"*
> *One of those red fortune-telling fish*
> *A pill of ecstasy*
> *A mix CD called "A KIT OF SONGS"*
> *The baggie was labeled "Kit" in black sharpie.*

Enclosed was also a note, which said:

Under NO circumstances can you break apart this kit.
Your Prince, Aidan.

I pull the "Balloonists Do It Better" tee shirt over my head and pad into the kitchen, once again berating myself for screwing things up.

∼

The morning is clear, and the view is stunning, but my heart is so heavy, it feels like it might slip down through the floorboards into the condo below.

With nothing better to do, I decide to give this whole running-positive-energy-through-my-body thing a try. I perch on the couch and plant my feet firmly on the floor. I close my eyes and imagine roots running from my feet deep into the center of the Earth, just as James instructed. My mind wanders, wondering what Aidan might be doing. My eyes fling open, and I go to adjust the curtains.

What the hell am I doing? Sitting alone in my house imagining things. Get a grip, girl.

Standing at the window, I graze my finger across my forehead, thinking back to my visit to San Francisco.

It was real. That bump was real.

James made it sound so easy. "Just sit down for a few minutes and imagine running a bright color through your body. Pull the powerful planetary energy up from the Earth."

I give it another try. I take a deep breath, and with great intention place each foot on the carpet. I take a few more breaths, and this time pull my hands over the top of my head, a step that I forgot the first time. Once again, I try to envision roots attached to the bottoms of my feet. I don't let them out of my sight as they penetrate the Earth's crust, spiraling down through the many layers of dense, dark soil into a big fiery orange ball at the center of the planet. I keep my eyes closed tightly, and my body silent, for fear even the slightest nudge will thrust me back into my lonely living room.

I focus on breathing as the roots transport this brilliant energy up from the Earth's core and into my body. I coax it up through the balls of my feet, through my veins and the membranes in my knees, and up to my first energy center—my root chakra. James told me that I had very dark, dense energy throughout my body, but it was especially dense in my first energy center, right between my legs.

After a few minutes, I get restless and hurry the energy through the rest of my body and up to my head. Then, holding my hands an inch apart, I visualize green inside my hands, because green is supposed to be healing, and say out loud, "I'm a beginner of life, giving myself permission to be and to heal," before pulling it into my heart.

I try and assess if I feel any different. I think I do. I at least feel better enough to get out of my pajamas and go get an overpriced latte. Driving to Washington St., I flip on the radio, and that song "Down Under" by Men at Work is just starting. I roll all my windows down and sing along, trying to mirror their accent.

"Traveling in a fried-out combie

On a hippie trail head full of zombie..."

I don't understand the Australian slang, but nonetheless, by the time I get to the coffee shop, my sprits have lifted considerably, and brewing in my head is the idea that the only way to get over Aidan is to get out of Los Angeles. Seeing as we have all the same friends, I see no hope of us successfully breaking things off otherwise. Australia, with its sunshine, surf, and location on the other side of the planet, seems perfect.

My mind starts churning, trying to figure out how to get past three big obstacles: I can't afford to quit my job; I have an apartment full of stuff; I don't know anyone in Australia.

I have always been happiest and most confident when traveling. Over the next few days all I can think about is Australia. I spend hours on the internet researching the best surf spots and daydreaming about all of the hot Australian guys who'll help distract me from the dull pain in my heart

As I'm walking out of Barnes and Noble with three guidebooks, my co-worker Janis calls, wondering why I didn't show up at our lunch meeting today.

I've been doing my best to keep my problems private, but now all of the secrets I've been bottling up come pouring out. That Aidan and I are on the verge of breaking up for good; we are having a trial separation right now and have been living in different houses for two months. I'm sobbing so hard, I can barely get out that I'm sorry I completely spaced the lunch meeting. When this is met with a long silence, I think maybe we've been disconnected.

"Janis?"

"You might want to think about going on disability," she suggests thoughtfully.

"Disability?" I repeat. "What do you mean?"

"You know, *disability*," she says again, slower and louder.

"How does that work, exactly?"

"It's designed for people like you who are going through some really hard stuff and need time to get your life back together. Although you aren't technically married, it's essentially like you're going through a divorce. You're totally justified in going on disability."

"Really?"

"Really. Plus, you've been killing it for this company for five years. They should be understanding when one of their best employees is having a mental breakdown."

"I suppose I kind of *am* having a mental breakdown," I say more to myself than to Janis.

And then it all comes together extremely easily: I find a psychiatrist on my insurance company's website and make an appointment for the next morning. I guess I really do look as haggard as I feel because without much more than a rendition of a recent panic attack, I get the doctor's recommendation to take a couple of months off for stress leave and a fresh prescription for Xanax.

Three days later, after another formidable battle with insomnia, which I finally won by popping that trusty pill at 3:00 a.m., I wake to my phone buzzing around on my wooden nightstand. It's Amber from work, one of my few friends in LA outside of my crew with Aidan.

"What time is it?"

"It's almost two. I just finished a lunch at Kierinian's office, and I'm heading out to Malibu to meet Robert and Scott. Want to come?"

I offer a weak excuse, but Amber says, "Come on! It'll be fun... or err, interesting at least."

"What does that mean?"

"Well, I guess Scott and Carrie are really on the rocks this time, and Scott hasn't been home in three days. He is holed up in their Malibu place with some bisexual Australian chick."

Did someone just say, Australian chick?

"Now that you mention it, I suppose I should get up." I open the curtains to a perfect blue sky. "And it certainly is a nice day for Malibu."

Within forty-five minutes, I'm drinking a mojito on Scott's deck overlooking the water and willing the sun to stay high in the January sky. Scott is playing bartender and looks like he hasn't slept in days, and a saucy blonde with huge fake breasts, who everyone is calling "the Australian," seems like she's known Scott for years even though I'm pretty sure they just met a couple days ago. When I tell her that I'm thinking about going to Australia for a few months, Scott drunkenly tells her my whole sob story.

"Love, you need to call Julian," she declares. "He's a great person to know down there."

"Who's Julian?"

"He's my ex. And if you are trying to get over a breakup, he's the *perfect* person to show you around Sydney. I wouldn't recommend him as a long-term thing, but he's fun for a little while."

"I think that's Ellsworth's friend," Amber chimes in.

"Ellsworth? Oh yeah, they are great friends," the Australian confirms.

"He told me that he was going to put you two in touch. I just forgot to tell you," Amber continues.

A friend! OK, well, maybe I'm getting a little ahead of myself... a mutual friend. Someone I can at least ask to just point me in the right direction!

Later that night, with the party in full swing, the Australian barrels into the bathroom and asks me if I want to do a "Stevie Nicks" with her.

"What's a Stevie Nicks?"

"You don't know what a *Stevie Nicks* is, Love? Well, ya know Stevie did so much coke that her docs told her nose was going to fall off. So she hired a guy to go on tour with her and blow it up her asshole."

"*What*?! That can't be true."

"Oh, it's a fact. So ya up for it?"

Everyone has a line, and *apparently*, this is mine. "Uh, no... I'm not really into that kind of thing," and excuse myself to get a drink.

In the kitchen, Amber says under her breath, "Scott and the Australian have been up to some kinky shit over the past few days. There's no way he can go back to Carrie now."

"Uh, yeah. Have you ever heard of a Stevie Nicks?"

"A Stevie Nicks?" she questions, her eyes quizzical.

"Well, if she asks you if you want to do one, the right answer is no."

"What is it?"

As I whisper the definition of my new slang term, her green eyes open wide before we both burst out laughing.

"I can't wait to hear about this Julian dude."

"You're telling me."

The following morning, I email Julian and receive a polite response the same day. He says Ellsworth had already talked to him about me and insists I stay with him for the first couple of days. Seeing as I have no plan, this sounds *amazing*. I decide to book my ticket. I can figure out something to do with my stuff.

Who knows? Maybe I just won't come back...

6.

*"Oh I hate you some, I hate you some,
I love you some... I love you, when
I forget about me"* —Joni Mitchell

I could never pinpoint the exact infraction I committed to change things between Aidan and I, but I'd certainly followed the crumbs of old conversations in search of anything to help me understand why he was once so madly in love with me and then suddenly began to pull away. I was convinced if I could just figure out where I went wrong, I could go back and fix it.

Was it when I told him that I wanted more affection or didn't want to party every single weekend? Maybe it was when I suggested that we figure out when the super-noisy street cleaners come to his house so we could sleep at mine the night before?

You would've thought I asked him to wear a tracking device.

"I'm not going to be on any type of schedule!" he fired back.

He'd never raised his voice like that with me before. We'd been spending nearly every night at each other's houses anyway, so I didn't understand his reaction.

Whatever the problem, it went down around the time he sold his first company and started his second. He was creating something that didn't yet exist on the internet on such a grand scale, and as the chief technology officer, the pressure was on him to deliver. This meant fifteen-hour days and tremendous stress that manifested in severe headaches and thoughts of giving up. When the weekend rolled around, he wanted to party and blow off steam. Our greater group expanded beyond Los Angeles, up to San Francisco and out to the mountain ranges of Colorado. When this collection of friends came together it was like New Year's Eve, Fourth of July, and Halloween all landed on the same day.

Everyone seemed to abide by the motto: work hard; party harder. We hit the slopes of the Rockies and Sierras, rocked out on front row to our favorite bands, floated down the Truckee River in Lake Tahoe, bet big in Vegas, and partied our way through Europe, Mexico, Hawaii, San Francisco, and Los Angeles for countless birthdays, weddings, and holidays, always enhanced with wigs, fake teeth, accents, alter-ego names, and, of course, the P.B. MAX: pot, blow, mushrooms, alcohol, ecstasy, and, of course, Xanax for when the off switch finally needed to be flipped. The guys were mostly whip-smart, successful tech entrepreneurs who shared an unapologetically inappropriate sense of humor. Not one person played an instrument, but we raged like debaucherous rockstars with little regard for tomorrow.

When we were all together, I never loved being with Aidan more. He'd be witty and ridiculous—in a wonderful way: pulling off a flawless "worm" in the middle of the cement dance floor in Tuscany with an entire wedding cheering him on, cracking jokes, and charming people with childhood stories about his cat, Wonder Woman, and her nephew, George. *A cat with a nephew?* Yes, of course, Aidan had one. But the thing I loved most was when were all out together, he said that he "loved having me by his side." During those moments, when he'd spin me around on the dance floor, ending with a dramatic dip and "movie star kiss," I let myself get wrapped in the illusion of the performance that we were putting on, believing that we were indeed perfect together.

Those nights we were a team, a unit, a tribe creating a world of amusement and adventure for ourselves that I suppose we believed didn't exist without drugs and alcohol. With our walls and insecurities stripped away, we danced freely, laughed hysterically, and showed affection openly. Our raucous behavior and inside jokes sanctioned an illusion of elitism and invincibility. Even chaos and danger (Chapter 4, urchins) spawned war stories that entertained us year after year. In manipulating our plane of reality so we could all have the same experience, we formed a bond so tight that when the sun started to rise, and the first person called it quits, it seemed painfully traumatic—like we were losing a decorated member of our platoon. It didn't matter that I was putting my well-being at risk; in my mind Aidan, Charlie, Courtney, and George were my family, and with them I had a sense of security and family I'd longed for my entire life.

Oddly enough, during that time, I worked harder at my job and exercised more than I ever had or have since. I must've instinctually felt the need to flush my body of the toxins I consumed during the weekends. And I justified, as long as I could put on that suit come Monday morning, pay the bills, and exercise, who was I really hurting? Never once did it occur to me that I was slaying my precious adrenal glands or that truly happy people do not destroy themselves on the weekend in the name of fun.

Despite Aidan slipping away from me emotionally, I still felt an almost primal connection with him. I suppose the feeling was mutual because from time to time, I would catch him staring at me, and he'd muse softly, "I want to breed you." Creepy, perhaps, but with his self-professed religion being science, I registered it as the highest of compliments. Aidan made me feel like if an asteroid pummeled the planet, or a tsunami hit, he would somehow be able to keep us safe. So we clamored along, our sharp edges grinding into one another, but come Friday, the party lubricated our disjointed relationship and once again we'd gel happily together.

As the weekend came to a close, and we found ourselves alone, it was as if sharp wind blew in, rattling its way through our relationship, causing him to withdraw. When I tried to talk about "us," he'd say everything he was doing was for "us" and our future together. He'd say I was creating a problem where there wasn't one. I started to believe that I was hormonal and literally crazy, making things up in my head.

How could there be so many problems when he says things are fine?

I rationalized that he wouldn't get so jealous of my talking to other guys if he didn't care so much.

I'd beat myself up for being too needy and wanting too much affection. It isn't normal to say I love you every day, and it's *ridiculous* for me to want to hold hands when we walk down the street or cuddle when we are going to sleep. I grew envious of my emotionally detached girlfriends, positive that they who wanted less connection were better off than I.

Even though our relationship had become a deeply lonely place for me, somewhere along the line, I got so dependent on being a couple and loved being a part of our group of friends so much, and I was willing to do anything to keep us together. I was in too deep; I was Augustus Gloop in the chocolate river, without Wonka, or anyone else, to point out that I have nobody to blame but myself.

Early in our relationship, which coincided with the beginning of my pharmaceutical career, I experienced real difficulty getting out of bed, lacking the motivation to complete even the most basic professional tasks. I confided in Aidan that I might be depressed because deep down I knew pharmaceutical sales wasn't my purpose, and I desperately wanted to discover what my purpose was. He laughed it off, saying, "That's all bullshit. Your life's purpose is to contribute to the economy and have fun."

"I think I need to go explore the world and find what matters to me," I insisted. But, like a skilled interrogator who knows his victim's weakness, he presented a different proposal: "I have a better idea. Why don't you give me a couple of years, and then we can travel around the world on a private jet and see the world in style?"

This is when warning bells should have rung loudly, drowning out such an extravagant scheme. Instead, I folded like a communist being offered a US passport, silenced my inner voice, and threw myself into selling pharmaceuticals, gleaning whatever satisfaction I could from being number one. Meanwhile, my identity floated unceremoniously off into the smoggy sky.

As our relationship continued to fray, and I voiced concern, he assured me that he was just stressed at work and once the company sold, we'd go on our year-long trip around the world, starting with a road trip across the US, ending in NYC where we'd kick off our adventure by breaking the sound barrier on the Concord. This inevitably prompted a stubborn case of the "when we's."

When we move in together, away from the influences of his rowdy roommates, then we'll be happy. When Aidan sells his company, and we go on our trip, then we'll be happy. When we get married, then we will be happy.

I pressed for us to move in together, and he rented us a gorgeous, minimalist-style penthouse condo on the Marina Peninsula, with high ceilings and unobstructed views of the beach. Unfortunately, the Brazil nut hardwood floors, sun decks, and brand-new Viking appliances couldn't bring us closer, but they did make it more difficult to imagine a life without him. I dove into the role of woman of the house, laboring over elaborate dinners and getting up early to make him breakfast before work, because acting like someone's mother is surely going to make him love you more.

I hadn't even changed my address with the DMV before one thing became crystal clear. Like all bright lights, Aidan had an "off" switch. I'd seen traces of it before, but it wasn't until we lived together that I witnessed how extreme it was. If you were lucky enough to be in his company when he was "on"— a mode reserved for friends, business associates, or people he wanted to impress—you got the double-double with the works and the secret special sauce: engaging and witty conversation, affection, lots of laughter, spontaneity, an exhilarating sense of connection.

On the flip side, if you are in the vicinity when he was "off," a mode only reserved for people he feels extremely comfortable with— namely his mom and dad, and me—you would find a restless and aloof man in search of the next party, shiny toy, or high-voltage activity, preferably involving high-powered machinery or scoring touchdowns, to make him feel alive again.

I'd beg him, "I want the Aidan that you give to all of our friends! Where does he go when he walks into this house?"

Every once and a while I could see the gears in his brain shifting and churning my words, but it only pushed him further away.

At times all of the hurt and rage I'd been swallowing would erupt, leading to a rip-roaring, sometimes embarrassingly public fight. Then I'd wake up tear stained and dehydrated, gushing remorse and begging for his forgiveness, when on the inside I was still pissed as hell over his rejection.

Other times it was the thread that seemed to stitch us back together because then I got *nice* Aidan back, no matter that it was a complete illusion with an impending expiration date. Back in the dejection of the work week, sitting on opposite sides of the couch, I would run on the memory of our drug-fueled promises like a car on its last drop of oil.

I don't know if he'd always had these two very different personas, or if they were exacerbated by our lifestyle. And, although I did little to discourage partying with two P's, as we liked to say, on a couple occasions I suggested that perhaps all the partying was the culprit of his irritability, and our lack of connection, but was met every time with, "I'm fine. I'm great, actually."

"In fact, I think that the drugs are making me smarter," he concluded with that shit-eating grin. And seeing as he was the CTO of one of the most groundbreaking companies to ever hit the internet, I had little evidence to combat his claim.

7.

"You can take a trip to China
or take a boat to Spain,
Take a blue canoe around the world
and never come back again,
But traveling don't change a thing,
it only makes it worse,
Unless the trip you take is in
to change your cruel course,
'Cause every town's got a mirror and
every mirror still shows me that I am
my own ragged company"
—Grace Potter

Curled up in my window seat, ready to take off for Sydney,
I can't remember ever being so happy at the beginning of
a fourteen-hour flight. The events of the past few weeks have
left me mentally and physically exhausted, and the idea of

popping a Xanax and waking up across the world is extremely appealing.

I'm barely fazed when a three-hundred-pound man sinks down next to me, oozing into my chair. I've shrunk so much that I fit in the seat like a lone jellybean in a big ol' jar.

Despite my fragility, I feel strangely powerful, bordering on a little out of my mind that, in a three weeks' time, I managed to: get a leave of absence from work, move all of my stuff into Amber's basement, officially end things with Aidan, and find a contact in Australia.

～

My heart throbs heavily in my chest, thinking about how just few hours earlier, I walked from Quarterdeck Street to Anchorage Street, happy for once to have seventeen blocks between me and the inevitable. My stomach swirled as I punched the code into the gate and walked down the narrow pathway to the side door into the kitchen.

The house we were supposed to move into together. The house we spent months searching for and many long hours working with the designer to remodel.

As I waited for him to come to the door, I knew that I'd never live there. Aidan greeted me with a quick hug, and I suggested we walk down to the beach. I couldn't bear setting foot in the house.

We fell into stride together as we headed for the beach.

"It's windy today," he said finally, filling the silence. We both knew what was coming. No matter how hard we both tried in our own ways, we were broken beyond repair.

"Yeah, it is," I agree softly.

Wind of change.

We sat on a bench at the edge of the sand facing the street, because it was too windy to face the water. February's muted sun warmed our backs.

"I want you to know that I love you so much," I started, taking his hand in mine, and for the first time in a very long time, he didn't shrug it off. "And it breaks my heart to say this, but I think that we both feel like we won't ever be able to make each other happy."

Relieved that he didn't have to be the one to actually verbalize it, he nodded his head and said, "I understand."

"I moved everything out of our place. I'm going to Australia tonight," I said, fighting back tears, sounding way more confident than I felt.

"Wow, really?" he said, raising his eyebrows in surprise. "For how long?"

"I'm not sure."

After that there really wasn't much more to say. We walked back to the house and clutched each other tightly in the middle of the street with the wind kicking up sand and dust and gravel all around us. I nuzzled my head into his red sweatshirt, wishing more than anything that it wasn't the end. When we finally pulled apart, we both had tears in our eyes.

"Bye," I said softy, squeezing his hands gently.

"Bye," he echoed. "Be good."

Sure... whatever that means.

As I headed back past the alphabetized streets, tears streaming my face, I blamed him for pushing me away and blamed myself for being someone he wanted to push away. The tall buildings blocked the sun, and the wind whipped down the corridor. When I got to Fleet Street, fear began to set in, and

I wanted to run back and say it was all a terrible mistake; let's give it one more try. But my feet kept moving. Past Hurricane, Ironsides, Jib, until I reached our nearly empty place. Empty except for an envelope on the counter with my name written in Aidan's handwriting. I must have just missed him. I didn't spend much time considering how he could have gotten there before me because inside I found a birthday card with a picture of a cat on it, and a check for $25,000.

~

"Make sure your seat belts are fastened low and tight across your lap," a female's voice interrupts my memory as I cocoon myself in fleece blanket.

~

In a moment of hot rage, I held the check in my shaking hands and almost did rip it up. *If you think $25,000 is going to absolve you from five and a half years of lies and broken promises, think again, buddy.* But then a line from a song that Arah used to sing popped into my head:

"Sy and I went to the circus; we hit with a rolling pin. We got even with that circus; we bought tickets, but never went in."

So, I pushed my ego aside and carefully folded the check and put it in my pocket, reminding myself that I could, in fact, really use the cash.

~

"Flight attendants, prepare for take-off."

I secure my sleeping mask and wait for the Xanax to beckon me into oblivion.

"We are nearing sixty miles outside of Sydney International Airport," a woman's voice, tart with an Aussie twang, wrestles me out of my slumber. I push my sleeping mask onto my forehead and turn to the large man who I've apparently been sharing a seat with and ask, "Did she just say that we are landing soon?" My throat is so parched, I sound like a frog with bad laryngitis.

"We're 'bout thurdee minutes out, lil' laydee," he chirps. "I'd say you've been taking a bit of a serious snooze this flight."

It's mostly great that I've slept for nearly the whole flight, but it's left me no time to mentally prepare for disembarking on an entirely different continent with zero game plan aside from spending the first couple nights with some bisexual Aussie girl's ex-model ex-boyfriend. During our brief conversation, he was very polite and nice. But since I've never met a male model before, all I can picture is Ben Stiller in *Zoolander.*

My head still foggy from the Xanax, I feel like I'm floating off the 747 and through customs.

"Passport and immigration form, please," says a pretty, twenty-something blonde woman. Then her ice-blue eyes widen. "You're going to Vaulcluuuse?"

"Yeah," I say uncertainly, "I've never been there before; I'm staying with a friend."

"Vaulcluse just happens to be one of the nicest neighborhoods in all of Australia."

"Really?"

"Very fancy. Have a g'day!"

Out on the curb, I immediately find a taxi. It's impeccably clean.

"Vaulcluse..." The cabdriver raises his eyebrows obviously impressed.

What is this place?

I roll the window down. The warm ocean air blows wildly through my hair. To our left, little white boats bob around Sydney's beautiful harbor. Fluffy pom-pom-like leaves perched atop long, spindly trunks sway side to side like characters in a Dr. Seuss book. I feel far, far away.

"Now we're heading into Rose Bay, Miss," my driver says. People sit at outdoor cafes under colorful umbrellas. Everything is perfect and clean, like a movie set.

We take a sharp, vertical turn away from the water. The houses get bigger as we climb. We reach a cul-de-sac near the top of the hill and stop in front of a huge wrought iron gate and a long steep driveway snaking around a cluster of trees.

I pay and get buzzed into the gate. Halfway up the driveway, the house comes into view. It's enormous—three stories with huge windows and a lush garden of magenta flowers and a big fountain in front. I reach the top, and my breath catches in my throat as I look out to unobstructed views of Rose Bay, the Opera House, and the elegant Harbor Bridge.

A tiny woman named Ming ushers me into a grand entry-way filled with colorful modern art. She says Julian will be back from his golf game in several hours. I follow her up a grand stairwell, two floors up, and down a long hallway, where she motions to a steep spiral staircase.

I open the door into a spacious corner suite with long panoramic windows with an even more grandiose view than from the driveway. Awed by my surroundings, I rinse off and then fall asleep.

A few hours later, Ming knocks to tell me she's leaving. I quickly dress and head downstairs to look around. The living room is formal, with spotless silk couches and a big mahogany table in the corner covered in photographs. I kneel down and scour the photos with the intensity of a homicide detective combing through suspects. There's one guy who's front and center in almost every frame; that must be Julian. He's attractive, with dark skin and defined features—totally my type. But all of the pictures seem like he's at a costume party.

Do they have Halloween in Australia?

He's wearing tank tops with bright patterns, tight leather pants, speedos, excessive hair gel, and even eyeliner in some of them.

I keep wandering, stopping short when I see a shiny silvery stripper pole in the middle of the great room. It's out of place in the light, airy space, like a tattoo on a child's body.

Eyeliner and stripper poles... what have I gotten myself into? Is "male model" code for porn star?

I pass through some ceiling-high glass doors into the huge, flawlessly manicured backyard. Sitting at the edge of the enormous pool, I marvel at how yesterday I said goodbye to the past five years with Aidan and now I'm at a stranger's house in Australia. When I hear the crunch of tires in the driveway, I'm filled with panic.

Flying through the house, I scamper up the stairs two at a time. I don't know why; I guess I don't want to look like I'm getting *too* comfy already.

The sound of his little dust-mop dogs gathering at the door to greet him ricochets through the house.

"Mila, you sexy thing you, and Gucc, where's your boll ol'man?"

I start down the stairs. "Julian?"

"Emily!" he calls warmly.

As we hug hello, I feel his contoured muscles underneath his piqué polo shirt.

"Thank you, again, so much, for letting me stay!"

"Of course! You're coming from the opposite side of the planet; you need to have a comfortable place to get your bearings for the first few days," he says with a wink. With his deep tan and boyish charm, he's like the love child of Ronaldo Cristiano and young Robert Downey Jr.

"Well, I do appreciate it very much."

"I'm going to shower up, and then my sister and her kids are coming by for a barbecue this afternoon. I don't know if you have anything planned or if you would like to join us?"

"That sounds great. I'd love to join you, thank you," I say, a little confused by how this nice, normal guy in golf clothes wears eyeliner and has a stripper pole in his living room, but I decide it doesn't matter.

About an hour later, his sister, her boyfriend, and her four children show up and begin splashing around in the pool. Julian is obviously close with them.

We barbecue chicken and drink a beer called Toohey's, and when I inquire where the Foster's is, everyone laughs and tells me Australians don't drink Foster's.

Julian and I dangle our feet in the deep end. I learn that he's of Armenian descent, he transitioned from model to real estate developer, spends winters in Ibiza, and the only thing he loves more than golf are his two dogs, who he won custody of from a past relationship.

I tell him I've just ended a relationship and am looking for peace of mind and hopefully some good waves. After a couple beers, I say teasingly, "I was admiring your pole in the living room."

"Oh, that..." he says, his cheeks turning pink. A friend of mine installed that as a joke for my birthday present."

"Does it get a lot of use?"

"Oh, here and there," he says nonchalantly, the corners of his mouth curling playfully.

When Julian invites me out with him and his friends in Kings Cross later that night, I happily accept. Julian takes forever to get ready. Finally, at 10:30 p.m., the guy from the photographs comes downstairs in a tight tee shirt and way too much hair gel and heavy cologne.

At least he isn't wearing eyeliner...

We take a taxi to a trendy, open-air lounge with a long line out front and paparazzi hovering. Julian sees some people he knows, and there's a flurry of introductions, smiles, and cheek kisses. Most of the guys are decked out like Julian, and my mental image of the burly Aussie surfer guy drifts off into the warm February sky.

"Are you ready?" Julian asks politely.

We gather behind him and, much to my surprise, bypass the line. Inside, Julian runs into someone every two steps.

The lounge is all limestone, white leather couches, and clusters of red candles. The band pumps out a blend of electro-house-funk as warm air breezes across the deck; the vibe is undoubtedly sexy. Tan, good-looking guys chat up gorgeous girls in flirty dresses under low-hanging chandeliers. Everyone's mixing into each other, more like a house party than a public space; a stark contrast to Los Angeles' disjointed social scene. Soon drunk, and convinced that Sydney is the best place *EVER*,

Julian leads me to the bathroom and pulls out a small bag of white powder. I watch in the mirror as he dips a key in it and holds it to my nose, then to his.

"Such a sexy gul," he says, leaning down to kiss me. I can't be sure if it's his lips or the blow, but the kiss is electric.

After hopping around to a couple more bars, a handful of people end up at Julian's for a swim. Stripped of his *Dolce and Gabbana*, and with his hair wet and sans gel, Julian is undeniably hot. And by this point, I feel like we have known each other for far longer than fifteen hours. He's witty and sweet, but it's his humility I find so appealing. After everyone else clears out, we stay up all night talking and kissing in the pool. The sun is coming up by the time we take refuge in his bedroom, blasting the AC, drawing the curtains down tight. The strangeness of being with a new lover after so many years is muted by the drugs and alcohol. We sleep for twelve hours, waking up to remember that in a drunken haze, Julian bought us and his other houseguests, a couple named Larti and Hans, who he met in Ibiza years back, plane tickets to Byron Bay, a little beach town known as a surfing hippie Mecca from the '60s. Our plane leaves in less than three hours.

Somehow we make the flight. I cross my fingers that I like Julian as much as I did yesterday because from the looks of things, we will be sharing a hotel room.

Byron Bay is a quaint little town with pounding surf set in front of rolling green hills. Three days of hiking, surfing, drinking, and romancing fly by, and although Julian is probably not my soul mate, there's a palpable chemistry between us.

Back in Sydney, crashing for a couple of days turns into an invitation to stay a couple weeks and then a couple of months.

While I'm usually attracted to outdoorsy guys, I accept the fact that hair gel, cologne, and Speedos are part of the package in Sydney.

I come to understand Julian is a celebrity of sorts, being that he modeled in his twenties in Milan and has managed to book a steady stream of commercials and small TV spots. But probably what he's most well known for are his New Year's Eve parties. Not to mention, his family's lucrative history in Australia and the wise investments he's made since they died.

He also happens to be the perfect person to stay with because with his latest real estate development project on hold, most of his days are wide open. We fall into a bit of a routine: going to the gym, walking his dogs on the beach, and partying with his friends. I manage to find an acupuncturist and sneak in cupping and needles whenever I can. When we go out, we are always treated as VIPs, and various young beauties vie for his attention. He's respectful and nurturing, and only every so often do I pick up on traces of *very* wild years I sense aren't too far behind him.

Cruising in Julian's convertible after a walk along Bondi Beach with Mila and Gucci in toe, he squeezes my hand and says, affectionately and almost shyly, "You know you can stay as long as you like."

"Thank you," I say sincerely, wishing more than anything that settling in with Julian is the answer.

A few days later, lounging by the pool, I take a few minutes to ground with my golden chords into the Earth and pop a few balloons. After three balloons, the question, "What is it, *exactly,* I'm doing here?" pops into my mind. It's hard to believe a month and a half has gone by. I'm not sure what I thought running halfway around the world would accomplish, but

I sort of envisioned cruising the coast for waves and regaining my confidence.

Instead, I've gone from living with one man to another, and although they seem different, I don't feel all that different.

And what has this accomplished, really? Aside from developing a good base tan, let's face it, not much.

My heart still feels like a charred piece of coal, and I need Xanax to fall asleep.

Tiptoeing barefoot through the airy house, I pause in front of the big bay window to witness the sun sinking into the baked blue basin that's Sydney Harbor. My gaze locks with the fiery orb, which is supposed to make your retinas bleed or something, but it feels so good, I can't tear them away. Suddenly, a little voice says, "Get it together. You're in one of the most beautiful places in the world, in possibly the most gorgeous home you've ever set foot in, with a hot, very wealthy, ex-model boyfriend who's told you to stay as long as you like. 'Stay forever if you want' is what he said... Okay, I get it—he wears hair gel and tight tee shirts, but clearly it's normal around these parts. You should be the happiest girl on Earth."

I am happy... I mean, of course, I'm happy. Who wouldn't be?

I stand perfectly still in the quietness of the house until the horizon swallows up the sun, then go to the office to check my email. I have three messages: one from my mom wanting to know why she hasn't heard from me, another from Amber saying she wants to visit, and one from James written in bright blue ink:

Hi Emily!

CONGRATULATIONS on your changing out of such a negative situation and going on your trip.

You made an immensity of changes very quickly!
You are doing great!

Here are some thoughts for you while traveling:

1. Take time each day for yourself to do a small meditation. It can be just a few minutes.
2. Ground yourself into the center of the planet with a bright new grounding cord.
3. Call your aura in and see a bright color surrounding you.
4. Transmute (pop a balloon) for anyone or anything that you may find in your universe because they should not be there.
5. If you are thinking of anyone from the past, then you should transmute.
6. Fill in with bright energy and an Element – Creativity / Awareness / Compassion, etc.

DON'T HESITATE TO CALL ME ANYTIME!

ENJOY the PRESENT MOMENT!

INNER KINDNESS TRANSLATES AS OUTER KINDNESS, AND THAT MEANS YOU ARE GRACE FILLED! WooHoo!

Light and Love,
James

Despite the fact it was just settled that I'm *obviously happy*, for some reason I feel the familiar stab of sadness in my heart and want to talk to him. It's 7:00 p.m., which makes it 12:00 a.m. San Francisco time, a tad late for a friendly chat.

He did say call anytime, didn't he?

Before I can talk myself out of it, I run upstairs to "my room," which is now basically just my stuff's room, and root through my backpack for his number. Laying down on the perfectly made bed that I haven't slept one night in, I dial his number.

"Hello?" he answers expectantly on the second ring.

"James?!"

"Emily? Is that you?" His distinctive voice is immediately comforting.

"All the way from dune unda," I respond in my best Australian accent.

"Well, howdaya like that?" he replies happily in his own version of the Australian accent.

"Is it too late to be calling?"

"Oh, no, not at all. What time is it?"

"I just read your email. Thank you," I say softly.

"What are you creating?"

"I've been staying in Sydney with this guy, Julian, and I've explored a little, but mostly just been staying in Sydney. It's so beautiful here, and you can see Sydney Harbor from his house."

"Ah ha, ha, Julian," he slides back into his Aussie twang for a second. "Hmmmm..." He pauses, and I can tell he is "looking" at Julian, me, and circumstances down here.

"Well, he looks like a really nice guy," he says brightly.

"Oh, he is! He is the nicest guy, very different from..."

"I'm happy you're having a good time."

"Yeah, I'm good," I say quietly. "I guess I'm just confused about what I'm going to do. I mean, I could stay here…"

"You could," he agrees neutrally. "What do you want to create there?"

"I'm not really sure exactly… I mean, I have a little money saved, and Julian says I can stay as long as I like. I know it sounds like I'm trying to run away from everything, but… Well, what do you think?"

"Well," he chuckles lightly, "you are trying to run away, but not in the way that you think. In fact, you've been running away for years."

"I'm not sure I'm following…"

"Tell me something; why did you put up with the misery that was your and Aidan's relationship for so long?"

"I think I was holding onto the good times… hoping that it would get better and we would be happy like we were in the beginning."

"*And…*"

"And, I suppose I was scared of change. I moved to LA to be with him, so we had all the same friends, same life, everything…" My heart tightens. "And it was frightening to break it all apart."

"This is all true, and it *did* take a lot of courage to finally walk away, but do you have any awareness that one of the main reasons that you stayed with him and endured such immense rejection was because sometime during your life's epic, you accepted an invalidation that just being you just wasn't good enough?"

"Hmph…" I give a little grumble, knowing he's right.

"And having high levels of competition like you do, you felt like whatever you would create wasn't going to be good enough to meet the standards you've created in your mind." His voice is filled with kindness.

"I'd never really thought about it that way." I can feel my face flushing.

"So this left you with only one choice: to find a successful man who you can hopefully make beautiful little children with, and then everyone will say approvingly, *ahhh... what a perfect life she has.*"

"It's not like I've spent the past five and a half years sitting around eating Bonbons and watching soap operas," I protest meekly. "You might be surprised to find out I kick ass at my job."

"Yessss, this is what's called competitive creation, which is very different from an authentic affinity creation inspired by a passion that burns inside of you. That is too terrifying. Aside from all the other disastrous things that go along with creating competitively," he adds lightly.

"What do you mean? All I've heard my whole life is that it's good to be competitive. I mean, doesn't competition drive success?" I ask, thinking of all the successful, competitive people I know.

"Of course, being competitive is a way to create money, but the problem with this is whatever you create out of competition will never, ever be truly satisfying. There will always be more to acquire and others that you view as ahead of you. And essentially this job you have is just *an illusion* that you are not part of the hardest working unions out there," he pauses, then says dramatically, *"The Crazy Goddesses."*

"Crazy Goddess?" I groan. "What's that? Wait, do I even want to know?"

He laughs easily and explains, "Only when we illuminate the truth, can we change and grow."

"Okaaaaay, lay it on me. What or *who* are the Crazy Goddesses?"

"I find the term Crazy Goddess appropriate because goddess is a widely accepted term for exquisite beauty. And I use it to refer to a certain type of woman who most likely was 'daddy's girl.' Because Daddy gave her everything, she feels entitled that her new daddy should give her everything too. But this ends up making her crazy because even *everything* will never be enough. And although she's beautiful, the majority of her self-worth is based on her appearance, which ultimately makes her crazy because she is constantly fighting a losing battle with the hands of time."

"It's not like I base *all* of my self-worth on my appearance," I object, quietly omitting the tens of thousands of dollars I've singlehandedly pumped into the beauty industry. "I've played sports my whole life, tap and jazz danced, surfed double over head waves, lived in foreign countries… Do you see me as someone spending my time matching my nail color to my shoes or something?"

"Nothing is bad or a wrong, and there are no mistakes," he says evenly. "Your path has led to here, where you're making recognitions about your creations. And let's not forget about daddy's little solider…" he warns ominously.

Oh jeez…

"Daddy's little solider is on a mission to prove to her dad that she's good enough, since she wasn't born a boy. So she sets out to find the biggest, baddest new daddy she can find—the senator, the congressman, the Super bowl hero, the CEO—and then puts on her camo undies and chastises him behind the scenes for wearing socks with his penny loafers or chewing with his mouth open. Of course, she doesn't know it, but she's unconsciously trying to prove to her real daddy she's OK. And although she's just as capable—if not more so—she ends up going crazy because no matter how hard she tries, the world still sees her as second fiddle."

"Yikes."

"Yikes is right." He laughs.

"Daddy's little girl believes that the only way she can amass a great deal of wealth is through a man. Daddy's little solider, on the other hand, is very skilled and can easily make her own money. While maybe she can't have the title of 'President,' she believes she can still do it better and will find other ways to prove that to her man."

"Can you be both daddy's little solider and daddy's little girl?" I ask, thinking I fall somewhere in the middle.

I mean, I don't wear camo undies every day of the week!

"Generally the groups are pretty distinct, but sometimes we do see some crossover. But keep in mind, both are in WE-ME mode, unable to see themselves whole without a man, and both believe being with somebody, no matter how unhappy they are, as better than being with nobody—more crazy behavior!

My mind is swirling with all of this new information.

"What is the longest amount of time you've been without a male in your life since... well, as far back as you can remember?"

Uh oh, buuuuuuuuuuusted!

Since high school, I've pretty much backed one serious relationship right up against another. With the majority of my girl-friends doing this as well, I never gave it a second thought. I'd always been drawn to relationships where my boyfriend was my best friend and we'd be nearly inseparable. And while I've been hurt before, after five and a half years planning my entire life with someone, this variety of a broken heart is new for me.

Then in an upbeat tone, he says, "So to answer your question of what I see for you staying in Australia, I see that you two make quite a good-looking pair, and that in the beginning, being in a new place will be exciting for you, with lots of new friends and a busy social calendar, and you will be the envy of many other Crazy Goddesses because being Julian's arm candy means something to a lot of people down there; but, after a while, even his mansion won't be enough, the parties won't be *fabulous* enough, and he won't be able to give you enough attention. Because as long as you have the Crazy Goddess mentality, *it will never be enough.*"

Aye, ye, ye. Crazy is right. Lock me up and throw away the key.

"Are you still there?"

"Yeah," I confirm glumly.

"Oh, don't despair!" James exclaims. "You've just been operating with the information that you've been programmed with. This is the exciting part—there's actually another way that most women don't know is available to them. You can start transforming into a *Vertical Woman.*"

"Vertical Woman?"

"Well, first of all, Crazy Goddess is not vertical because she has to lie horizontal and use her sexuality to get what she needs. A Crazy Goddess runs around trying to heal and make it ok for everyone else on the planet, especially males, with the belief that by doing this, she will then be OK, which you now know is just illusion healing."

An image of father floats into my mind.

Were my attempts to make it OK for him really just an attempt to make it OK for me?

"She puts her life on hold for males. She does everything in her power to prove she's the right woman for that man, and most devastatingly, she changes herself for a man." Does any of this sound familiar?"

"Unfortunately."

"Conversely, a Vertical Woman is complete and whole without a man. She doesn't lose her affinity for herself if she doesn't have a man. And understands what her man does or doesn't do isn't *about* her because she is simply navigating with a man, not making him the reason for her existence. She is a passionate creator and manifests her own money. She doesn't compete with her sisters, nor would she throw them under the bus for a man. And—very important—a Vertical Woman has the ability to heal her own body without drugs or surgery."

"When you say she can heal her own body, what exactly do you mean?"

"Well, as I've mentioned, we have the ability to heal our own bodies. Most people are just so disconnected from this capability. When I look at you, I see that you have very high healer levels."

"Now that sounds crazy!"

"Oh, I'm sure that I will tell you a lot of things that sound crazy, but in time you will see," he says with eerie certainty.

"Can a woman be Vertical *and* have a man in her life?"

"Yes, a woman can have a partner, but she will not see him as the sun in her sky. Instead of him being the number one thing in her life, he will be one of the *many* passions she has in her life."

"I see... I think." From as early as I can remember, it's been very difficult to avert my attention from whatever boy is in my life.

I hear the gate opening and the dogs barking; Julian is back from golfing.

"Well, you've certainly given me a lot to think about. Julian's back, so I should probably get going," I say in true Crazy Goddess form.

"Oh, OK. It was great talking to you!" he says enthusiastically. "I look forward to seeing what you create."

"James?" I ask softly.

"Yes?"

"Thank you."

8.

"I can make a bad guy good
for a weekend..."
— Taylor Swift

The airport in Los Angeles welcomes me home with the familiar stench of car exhaust and cigarettes. I squint down the galley and see Amber's white Jeep pulling up to the curb.

"Welcome home!" she cries from the front seat, her wheaty blonde curls gathered in a high ponytail. "How was the rest of your trip?" She gives me a hug, but before I can say anything, she says, "You're going to kill me... we didn't have time to do the room."

"That's alright," I say, but I can feel my chest tighten and the backs of my eyes prick with tears.

Disclaimer: I'm still so unstable that a Downy commercial could probably have me using up a box of tissues. It's not pretty, it's not fun, but these are the facts, people.

"You know how Robert is; he has some sort of resistance to fixing up that room, but we'll set you up on the couch for now, and you and I can get the room together ourselves."

A week or so before I left for Australia, and halfway through a second bottle of red, Robert asked if I knew where I would live when I got back. To this, Amber cried, "You'll move in with us! I've always wanted a sister!"

Her (much older) husband shot her a dubious look, and I interjected nervously, "Are you sure? It would only be until I can figure something else out."

"Of course, you can stay," he said with a forced smile.

"It will give us a reason clean out the extra room, and we'll put a bed in there for you," Amber enthused.

Amber had become my closest friend and moving in with them seemed like a good idea. Then again, when you're twenty-nine and homeless, your only offer is your best offer.

Now I feel paranoid that Robert doesn't want me staying with them and I need Amber to reassure me about ten more times before we get to her house that it is, in fact, OK.

If I'm ever prosperous enough to have a guest room again, I'll offer it to every friend I know. Friends of friends and their friends' friends will all be welcome!

I also wonder if she wants me there because she doesn't want to be alone with Robert, but I keep that theory to myself.

Arriving at Amber's house, my fears are confirmed by Robert's tepid reception. Fortunately, Robert's friends have organized a weekend trip to Vail and invited me to come along, so reality can be put off for a few more days.

I've spent a little time around a few of Robert's friends but never really connected with them. I know their circle rang in the new year in Aspen, "summered" in St. Tropez, and had courtside seats for the Lakers.

Despite a blizzard we land on time. A driver picks us up, and we make the short drive to the cabin one of Robert's friends has loaned him. Stepping into a grand room with walls a deep shade of red and rich, exposed beams crossing twenty-foot, vaulted ceilings, I see my idea of "cabin" is a little different than theirs.

"They built the house from the ground up and imported all this Douglas Fir timber from an old mine," Amber offers. "There's even a staircase from an old railway in England."

"Beautiful. Stunning, actually," I say, mesmerized by all the unique touches.

Amber's tour includes the screening room, a couple bridges with ponds beneath them, a steaming hot tub, and the bowling alley. My room has a king size bed, a sitting area with a view of the mountain, and an enormous bathroom with a Jacuzzi tub. I quickly change into fitted jeans and a nubby sweater, grateful that my Australian tan gives the appearance that I'm far more carefree than I feel. We head to the restaurant to meet the rest of the group.

Someone has rented a private room at the restaurant. There are roughly thirty people, and it looks like a scene from the TV show *Entourage*. A bunch of average-looking guys who are clearly "somebodies" and countless gorgeous model types looking bored.

I feel drab in comparison. I exchange a look with Amber, who, judging from her expression, is having a similar experience. We order glasses of sauvignon blanc and try to blend in.

Tommy, the good looking and unofficial leader of the group, who has female and male worshippers alike, gives me a warm hug.

"Heeeey, Emily, I didn't know you were coming on this trip."

"It was kind of a last-minute thing."

"You were just in Australia, right?"

He's asking about me?

"Just got back yesterday."

"That explains the tan," he says approvingly.

"I think you still have me beat," I say, pushing up my sleeve to compare.

Damn is he cute!

"Well, *that* is not a fair contest," he protests, his eyes not leaving my face. My parents are from Iran," he says easily.

Out of the corner of my eye, I see a couple models staring.

"What's your heritage?" he returns the question politely.

"My father is 100 percent Portuguese but born in the States."

"Then that explains your nice coloring."

"Well, he has dark skin and black hair, but my mother is as blonde with freckles all over her body. So I'm so thankful that she decided to marry someone with a little pigment in his skin, or I'd really be in trouble."

He laughs. Now I'm certain some girls are staring at me.

"It looks like a perfect combination to me."

A few hours and a few drinks later, everyone is acting like old friends, and I'm trying to remember why I never took an interest in Robert's sweet and hilarious friends. Tommy hasn't left my side for more than ten minutes. Turns out he is more than a pretty face; he graduated Johns Hopkins in three years pre-med before entering the family business of building luxury hotels around the world.

He is disarmingly funny in a mildly self-deprecating way, while still maintaining an air of total self-confidence. When the bill comes, he casually throws down his credit card for the entire group. If this was *Entourage,* Tommy would be Vince.

I'm already completely smitten and envisioning an amazing life with my handsome Iranian husband, traveling around to exotic locations to scout for new hotels. I even manage to envision our beautiful tan, high-cheek-boned children.

It doesn't even faze me when Amber pulls me aside to warn me that he is a *playa* above all *playas* and she has seen him with more girls than she can count. He probably just hasn't met the right girl yet, I rationalize as I switch from wine to vodka.

Clearly, he's ready for something different if in a room full of LA model types; he's talking to me, right?

Hours later, Amber suddenly remembers that there's a bowling alley at the cabin and announces that we're going bowling, now.

"Can I come?" Tommy asks, fully aware that he can do whatever he wants.

For the rest of the weekend, Tommy and I ski together, then spend the evenings drinking, dancing, bowling, and making out like eighth graders before falling asleep in each other's arms. Even though it's probably because there are no drugs, so we get so drunk we just pass out, I decide this is evidence he isn't really the player Amber made him out to be.

I wasn't very excited about coming home, but it seems like after this weekend, I have a new group of friends *and* maybe even a new love interest. For the first time in a very long time, I think things might just be OK. Maybe even *good*.

Then we get back to LA, and Tommy doesn't call. A few days go by. Robert, Amber, and some of the Vail crew are going to a fashion label launch party for Hudson Jeans, and Tommy does at least ask Amber if I'm going when they bump into each other at the gym. So, I get an overpriced blow out, slither into a pair of tight black jeans and an off-the-shoulder top, slide on black Louboutin sandals with a corked heel, and cross my fingers that he'll show.

The party is in the backyard of a massive house perched at the top of Benedict Canyon. When we walk in, my stomach does a couple somersaults in anticipation of seeing Tommy, but he's nowhere. A cool blue light illuminates a beautiful Olympic-sized pool with candles floating in it. People are standing around, trying to look as though they didn't put that much effort into getting ready, even though I know they did. I see a few of the guys from Vail, who are cool, but it no longer feels like we're the best of friends. A couple hours go by, and still no sign of Tommy. I'm getting ready to leave, when I see him come up the driveway in a suit.

"Hi, Em," he says, giving me a casual hug.

"You made it!" I exclaim, trying to keep my cool.

"I came straight from a work dinner," he says, flashing me a big white smile.

Then his attention is turned towards the endless train of people who want to talk to him. I chat with a girl I met on the ski trip until he finally makes his way over to me. We chat for mere seconds before he looks like he just saw a ghost.

"Will you excuse me for a second? I need to, um, deal with something."

"Sure," I say, hiding my disappointment.

"Promise you'll wait here for me?" he asks, squeezing my hands and searching my eyes. "I will only be a few minutes." A tall brunette is glaring at him from nearby. I watch as they head toward the driveway.

I wander aimlessly, looking for Amber and Robert. When I find them, they are getting ready to leave. It's been nearly an hour, and no sign of Tommy.

In the back of Robert's car, feeling like a complete idiot, I get a text from Tommy: **Sorry I had to leave. That girl and I had to deal with a very bad situation, and that was the first time**

I had seen her since. I walked her to my car, and we discussed it. After that, I couldn't go back to the party.

I silently pass the phone up to Amber.

"Abortion?"

"Who knows?" I ask, relieved that I'm not that glaring girl. "Either way he's obviously pretty shady."

"I tried to warn you," Amber says helplessly from the front.

"I know," I agree, annoyed with myself for thinking I could change him.

Back at their house, I get ready for bed and make myself as cozy as I can on the couch. Cocooned inside my fluffy, down comforter, I take a little nibble of a Xanax and wait for that warm feeling of nothingness to come for me. Just as I start to drift off, my body bristles and my eyes fling open. For the first time since James and I talked in Sydney, the conversation comes flooding back.

Shit. The Crazy Goddess strikes again!

9.

*"Can't talk to you without talking to me,
we're guilty of the same old thing
Been talking a lot about less and less and
forgetting the love we bring"*
— The Grateful Dead

In the months following my return from Australia and the whole Tommy incident, the reality of my "new life" starts to set in. Of course, I pretend, to anyone who's paying attention, that everything couldn't be better; a role I've become accustomed to playing. I'm not sure why I put being pitied by others in the same category as cleaning porta-potties at the end of a three-day music festival, but for some reason I do.

As luck (*or as James says, luck has nothing to with anything*) would have it, my friend Rachel's roommate decided to move out, leaving me homeless for only a month. The apartment is just around the corner from where Aidan and I used to live—and where he still lives. When I tell James this, he says, "I hope you're *amuuuuused!*"

Amused isn't quite the emotion I feel as I drive several miles out of my way each morning to avoid passing our old place; or as I carry my clothes down three flights of stairs to a laundry room shared by one hundred residents when just half of a mile away I used to do my laundry while watching the waves break onto the shore; or as I pass by the neighborhood Starbucks and see Aidan's arm draped around another girl. When I'd try to get him to come to Starbucks with me, it was always met with a "Sorry, it's not efficient enough."

Fortunately, Amber and Robert seem to like having me around and insist that I can hang with them whenever I like. Welcoming the opportunity to not be alone, I eagerly become their third wheel, or more like they become my oxygen mask in a building being devoured by flames. From my vantage point, their relationship appears to be stable at best, and my presence seems like a welcome distraction. It isn't long before I'm spending most of my time with them and their friends. Tommy apologizes for his behavior, and I manage to let it go, knowing that I got off far easier than most of his conquests.

On one hand, their gang is a nice reprieve from all the loved-up, married, and engaged friends that I'm used to being with, but at the same time, I miss my old friends desperately. Since Aidan and I broke up, Courtney has only initiated contact with me once, and none of our other friends have bothered to check in on me. I'm aware of birthday parties, trips, and events that he's attended, and I haven't even been invited.

I distract myself from the pain of losing Aidan and all my friends by going out constantly, forming superficial friendships and getting acquainted with a side of Los Angeles I'd never known. I find that in the years I was with Aidan, the boys in our dating range have risen from intern to partner, and the economic boom has blown up people's egos to match their inflated bank accounts.

Suddenly, things like summer rentals in the Hamptons, invitations to swanky parties, and an endless stream of group dinners at Madeo, Mr. Chow, Dan Tanas, and Mastros are extended my way. Apparently, a twenty-something single girl is always welcome.

One moment, I find myself top gunning through the air with a pack of raucous "road trippers" on the jet of a billionaire's son from LA to Vancouver and then Montana to catch a football game and back. The next, a famous baseball pitcher has a private sushi chef slicing up sashimi for us in his Hollywood Hills mansion while he's serenading me on his guitar. Everything has a silken sheen, stitched with unsettling threads of transience.

Despite Aidan's success, this is a whole different reality. This intoxicating new scene contrasted with the existence I'm discovering with James makes my head feel like a ball bouncing haphazardly on the roulette wheel. I want to share my new life with Courtney, but she seems purposely disinterested.

Nearly five months go by, with nothing more than an occasional forced conversation, before I end up over at her and Charlie's house for the first time in almost a year. It's late, and I, the ever-emotional one (especially with five vodka-sodas and a line of blow under my vintage belt), corner her in the guest bedroom and tell her that I know we aren't as close as we used to be, but I love her and I'm very happy that she and Charlie are getting married.

"I just can't relate with you anymore; *you've* changed, and all you care about is money," she retorts.

I practically buckle at the knees; not just because of her frosty self-righteousness, but because it's exactly, to a tee, how I've been feeling about her. She has no time for friends because her job is too important; all she talks about is how big her commissions are, her expensive shoe addiction, and her over-the-top, extravagant wedding. Then, she says, as if she's accusing me of an unforgivable crime, "You are a *gold digger!*"

Whoa.

It *is* true that things have changed dramatically for a single gal compared to the last time she was single over six years ago, but gold digger is pushing it.

Isn't it obvious I'm longing for someone I can build a real partnership with, rather than just going through the performance of happiness? I suppose there's no reason for her to know that, as the spiritual work I've been doing with James is so sacred to me and I'm still so fragile in my understanding of everything that I haven't shared very much information with her about the mackerel-slap-in-the-face dose of reality I've been bringing upon myself lately.

I take a deep breath, searching for some words I won't regret later. "Funny, that's the exact same way that I've been feeling about you. Aside from the gold digger part," I tack on quickly.

Our relationship has become so strained, conversations have become limited to what we do, whom we meet, and what others do, neither one of us daring to dip beneath the surface where intuitively, we know something terribly wrong has been brewing in our friendship for some time. There's also my aversion to other people's pity, and I'm doing my damnedest to let everyone know that I'm just fine without him.

I want to scream in her face, "If I was such a gold digger, don't you think I would've found a way to stay with Aidan?

I had hundreds of chances to get pregnant and never have to worry about money again—isn't that what gold diggers do? Or I could've easily stayed with Julian. Actually, it would be a whole lot easier if money was all I was after because these days money doesn't seem hard to find!"

Instead, I lock myself in Courtney's guest room and curl up into the fetal position on the bed. I'm interrupted by Charlie's soft knock on the door. I lean over and let him in. With his open and affectionate nature, I've always thought Charlie was a good balance for Courtney, who's naturally reserved and would be perfectly happy never talking about her emotions.

He comes in and gives me a hug. "We both love you and know you are a good girl," he starts off. "You're just going down the wrong path."

What the hell has Courtney been saying about me?

I try to explain through my drunken sobs that he has it all wrong; that finally, now, I actually am on a better path, but I'm too drunk to make any sense.

Who knows who else she has been talking to? Is this character assassination why none of my friends are talking to me anymore?

Mascara bleeding down my cheeks, I stumble out of their front gate without saying goodbye. Hugging myself tightly under my coat as I wait for the taxi, I can't remember ever feeling so alone.

~

The sun makes its way through the plantation blinds that line the eastern wall of my bedroom, and I pull a pillow over my face as a shield. My mouth is suctioned shut, my eyes are stitched with crust from the dried salt of my tears, and my head is pounding rhythmically. The alcohol-fueled fight with Courtney comes barreling back.

I stay there for I don't know how long. I hear Rachel leave then come back, and then leave again. I listen to the people who I share a wall with talk about how beautiful it is outside, but I can't bear to remove the pillow from my head.

Finally, my bladder coerces me out of bed, and as I catch a glimpse of myself in the mirror, it's confirmed that I *will* be spending the rest of the day inside.

A familiar buzzing lets me know that my phone is buried somewhere in a tuft of pillows. I dig around half-heartedly for it and see that it's James.

"Hello?" I answer, trying to sound perkier than I feel.

"How we dooooo-ing?" His typical I-know-there's-something-wrong greeting.

"Oooooh," I groan, "where do I even begin?"

"Lemme guess... you and your hubby are having marital problems."

"Oh, no... I haven't talked to Aidan in I don't even know how long."

"Let the court record show that I clearly stated "hubby" as in husband, not "ex-boyfriend," he jokes. "C'mon... you mean to tell me that you don't know who your hubby is? I mean, when I look at the two of you... yeeeesh! You two are still *sooo* married."

I sit silent, puzzled for a second. The booze haze has my synapses snapping like a fly caught in honey.

"*Courtneeeeeeeey.*"

"Hmph," is all I can muster.

"I love it when you do that!"

"I love that I amuse you," I respond dryly.

"When I look at the two of you, it's like World War Three, but neither one of you has any intention of letting go," he says, obviously looking at my "pictures."

"You have just *a few* lifetimes together as husband and wife."

"That doesn't surprise me. We had it out last night," I say, filling him in on the details.

"I hope that you're very amused right now," he says in a cautionary tone.

"I wish I could say that's how I feel right now."

"Oh c'mon! The spiritual mirror is one of the most amusing things around."

"The spiritual mirror?"

"The spiritual mirror. If something or someone really irritates you or gets under your skin, you want to take a look inside of yourself and see where that sits inside of you. Because if something doesn't sit inside of you, it isn't going to ruffle your feathers when someone else does it."

"Really?" *My brain function is limited by my hangover.*

"No, I just made that up," he jokes. "Yes, really. Basically, if you point your finger and call someone out in an energized way, you're essentially calling yourself out."

"Well, her argument is that it's *completely different* because she makes her own money, so it's OK for her to talk about it."

"Well, that's terrific that she's making a lot of money," James says earnestly. "But when you see what I see, that argument doesn't hold a lot of weight. I don't care if you've won the lotto, robbed a *Wells Fargo*, or you're Bill Gates; net worth doesn't equate to self-worth. Pontificating about money—your own or otherwise—is a veiled attempt to feel worthy. You could have all the gold in Dubai, but without integrity, authenticity, and vulnerability, you're not going to feel very good about yourself. It's this absence of self-worth that you're mirroring in each other, and it's registering for each of you as annoyance."

It is pretty amusing that we're irritated with each other for the exact same thing.

"If you are *conscious*, and becoming more conscious is what you are working towards," he says carefully, "the next time you feel adversarial towards someone, you can make a recognition of where that sits inside you and take it for the *true gift that* it is. True consciousness is the awareness that all relationships are really only about the understandings you make about yourself. And the spiritual mirror is a valuable tool in your toolbox. It will help you to separate truth from illusion, and in turn will make you more compassionate to yourself and to others."

Merry fucking Christmas. A gift indeed.

"Wow," I say, flashing back over the course of my life, all the times I was too busy feeling self-righteous and irritated to consider that on some level I was mirroring the very thing that was pissing me off.

"This unfortunately isn't usually what people do. Because we have judgments, programmed into us by society, that say we aren't supposed to think or feel a certain way, we become closed to truth," he explains. "When we are able to shut down those judgments, we can open up spiritually to receive communication, inspiration, and love."

"Wow," I repeat softy.

"Truth is simple. It's illusions that are complicated. When our illusions overtake the truth, they form agendas, and yeeeeesh... it's a slippery slope from there, little lady," he says with a false chuckle. "Once you are working with an agenda, you've lost any and all affinity for yourself because that thing becomes greater than you. If something is greater than you, you are basically saying, 'I'm not good enough as I am, so I must perform in order to pull this agenda through,' which cannibalizes your authenticity. And that is the last place you want to be."

Yikes.

"Can you define agenda?"

"An agenda is when you're out of acceptance of the situation and want something from someone else. It can be as simple as wanting someone to love you, or as complex as wanting someone to be your provider, your lover, your best friend, your protector, your entertainer—you know, create your life for you... nothing that you'd be familiar with at all." I can hear him smiling.

Oh me oh my.

I suppose in an effort to maintain harmony as our interactions became more agitated, I began editing and agreeing with what Aidan wanted. Although I burned inside with anger and rejection on many occasions, I was rewarded by a day without fighting. And because the little competitor inside my head had decided that Aidan was the prize, this new technique I devised of letting him win would in fact help me win in the long run. Never mind the fact I was on my way to winning a loveless life, where I wasn't appreciated and wouldn't even rub up against concepts like "seen," "supported," or "celebrated;" I was in it to win it, *damn it!*

Just your garden variety Crazy Goddess agenda.

"Aye ye, ye! Why am I just learning about this now?"

"Because you are finally ready to start seeing truth and your life is going to start to change."

I close my eyes and think of Courtney and our terrible fight and the disaster that Aidan and my relationship became and whisper, "I sure hope you're right."

"You may have heard about it before, but you weren't ready to separate truth from illusion yet," he adds. "Many people go entire lifetimes never seeing truth and end up really damaging themselves in order to carry out very intricate agendas." He pauses. "I have a few minutes before my next session; if you want, I can give you a little healing."

"Over the phone?"

"Yes."

"Uh, sure..." I agree, not really knowing what I'm agreeing to.

"OK, pull your hands over your head and hold them an inch apart," he says, business-like.

I switch to speaker-phone mode and lay my phone on the bed, then pull my hands very slowly over the back and then the top of my head to clear away all the energies surrounding me that James says "aren't me," and then I hold them an inch apart.

"Okaaaay, repeat after me," he commands. "I'm in alignment with James to do this healing. I'm a beginner of life and I give myself permission to separate truth from illusion so I can change and grow and vibrate in my highest affinity, compassion, and grace."

James begins to direct me to different areas of my body where densities have been gathering, then instructs me to apply pressure with my hands as he assists me in releasing what he describes as a charcoal-grey energy.

"We hold energy from the judgments of others in our hips."

"Does that mean a lot of people are judging me right now?"

"Bingo. I see that several people in your life are trying to make you the problem—which you are not."

"Now, don't analyze this; just repeat after me," he commands, "I accept myself, I accept Courtney, Courtney accepts me."

I do as I'm told.

"Now do the same for Aidan."

With great purpose, I say, "I accept myself, I accept Aidan, Aidan accepts me."

"You can do this for anyone in your life who you are having difficulty accepting or who you sense is having difficulty accepting you."

The murky hangover feeling seems to have lifted significantly.

"You're brightening up; you know that?"

"I feel different," I admit.

"Well, I have to run into a session here, but let's talk later and you can let me know how you are doing, OK?"

"I will."

"Good job. And don't forget to fill in!"

"Ugggh." *Filling in... so much harder than it sounds.*

"Remind me again why filling in is so important?" Before he can answer, I interject, "Wait, let's see if I've got this right. The way I understand it is, you helped me release some of the toxic, negative energy that was stored inside of my body, and if I don't fill in with a bright color that has a positive vibration, then everything will just go back to how it was before the healing."

"Very good! *And...*"

"Well, is it that each thought, action, and interaction has an energy vibration attached to it, so if I think negatively or competitively, those thoughts will deposit dense energies into my body, which can lead to more yucky emotions and eventually illness into the physical body? Conversely, the more I remain positive, the easier it is to keep the dense energies at bay."

"Well, remember that like attracts like. And essentially, it's as if each emotion or thought form has the ability to attach itself to us, if the vibrations match. So, let's say that someone cuts you off on the freeway, honks their horn, and flips you the bird. If your vibration is negative and dense, firstly you will *react* by honking back, shouting, and maybe giving the finger too. Then, because your energies match, it's like there are little hooks hanging off your aura for that negativity to latch onto. And then that negativity compounds inside of you and makes you even more negative and unhappy. On the other hand, if your vibration is high, the interaction won't really faze you, and although you have hooks hanging off your aura, the energy that is being thrown your way doesn't fit on those hooks, so it can't stay with you and just breezes on by. Your hooks are looking for higher vibration energies to latch onto them. Which then will manifest into all sorts of wonderful things."

"Really?" I say more to myself than him.

"So the goal with these healings is to remove the dense energies you've generated, and also those that aren't you that you've accepted from others. That's why after healings, folks feel so much better. And filling in with bright blue, green, yellow, orange, I don't care what color you use... helps you to increase your vibration and keep the negative energy out. But I can do marathon healings for individuals, and they can go out and engage in destructive behaviors, and the next time they come to me they are filled up with dense energy all over again. That is why we are going to start doing charts one of these days to complement the healings, but we can talk about that later."

The word *chart* evokes intimidating images of math class, but I say, "OK," happy that he said, "we can talk about that later."

"OK, running into session. Great job today!"

"Thank you so much," I say, wishing I had stronger words than thank you to show him how grateful I am. I suppose that he already knows all of this, I rationalize.

"After we hang up, I quickly ground myself in to the Earth and pull up an emerald-green color like the one he just spoke of, through my feet, up my legs, directing it up through my first energy center all the way to my crown.

I'm interrupted by the rumbling of my stomach, and suddenly food, which was about the least appealing thing I could think of a half an hour ago, sounds amazing. I head for the kitchen for a bowl of cereal.

I no longer feel condemned to an all-day hangover, and in the mirror, a considerably less puffy, brighter face stares back at me.

I brew a pot of Detox tea and send Courtney a text: **I'm sorry we fought last night. Do you want to talk face to face this week?**

I'd like our fight to just fade away, but the pressure is on for us to clear the air with her wedding only two weeks away and me being one of her bridesmaids.

I wait anxiously for her reply as I flip through the channels, looking for something to distract me from, well, myself. Minutes turn into hours, and I wonder if maybe she just won't reply. Maybe this is it; the end of a sixteen-year friendship. My mom calls twice, and I brush away a pang of guilt as I send her to voicemail each time. I can tell she feels me pushing her away, but I find it hard to talk to her when I don't have anything good to report. Finally, my phone vibrates with a text from Courtney.

How bout dinner tomorrow night at Hal's?

For the rest of the night, I try not to think about the cruel words we threw at each other and roll this concept of *the mirror* over in my mind.

The next morning, I wake up early with a rock of anxious anticipation planted firmly in my belly. I take a few minutes to ground myself, running emerald green throughout my body and breaking plates of glass in my mind with Courtney's face on them, then ones with my face, and, of course, the C word. *Competition.* The ubiquitous third wheel that has been tagging along with our friendship for a long time.

It's hard to know when it first showed up because the first four years of our friendship were so easy; it was like a high. In boarding school, we lived down the hall from each other but would often have sleepovers in each other's rooms, borrow clothes and makeup, and shower in adjacent stalls, singing *American Pie* at the top of our lungs. She taught me all of her camp songs because, *of course*, our children would be going to her childhood camp together. We were always looking for mischief and adventures; we called them quests. We'd sneak into the kitchen in search of snacks, pretend to be detectives on important cases, raid the theater room wardrobe and masquerade downtown in our costumes, speaking in thick British accents, never once stepping out of the characters we'd invented. We'd crawl along the damp soil under the eucalyptus trees or climb the trunks of ancient oaks, searching for old hideaways from students that came before us. Sometimes we find old records, pipes, or books dating back to the 40's. I'd help her with her English homework, and she'd do my math. We were always laughing, even when we were crying. She was the sister I always dreamed of having, and with our petite frames and delicate features, we often were mistaken for twins. Come vacation time, we refused to separate and would rotate between her parents' house, and mine. Our parents became good friends. When college rolled around, *obviously*, we were going to the same school.

Since we didn't request to be together, we were shocked when the University of Colorado paired us as roommates, which we were both rightfully nervous about. It didn't take long for competition to wreak havoc on our relationship. Despite the conflicts, the pull of our friendship was stronger than the pain, so we went on living together three of our four college years, moving to Lake Tahoe one summer and then to San Diego after we graduated. And now, almost seventeen years later, we're pointing fingers at each other.

Uggh!

Using the tools James has given me, I manage to keep my anxiety at bay for most of the day, but on my way to the restaurant, my stomach starts grinding again.

Courtney is already sitting down at a corner table with a glass of chardonnay. Courtney only drinks chardonnay. It doesn't matter if she's in a dive bar connected to a gas station in Vegas; girl is ordering a Chardonnay.

I lean down for an awkward hug, and we talk about the weather longer than the weather deserves to be talked about. I order a glass of red.

"I suppose we've needed to talk for a long time," I start out nervously.

"Probably," she agrees, picking nervously at the cuticle around her thumb.

"I'm sorry that we fought the other night."

"I'm sorry I wasn't there for you when you and Aidan broke up," she says quickly, "but I just felt like I couldn't relate with you anymore. I feel like all you care about is money, or staying at someone's mansion, or a guy buying you something. It just *disgusts me* how money hungry you've become."

I don't become reactive, instead focusing on her words through my new lens.

"It's too bad that you view my sharing those things as so offensive; I see it as part of the story, and that's what friends do—share stories that happen in their lives. I've just needed to branch out a little; if anything, I wish you'd join me once in a while."

She shrugs, not really sure how to respond, then says, "I know you think that all I talk about is money, but I make my own money. It's *completely* different. You basically don't work and just hang out at rich people's mansions."

"Hmm..." I pause, remembering what James said about people's judgments about what is "right" and what is "wrong" preventing them from seeing the truth. "In five years at my company, I've won three President's clubs and the International Sales Excellence Award, which means I was ranked number one in the nation of five hundred people. Just because I'm not working twenty-four-seven and I don't talk about how busy I am and my work; doesn't mean I don't work. I actually think the fact that I'm not willing to sacrifice my life for work is more of a testament that not all I care about is money."

We go back and forth like ping-pong. The waitress hovers around us but can't find an opening.

"I loved you when you used to be so carefree, but now it seems like you are just trying to be with people so you can better your situation," she says, unwilling to see it any other way.

"I guess I only share the parts of my life that I think would be interesting to you. And since the only things that you talk to me about are making money, shopping, and your wedding, maybe I feel like it is a place to connect. You have no idea what is really going on with me because you don't ask how I'm feeling. You just ask what I'm *doing*."

Courtney takes a long sip of chardonnay, her shoulders relaxing a little as she considers what I just said.

"I've actually been doing some spiritual introspection lately," I confess. "Which means I've been taking a good, hard, and painfully honest look at how I've been creating my life."

Grazing right over the bit about my doing spiritual work, she concludes, "I guess I can see how maybe we both talk about material things when we are in the presence of each other because we feel like that is the point where we can relate."

I can't be sure if she really believes that or if she thinks this is the only way we are going to come to any sort of resolution with her wedding two weeks away.

"And, I don't want people to pity me so I probably emphasize details that make it seem like everything is so fun and exciting, so nobody will know how hard breaking up with Aidan has been," I add.

"You act like everything is great and you don't have a care in the world."

"That couldn't be further from the truth."

"Well you could've fooled me," she says with a small smile, and it feels like the worst is behind us.

10.

"One good thing about music,
When it hits, you feel no pain"
—Bob Marley

As winter speeds into early spring, I fall in love again. Except this time it's with a very unsuspecting character—the city of Los Angeles. I guess you could say that our relationship got off to a slow start, considering I've already spent the last six years living everywhere from Westwood, Venice, Marina del Rey, and the Hollywood Hills and never really progressed past the "like-like" stage.

I'd been seriously considering making the move back up to San Francisco, where my family lives just across the bay, but now it seems Los Angeles is determined to get me to stay, persuading me with all her many charms. Come March, my eyes feast on vibrant green hillsides covered in wild magnolias and tangerine-colored poppies. Not an inch of brown can be spotted for miles around, and spontaneous waterfalls sprout up on the otherwise dry hiking trails.

With ten million-plus people pumping carbon monoxide out into the atmosphere, Los Angeles isn't really the place that comes to mind when I think of a city teeming with nature, but I discover canyon roads that feel almost tropical with their canopies of bougainvillea and thick banana plants fanning into the sky.

With all of these signs of change, and seeing that I'm in *loooooooove* and all, you must be thinking that surely things are on the up and up, right?

Actually... I feel inclined to provide you this WARNING: IT GETS WORSE BEFORE IT GETS BETTER. *MUCH WORSE.*

Not worse in the way that I recoil to my apartment keeping myself company with old *Friends* reruns or anything, although maybe that would be preferable. I'd compare it more to tossing a book of matches into a bundle of spindly, gasoline-drenched wood. It's amazing, really, what a dash of newfound confidence, mixed with a healthy serving of liquor and a bunch of unresolved issues, can produce. The phrase *hot mess* comes to mind.

And just as James always says, "like attracts like," it's no wonder that as the cracks in Robert and Amber's marriage widen into a deep crevasses, she and I become even more inseparable than we already were. Since we work together, we arrange our schedules so we can make our calls together. And even though this is "frowned" upon, we're both leading the nation with our respective products, so nobody seems to care. After work, we hit up a spin class or yoga together before seeing what's happening for the night.

On good days, we pump ourselves up as talented and successful businesswomen not only driving the business in our company but dominating the industry as well. Our bosses think we can do no wrong; our customers love us; we're young, connected, and attractive.

I mean, who are we?

With this ridiculously entitled frame of mind, we ditch work to hang out at friends' Malibu beach houses, wrangle invitations to trunk shows, sip champagne at lunch, lay out by the pool at the Mondrian, or soak up the sun on the patio of the Chateau Marmont.

On bad days, we bemoan our lame jobs and feel completely inferior to the talented and beautiful women in this town finding success as musicians and actresses, which prompts us to escape from our mundane existences, in need to feel more "special," by ditching work to hang at friends' Malibu beach houses, wrangling invitations to trunk shows, sipping champagne at lunch, laying out by the pool at the Mondrian, or soaking up the sun on the patio of the Chateau Marmont.

Whether we're high or low, we are thick as thieves and bound together by our faux happiness, or real unhappiness. Hot mess to the power of two = *very* messy.

Although my Hollywood crew has lost a little of its appeal, like a shiny new toy the day after Christmas, I can still appreciate that they do know how to throw a good party, and seeing as they are pretty much the only people I know outside of the mutual friends I had with Aidan, I'm grateful that they spend of good chunk of their lives distracting themselves from themselves. As the days stretch out and the temperatures begin to rise, they rent cabanas at the Four Seasons on warm spring afternoons, get VIP tables at the hottest clubs in town, take turns hosting parties at their various sprawling homes nestled in the hills, and charter jets to Vegas or Napa at a moment's notice. With the internet still in its infancy, there are no conversations about carbon footprint as we spiral, unaware, towards an impending economic crash.

Most of the other girls at these gatherings are either models, actresses, or trying to be models and actresses and somehow always seem to wear the hippest, most effortlessly chic outfit for the occasion, which, of course, leads me to feel like I have *nothing* to wear and end up spending money I don't really have on that "perfect" dress, pair of shoes, bag, manicure, and blow out.

I mean, when did looking perfect become so... expected?

One Thursday night, the guys have at a table at Goa, the latest LA hotspot. After some debate, Amber and I decide to stop by the Indian-inspired nightclub. Standing around, watching a throng of beautiful young women vying for the attention of Tommy and his circle, as bad hip-hop plays too loud to have a real conversation, Amber rolls her pretty eyes. "Is this supposed to be fun?"

I scan the twenty-and-thirty-somethings standing around the packed club, looking for indications that this is indeed "fun," unable to find any convincing proof. I slurp a tinge of sadness through my straw, remembering the long nights of laughter, classic rock, and competitive Cranium with Aidan, Courtney, Charlie, and George fueled by magic little pills that made everyone love each other more.

"Let's get out of here," Amber declares, downing the rest of her vodka soda in one long gulp.

We burst out through the exit, passed the surprised looks of the, at least one hundred people, waiting in line, seemingly willing to offer up a kidney to get beyond the velvet rope.

What am I doing with my life?

We wander up Hollywood Blvd., past tourists snapping photos of Marilyn and Elvis impersonators, by a seedy tattoo parlor with a flickering neon light, crossing to the other side of the street where men dressed as women start directing their cat calls our way. Turning onto Vine St., with no real idea of where we are going, Amber stops in her tracks below the kiosk of the Avalon Theater and shouts out, "*North Mississippi All Stars!* These guys rock! I used to see them in college."

"They passed through Boulder a few times..." I trail off, remembering how the better part of my college nights were spent dancing to live music.

Wait, why don't I do that anymore?

"We have to go!" she decides impulsively, tugging my arm towards the entrance.

"Looking like this?" I stall, glancing down at my cocktail dress and Louboutins. Amber hesitates for a second, a subtle admission that we are undoubtedly overdressed for the occasion. Unwilling to admit it and empowered by the three vodka sodas she took down in less than thirty minutes, she announces in her slow Southern drawl, "I couldn't care less."

Following her lead, we head for the box office, and because the show is more than half over, the guy waves us in for free. Amber slides her wedding ring into her purse, giving me a wink as I follow her inside. At first, I feel a little self-conscious; after all, my normal concert attire is usually jeans and a tank top, but we're quickly reminded of a universal truth—even in the gritty jam-band scene—girls in short dresses are always welcome. Guys are nearly tripping over themselves to buy us drinks, leading us into the front row, and just trying to have a conversation with us—a stark difference from the scene we just abandoned.

A tall guy with sandy blonde hair and a square jaw strikes up a conversation: "How you girls doin' tonight?"

It's only a tenth of a second, but I watch as Amber's catlike eyes flicker over the All-Access laminate hanging loosely from his neck.

"Couldn't be better," Amber purrs into her whiskey, looking up at him from under her eyelids.

Oh, Amber, I love you...

"Do you ladies wanna check out the show from backstage?" he asks with a friendly smile, and I notice that he has very long eyelashes that curl up at the tips.

"Why wouldn't we?" Amber says, flipping her golden curls over her shoulder and taking a long sip of her cocktail.

As we trail behind him through a sea of people, Amber turns around and hisses, *"Seeeeeeeeee!"* in my ear.

So, just like that, getting wasted and shaking our stuff on front row becomes the perfect antidote for our ailing hearts. Moving my body to music was something that always came naturally, and when you add a live band, a few whiskeys, and a seemingly endless supply of free drugs, I found it was a lot easier to not think about how much I missed my old life. When I share sound bites of my new life with my family, it seems like they aren't sure if they should be happy for me that I'm having fun, or appropriately concerned. I, of course, assure them that things couldn't be better, and at fleeting moments even believe it myself.

Robert and Amber's marriage continues to chug along, but mentally, she is somewhere else—somewhere like front row and, if we work it right, backstage. After several months of Amber forgoing date night with Robert to rock out with me, Robert gets smart and decides to set me up with one of his old football buddies who lives up in Oregon named "Super Bob," but from what I can see, he's not a real superhero. He is, however, in his early forties and good-looking in the traditional sense —6'3" with a fit body thanks to muscle memory from his years as a college football star, a defined jaw, bright blue eyes, and a thick head of silver fox hair. I quickly discover, once you work your way into dating guys in this decade, hair becomes a red-hot commodity, like owning a few hundred ounces of gold in a crashing economy.

Although he's thirteen years older, he behaves like a guy in his twenties—backwards baseball caps and drinking on roof-top bars. Part of the reason he's able to come down to LA for extended periods of time and party all day is because he owns a property development company, and apparently things are going well to the point where other people are working hard while he gets to play.

The only thing that gives his age away—aside from the grooves in his forehead—is that he refuses text or use a computer. Oh, and that little detail that every time we have sex, he thinks he's the star of a bad porno movie—shouting out phrases and questions that make me feel like a Puritan at a free love rally. I've decided dirty talk, like pickles, has a wide range, and Super Bob is getting dangerously close to those dark green, slimy pickles that don't crunch. I politely tell him that this talk is distracting and ask him if he wouldn't mind toning it down a little. He's a little taken aback by my request, but agrees, although not before informing me that he's never gotten any complaints before.

Right.

But since he's a genuinely kind, fun-loving guy, I embrace the idea of a long-distance romance. He whisks me away on adventures to Mexico, Lake Tahoe, Oregon, and San Francisco that usually include Amber and Robert and a few of his other friends. Super Bob turns out to a terrific playmate. Since he spent the past twenty years working his tail off, all he wants to do now is travel and have fun. He's free and open with emotions and after just a few months confesses that he's really *feelin'* it for us. With this admission, I'm forced to think about how I feel for him and I realize if I really have to think about it, I'm probably not *feelin'* it the way I should be, but I can't pinpoint why not. I'd spent hours thinking if only Aidan adored me and wanted to travel and have fun, I'd be the happiest girl on Earth.

Wasn't this what I wanted?

The next time James and I talk, I ask him about my lack of love for Super Bob, but he brushes me off, insisting, "You must call my friend Jody."

"I must?"

"She's expecting your call. It's important that you get a female perspective on things. And I won't take it personally if you decide that you love her so much that you stop calling me," he jokes.

"Well, who is she?" I stall.

"I met her in my clairvoyant class over twenty years ago, and we fell in love and lived together up in Trinidad, and I helped her raise her son... and we owned an art gallery together, and now we're best friends, and she's a Vertical Woman that can help you immensely."

"Wow. OK, I'll call her."

I feel a little awkward calling a complete stranger, but I do it anyway.

"Hello?" a very sweet voice answers on the third ring.

"Hi, Jody? This is Emily, James' friend."

"Why hello, Emily!" she says warmly.

"James told me that you'd be expecting me."

"I'm glad that you called." Her voice has a girlish quality to it, even though I know she's closer to James' age than mine.

We make friendly small talk for a few minutes, and I discover that she also grew up in the Bay Area and stayed local to attend college at UC Berkeley before starting a few businesses of her own.

Vertical indeed!

"So I see you've been going through some big changes," she says, reading me.

"Hmmmm..." I pause, "where to begin?"

"Why don't you start at the beginning," she suggests kindly.

I take a deep breath and fill her in on Aidan and my saga, the breakup, desperately missing my friends, especially Courtney, all up to my confusion over Super Bob.

"Why, after all, don't I want someone who's smart and prosperous and adores me and wants to have fun?"

"You want to have a partner you can talk to." She starts reading me like a book. "Like, *really* talk to about any and everything. Deep stuff. That is your biggest attraction."

When I hear her say this, I know instantly that's what's missing. I want to be able to discuss wild theories and ideas, books and films, music, and, more than anything, spirituality. Bob *is* super, but he's not really down to get super deep.

"I guess someone can only meet you as deeply as they've met themselves?"

"This is very true. Try to be in great gratitude for the fun you've had together," she advises. "This gratitude will help you create the partner you really want."

"What do you mean?"

"When we get into gratitude, we're in a state of mind to accept the present as the gift that it is, and this acceptance has a vibration of abundance. This has a very different vibration associated with it than the vibration of lack. Since we know like attracts like, if you are vibrating in a place that is giving to you, you will create a partner that wants to give and share with you. On the other hand, if you are to hold onto what is lacking in this relationship, there will be lack in the next one too."

Shittttttt! He has very nice hair, I swear! And is sweet, and fun, and likes to travel...

"I see you're very capable," she remarks, validating me.

There is that word again. Capable.

"But, I see that you're in a lot of fear, and this means you want to control things. Control carries a masculine frequency, which is toxic to your body and makes it difficult for you to create what you want."

"Eeek." I didn't know I was doing that, but it doesn't sound good.

"Just sit for about ten minutes a day and see a bright feminine color running through your first and up though all of your energy centers—a bright orange or hot pink will do you very well. Trust that everything that shows up on your path is there to teach you."

She says that her younger self wasn't always so vertical and she and I actually have some matching pictures.

"You know, Emily, small shifts can make big differences," she says before we hang up, the encouragement in her voice so sincere I feel an immediate kinship with her.

So you're saying... there's a chance!

~

Things between Amber and Robert suddenly slide downhill. What begins with a few white lies to her husband that she has an unbelievable amount of work dinners to attend snowballs into staying out with me and turning up to her house a couple days later. Since Robert is unwilling to pick up on the hints that Amber wants out of the marriage, she finally tells him that she can't do it anymore.

As to be expected, this goes over like a drag queen doing a burlesque show at the Republican National Convention. Despite the fact that he's been throwing verbal punches her way since they got home from their honeymoon, now that she finally is getting up the courage to leave him, he becomes a model husband. Her parents, whom he never called or visited once in five years of marriage, are suddenly his new best friends and allies in his attempt to get her to stay. Amber hails from the deep, religious South, and her family doesn't understand why she isn't trying harder to save her marriage, when in actuality, she's been living in a secret hell for years. I can't help but wonder...

How many women are living in a secret hell to keep outward appearances intact?

I helplessly watch her wade through an enormous amount of guilt about leaving him before eventually petitioning for a divorce.

Of course, none of this drama slows us from going to see as much rock 'n' roll as possible. And ever since that reception we got at the Avalon, we've long since ditched our flip-flops and tank tops in exchange for attention-grabbing outfits: short dresses, sequins, and boas that are probably a little much to everyone except us and the guys checking us out.

With Robert out of the picture, it's easier to arrange our entire social schedule and paychecks around going to as many shows as we can. We become regular fixtures at the Black Crowes, Tom Petty, Dirty Dozen Brass Band, The Dead, Phish, Further, Robert Randolph, and, the big daddy of the jam band scene, Widespread Panic. We travel to San Francisco, Lake Tahoe, New York, San Diego, Vegas, Chicago, Atlanta, Birmingham, and, of course New Orleans just to catch the next show.

Whatever problems I have are easily forgotten, imbibing my happiness and shaking my stuff on front row. We scour all the vintage shops, looking for just the right, rock 'n' roll look, and when we walk into Tipatina's, a legendary New Orleans bar, decked out in our signature purple feather boas, someone shouts out, "It's the boa girls!"

Which prompts Amber to turn to me and slur in a low, gritty Southern drawl, "Let the Hilton sisters have LA; I'd rather be famous here."

Sure, it wasn't the most comfortable or practical of get-ups, but we looked hot, or at least we thought did, and after a few drinks and a pill or a line, we couldn't feel our feet anyway. Like I said, *it gets worse before it gets better.*

During this time, Amber meets, err... runs into, Chad at a Black Crowes Concert. Turns out he saw her dancing on top of a bar at a party back on NYE and was immediately smitten.

With his easy Texas charm and dark good looks, Amber is instantly infatuated. It also doesn't hurt that he hails from a well-heeled Houston family and his top priorities are the same as hers—partying and rock 'n' roll.

At first I'm thrilled that she has met someone so sweet to take her mind off the dissolution of her marriage, but when the truth comes out that Chad has another girlfriend, it sends her reeling into a shell of the friend I once knew, trying desperately to prove that she's the right one for him. Like a peacock strutting her most decorative feathers, she puts on an exhaustive campaign to convince him that she is the coolest, skinniest, richest, wildest, sweetest, most adventurous girl in existence in an attempt to live up to the image she *thinks* Chad has of the girl dancing on the bar the night he first saw her. Meanwhile, eclipsing the genuinely cool, quirky beauty I'd come to love so much.

And because he can't be trusted, she decides that every single girl in her sphere is competition, *including me.* On a weekend trip, when we're deciding what car to rent, I suggest getting an automatic because Amber doesn't drive stick—which earns me a glare worthy of junior high school playgrounds everywhere—because, *obviously,* Chad won't like her anymore if she can't drive stick shift.

One night at a Widespread Panic show, a tall, sexy guy with a Southern accent introduces himself and asks, "Are y'all sisters?"

"Yeah, twins; I'm older," Amber slurs, as if being older is something very important, before grabbing my wrist and pulling me down the aisle. Before he's out of earshot, I glance back with a wink, "but I'm wiser."

Cleaning up the remains of her divorce and this erratic performance she's putting on pushes her to the edge, and her once-enviable figure shrinks fifteen pounds lighter almost overnight. Fueled by alcohol and drugs, Amber blows like a volcano at anyone who steps on the wrong side of her path. Unfortunately, that person is often me.

Night after night, I find myself escaping her wrath in fear as she rips into me for talking to a girl who is flirting with Chad or not substantiating some story she is weaving to him. Chad is the prize, and she is a contender of Olympian proportions, and nothing or nobody will stand in her way.

Where, oh where, has my dear friend gone?

One night something happens that I can't quite explain.

Perhaps it's because of the spiritual work I've been doing. Maybe it's that I'm now aware of an undercurrent of energy—a sort of invisible magic only available to people with sharpened senses not dulled from the synthetic substances?

Whatever the reason, the prospect of ingesting cocaine, ecstasy, or even my trusty little helper Xanax starts to feel like an obstacle in my pursuit of genuine happiness.

But just because a light bulb went off in my head doesn't mean it went off for anyone else, and the party, and Amber's volatile-behavior, rages on. I begin making excuses so I can avoid her, and she's so wrapped up in Chad she doesn't even notice. But one thing I can't avoid is the party we've been planning before the Widespread Panic Show at The Outside Lands Music Festival in San Francisco at the house she and Robert used to share in Pacific Heights.

The party is pretty much her baby, but a few long months ago, when we were still "peas and carrots" as she liked to say, she asked if I'd like to host it with her. Call it the proper Southern hostess in her, or just wanting to impress Chad, but she decides to make this a party to remember. She has invitations printed with an old-school photo of the band accompanied by a lyric from their song "Heroes."

Old friends, lifetimes, don't let a single memory fade away.
PARTY BEFORE THE SHOW

We send invites to just about every music lover we know and come the day of, we have all the ingredients for an amazing party: sunshine, an ice luge carved into an electric guitar, a piñata, custom-made cups with another lyric printed on them: *melted whiskey in my hand*, and all to be served by a "hot chick bartender wearing a sexy tee shirt"—Amber's orders. And for people drinking beer, no problem: Amber has custom-made koozies that say, *sippin' on a tall boy*—a lyric from yet another song. Only problem is that Amber and I are tense at best.

The house, an old San Francisco Victorian she and Robert had planned on restoring before their relationship went the way of the dodo bird, has views spanning from the Legion of Honor, to the Golden Gate, and all the way over to Alcatraz. She rents tables and chairs that we arrange on the deck, and we slice up the sub sandwiches we'd picked up on Union Street, turn on some tunes, and wait for our guests to arrive.

As people make their way out to the deck, everyone is blown away by the level of detail we put into the party, which serves as a nice big and much-needed Band-Aid over our problems.

By two o'clock, the party is in full swing and I didn't even notice the tall guy who'd asked Amber and I if we were sisters at the Los Angeles Widespread Panic show arrive. But there he is, casually leaning against the railing of the deck, sporting a tee shirt that says *Hugs not Drugs* and shiny, rainbow disco pants. His skin is the color of caramel ice cream, and his eyes are greyish blue.

Suddenly, Amber yanks my arm and drags me over to him and his crew. "Do you remember Emily from Panic LA?" she asks him.

"Of course," he responds easily.

"We bumped into him at the Boom Boom Room last night, late night," she informs me, "and he's from the same place in Houston that Chad's from!"

"Small world." I look up at him with a smile. "You guys just up here for the shows?" I ask as Amber flitters away.

"We are on a road trip," another guy pipes up. "I'm Billy, by the way."

"Nice to meet you," I raise my cocktail to his and give it a little cheers.

"Great party," he comments appreciatively.

"Happy to have you guys here!" I exclaim. "Where are you headed next?"

"Vegas and then Aspen for the jazz festival," Billy responds.

"You should come to Vegas with us," Walker suggests with a flirtatious smile. "We head out tonight after the shows."

"I would..." I say, "but I don't think I can swing it this time," I explain flirting right back.

The three of us hang out in the sun, joking around up until it is time to head out for the show. I find out that Walker lives in Newport Beach, is in the process of opening a high-end residential treatment center for teenagers who have drug and alcohol problems, and that he indeed prefers hugs over drugs... well, at least as of the past three years.

With his open and fun-loving demeanor, and the light blue boa he's picked up off the stairwell and wrapped around his neck, I'm having a little difficulty believing that there isn't a cocktail in his cup.

"Will I see you later?" he asks as we exchange numbers.

"I hope so," I respond. And I do.

On the way to Golden Gate Park, my throat begins to feel raw and dry.

I will not be sick. I will not be sick. I will not be sick.

As much as I try to enjoy the show, I can't fight it; I know I'm getting sick and instead of joining the others for late night, I head back to my friend Carrie's house, where I'm staying, to go to bed.

The next morning, I'm sure microscopic razor blades have infiltrated my throat. I prop myself up with a pillow in Carrie's bed and dial James. Fortunately, he answers on the second ring.

"Hello, Sweet Pea!"

"Hi," I grumble.

"What have *you* been creating?"

"My throat is killing me," I croak out. "Amber and I had our party yesterday. I think I had too much whiskey."

"That may be true," he agrees with a chuckle, "but that has nothing to do with why your throat hurts."

"What do you mean?"

"I see a gooey grayish energy stuck in your throat," he says, reading me. "True or false—you've been editing yourself? Not communicating thoughts that you're feeling?"

My thoughts float back to Amber and how I've been withholding things that I want to say to her because I'm basically afraid of having another confrontation. I finally break down on the phone to James about Amber, and how the friend I once had has vanished without a trace.

"Your throat is your fifth energy center and is responsible for communication. The frequency of these thoughts is attracting a very dense energy into your throat and without assistance this will manifest into an infection."

"It will?" I ask dubiously.

"This may be difficult to wrap your head around, but the medical community knows very little about *why* our bodies break down and get sick. They are great at labeling and even stabilizing conditions, but there's just so much about how these bodies function that most people don't know."

I let out a helpless groan.

"Scale of one to ten, where are we?"

"Eleven," I whisper.

"OK, clean your hands off, and start pinching the skin in your neck lightly, and let's see if we can pull this out," he says kindly.

I pull the skin away from my neck for the next few minutes, still unable to swallow.

"OK, now say, 'I'm in alignment with James to do this healing,' and clean your hands off again, then you want to circle in a clockwise motion right in front of your neck."

I do as I'm told, and after about five minutes of circling, James explains, "This is like an oatmeal consistency of a dull grey color all coming out of you. A very dense energy. Oh! There you go!" he exclaims victoriously. "You are now bringing in some green. *Goooooooood job!*"

He's quiet for a few more minutes and then he says, "OK, let's monitor. It's gotten better, worse, or stayed exactly the same?"

I try to swallow and assess. It is, without a doubt, considerably better. Not gone, but better. I can actually swallow without too much difficulty. I lean over and take a sip of my water.

"Better, but still hurts."

"So if it was at a pain level of eleven before, where is it now?"

"Hmmm... probably a five."

"Wow, you must be really capable," he says, validating me

even though from what I can see, he's doing all the work. "OK, clean your hands off and circle again."

"There is something confusing me about this whole situation with Amber," I start out.

"Yes," James replies calmly.

"From what I know about the spiritual mirror, if her behavior is driving me so crazy, then it should be mirroring something inside of me, right?"

"Yes, it is lighting up energized pictures that you have," he confirms.

"Even if I take a really honest look at myself in the *harsh* light of day, I do not see matching behaviors here," I insist, thinking of her recent behavior.

"Really?" he asks, amused. "You can't think of a time when you were trying to *prove* something to someone?"

And just like that, after months of trying to figure out why her behavior is grating on my last nerve to the point I can't even be near her, he strips it down with such a simple question.

How could I have missed it?

It's not necessarily about trying to find the match between the things we do; it's *the source* of the behavior. It is about being inauthentic and trying to prove something, and yes, for that I'm guilty.

Shit, very guilty.

I certainly tried to prove I was the perfect girl for Aidan. Then the second wave of recognition whacks me in the face like walking into the SAE house and being hit with the overwhelming stench of Abercrombie and Fitch cologne. Come to think of it, we've been mirroring each other more than I'd even allowed myself to see. Sure, she's been trying to prove how great she is to this guy; now that I'm open to seeing it, I see I'd been trying to prove something to my old friends.

Rather than being honest with them and showing them how badly I've been hurting inside, I've put on an Academy Award worthy performance to show that I'm just fine, *dammit*. When in reality, I've wanted nothing more than their love and support, especially from Courtney. How can I blame them for not being there for me when I haven't let them know how much I've needed them? My cheeks burn in shame over how obnoxious my pursuit to not be pitied must've been.

"Well, when you put it like that," I admit sheepishly.

I quickly relay my thoughts to him.

"Ah ha!" he exclaims jubilantly. "And how does this recognition make you feel?"

Like a life-size Gumby riding a life-size Pokey has been removed with a crane from my shoulders.

I ache, realizing what a terrible friend I've been.

"Compassion," I acknowledge softly.

"Feels different, doesn't it?"

"Very. She's just trying to be OK... probably terrified about being on her own after so long."

"If you feel like you need to *prove* something to someone— that you are smarter, more successful, a better trapeze artist, whatever, you have little real affinity for yourself," he informs me. "But making recognition of truth is very powerful and transformative."

"I've been rejecting her when she probably needs me most, just as Courtney and my old friends rejected me when I needed them most. But the thing is I now understand *why* they weren't there for me."

"Um, yes, United Airlines," James chirps into the phone. "I'd like to book a one-way ticket to the Bahamas for a very, *very*, extended vacation," he jokes, working himself into a hearty chuckle. I smile at his corniness.

"We create relationships for a very important reason," he declares. You wouldn't happen to know what that reason is, would you...?"

"To learn about ourselves?" I guess meekly, recalling a time he said that.

"Young grasshopper," he says in his best Mr. Miyagi voice, "dis is *huge* recognition."

Then, swapping back into his regular voice, he continues, "With this understanding that you create each and every person to learn about numero uno—you—you remain in the vibration of gratitude rather than victim nature, which is a very powerful vibration that attracts what you want into your life rather than the other way around."

"Jody mentioned the power of gratitude when we spoke."

"It's one of the most important spiritual superpowers," he says very seriously.

"It's kind of amazing how all of a sudden things can look so different than they have for so long," I reflect, even more surprised by how my throat, which felt like it was being slashed with razors less than twenty minutes ago, feels perfectly normal.

Energy healing is CRAZY! Or wait, maybe everyone else is CRAZY to think that this is CRAZY and taking expensive drugs that don't actually cure your sickness is NORMAL?

My mind hurts like I'm trying to solve a complicated mathematical word problem as I try to wrap my head around what just happened.

"This is called growth," James informs me.

"Well, all I know is I want to keep growing," I say determinedly.

"Well, looky here," he slides easily into his Trucker James twang "we gotta hot one."

PART II:

PERMISSION

TO BE

FEMALE

11.

"And I'm a million different people from one day to the next..."
— The Verve

September rolls in "hotter than one hundred pigs in a blanket," as my cousin's four-year-old likes to say, and I do what I was sure I'd never do—move to the eastside of town, farther away from my beloved ocean and everything familiar. Without much effort, I find a charming Hollywood bungalow tucked into the folds of leafy banana plants and shaded by sagacious old palm trees at the base of Beachwood Canyon, known more for the hordes of Japanese tourists snapping shots of themselves in front of the Hollywood sign than its wild beauty. Maybe it's the proximity to such an iconic Los Angeles monument, but I'm aware of a distinctly different energy in this little canyon—an energy that anything is possible.

"Woooo hoo, congratulations!" James exclaims slowly as I open the door to let him in. He hands me a square glass vase half filled with sand, with a few dozen blades of tall dry grass reaching out in all different directions. The effect is artsy, dramatic, and unique.

"Thank you," I stammer, surprised.

"Well, of course!"

"What do you think?"

"Fabulous, Sweet Pea! Give me a tour!" If he notices that my bungalow feels like a sauna tucked inside a steam room in the middle of Thailand during the summer solstice, he doesn't mention it.

"This is the living room. These bungalows—there are only six in the complex—were built in the 1920's as mountain cabins for the wealthy who lived in Beverly Hills."

James' eyes travel up the white stucco walls, to the vaulted ceilings, and down to the little round fireplace. I can tell he's reading the energy in the room. He yawns deeply, then says that the guy who lived here before is still here—well, his spirit is anyway—and I had a lifetime in Hollywood in the 1940's as a B list actress, who never quite made it.

Great.

"Lots of great art walls!" he says, breezing into the dining room.

I open one of the French doors leading out to my private red-brick patio, which—thanks to the guy before me—has a luscious garden teeming with bougainvillea, oversized banana plants, fresh rosemary, bushels of lavender, and even an exotic little cactus garden. I crisscrossed a few strands of thick Italian light bulbs across the patio.

Sitting in a faux wicker chair, James slips into "French": "Bonjour mi ami, ze flores are biutiful, oui?"

A bright orange butterfly dances atop the bougainvillea before swooping around my face.

"Good sign," he says with a wink.

The kitchen is big, but I lament the lack of dishwasher, garbage disposal, or washer and dryer.

"Oh, you just need to find a nice laundry place nearby. For years I had this nice laundromat just down the street from the boat. And when I'd go to pick it up, it would be all folded so nicely and wrapped in this great brown paper."

How does this man find fun and gratitude in everything he does?

"What an amazing creation, Sweet Pea," James remarks when the tour is over. He plops down on my new red sofa and rests his blue and green Sperry Top Siders on the edge of the coffee table. I get a glass of water and plunk down beside him.

"So what are we doing today?" I ask expectantly.

"Well, how are we doooooooing?"

Relatively speaking, I'm doing great. Amazing, really.

But I did say relatively, didn't I?

"OK, I *do* feel dramatically better than when I saw you at my sister's apartment in San Francisco."

"That day when your aura was grey and you were dead on arrival?" he jokes.

"On the one hand, in less than two years I've managed to: no longer need pharmaceutical assistance to sleep, distance myself my Aidan, meet some new friends, and create a beautiful living space, and—possibly most importantly—I've started to believe I haven't made terrible mistakes."

"You've made an immensity of changes." James takes my hand and digs his thumb into my palm. "You are starting to vibrate differently."

"On the other hand," I confess, "I'm just not enthused about my job the way I once was, and my new boss seems way too interested in my every move, I still feel the sting of abandonment from my old friends, and why is that I'm drawn to guys who are initially infatuated with me only to... well, let's just say, I finally understand that show *Sex in the City*. And even those women, who thought the dating scene in Manhattan was a battlefield, had an *even worse* experience when they came to LA for the weekend!"

"I must've missed that episode," James responds dryly.

I tell him about the cute DJ surfer who I've been seeing: "One day he's into me, the next he isn't."

"I see you two do have an epic. Sometimes we have an epic, but only one person can recognize the connection, and it isn't until years later that the other person recognizes you."

I let out a long sigh. "Then, when it comes to the sweet and loving guys like Super Bob who want a sincere connection, I'm just—"

"Lemme guess, you're just not *feelin'* it?"

I laugh out loud at his imitation of me.

"Yes... we are going to talk about that," James affirms seriously.

"I mean, I know enough to know that I'm responsible for creating these people, but why?"

"Oh, these guys are just..." he pauses, looking around before deciding on, "the palm tree boys, dropping into your life the way palm fronds fall to the ground." Remember, like attracts like, so the boys you are attracted to are going to match your vibration. We don't attract who we want; we attract who we are.

"Well, I'd like to create a partner of a little more significance then a palm frond."

"In some time, you will create a very different kind of man. But you need to shift your vibration a little more before you bring him to you. As your vibration moves into one of greater love, acceptance, and respect for you, you will attract a man who also has more love, acceptance, and respect for himself. And only a man who loves and respects himself can love and respect you.

"Well, when you put it like that..." I smile sheepishly. "I've really tried to remain in gratitude about Super Bob," I add, hoping it will help my cause.

"This is goooood. And I do wish it was that simple..."

"Uh, oh, what does that mean?"

"Growing up, were you happy that you were a girl, or did you think it looked more fun to be a boy?"

"*I think* we both know I think it looks a lot more fun to be a boy," I say with a crooked smile. I've enviously watched guys enjoy drama-free friendships, freedom to behave anyway they want without ridicule, and being included at dinners and vacations with couples even when they're single. All my life, I wanted to be a boy and hang with the boys.

"Just be happy this ain't the 15th century," he jokes with a faux Southern twang. "Back then it *really* wasn't fun to be a girl."

"Hmph."

"What I'm getting at is that you've given yourself very little permission to run your feminine energy this lifetime, and disastrous things happen to female bodies when they are full of male energy. Not to mention it's more difficult to create in an effortless manner—which is something females have the power to do."

I must look totally confused because he continues, "Females vibrate five times higher than males, considering the fact that your body has the ability to create another life inside it. You should be vibrating here," he stands up and reaches his arm high in the air, "but as long as you're running this male energy, you're going to vibrate here." He lowers his arm down about five feet.

"But I thought you said that I'm vibrating differently!"

"You are because you, as spirit, are taking more ownership of your body, which is allowing you to run more female energy. The more you do this, the more you will come into your true female and healer-girl powers."

"And on one level, when a guy is infatuated with you, he is responding to your feminine vibration. Then when you get fearful that you aren't enough, you call in more masculine energy from your entourage, which tends to be more controlling, manipulating, proving, and performing—believing it will keep you safe. This has a completely different vibration and can impact someone who you are intimate with."

"Wow."

"What most people call 'moody' is many times different spirits coming through the physical form. And keep in mind these guys have entourage too. So one minute a guy is in his body and can't get enough of you, and then he channels his mama or an ex-girlfriend, and suddenly he feels like he wants to punt you off the Brooklyn Bridge. This is the essence of trans-dimensional nature. It's who we are as human beings, and *nobody* is exempt."

"Do beings from people's entourages ever connect more than the actual true spirits?"

"Hmmm... I wonder why you are asking this?" he asks sarcastically.

Then his voice softens. "This is common for people who drink a lot of alcohol and do drugs because these send you even farther out of body. You may recognize that people have different personalities when they're engaged in partying. This is because going out of body leaves you open to a number of spirits.

Is this why indigenous cultures called alcohol spirits? Did they know?

He continues, "The sensation of lacking control, known as addiction, is a result of literally not being in-body enough to maintain ownership. Then any Dick, Bob, or Harry from your entourage directs through your body, making you feel like you have an insatiable appetite for more."

"Spirits with and without physical bodies?" I clarify.

"Correct. And the more emotional pain someone is in, the more they will be out of body because they're living in a pain body and it doesn't feel good to be in that body!"

"True or false, as you've been able to heal and get more in your body, your desire for drugs and alcohol has subsided?"

"Whoa... is that the reason?"

"Yes. As you heal your emotional pain, it makes it easier to be in your body more frequently and maintain ownership."

"Growing up, my mom labeled me 'moody,' which made me defensive because most the time, I didn't have control over my rollercoaster of emotions."

"That's just entourage."

"I guess, I know entourage well then," I acknowledge with a wry smile.

"The key is identifying when it's not you so you can come back in and kick your entourage out."

"How can I tell?"

"Generally speaking, cold hands and feet and forgetfulness are signs you're out of body. But for you personally—your true self is very soft, easy-going, and silly. When you channel your entourage in, you get more abrasive, argumentative, and impatient."

Eeeeek.

"I know people who don't remember what they said or even did because the original spirit that is them wasn't actually doing it."

"But I remember stuff. I mean, maybe less stuff when I've been drunk, but I have a good memory."

"The spiritual realm isn't black and white, Sweet Pea. There are so many variables at play. The strength of your life force is also a factor, and I see when you go out of body, you aren't very far away because you have very strong spiritual will. Your spiritual will is the reason you were able to transcend the entourage controls enough to call me again after so long. Some people I work with are so far away as spirit that they can't remember entire decades."

I watch his gaze shift slightly and can tell he's reading my pictures.

"I also see you really liked how kind and loving and more willing to connect everyone else was when you partied. You've been searching for a familial security that you didn't feel growing up, and you sacrificed a lot to be accepted by this group of people who you wanted to believe were your family."

His words ring very true.

"Throughout the course of a day, we unconsciously channel any number of energy beings from our entourage through our physical bodies. In fact, many of the wealthiest people I've worked with have created their fortunes by bringing other spirits in to do the work for them."

"That doesn't sound like a bad gig to me."

He chuckles at this; "Yeah, it's a great gig, just as long as you don't mind being numb and getting no fulfillment from your creations. If it's not your real spirit creating, it is difficult to gain any real meaning from much of anything. This is another reason why so many people turn to annihilating behaviors. While many people do drugs and alcohol to escape, an equal amount are searching for a way to feel alive. These are all conditions that stem from disconnection to our true spirit."

I cringe, thinking of how I abused my body with drugs in the not-so-distant past.

"However, the more you can get in the body, the more quickly your life will improve. You will have little desire for drugs and alcohol, you will age more slowly, have a surplus of energy you never knew existed, and your creativity will skyrocket."

Well, who wouldn't want that?

James gives me an odd smile that seems to say this is just the tip of the iceberg.

"So much of whom you've thought you are as a person hasn't even really been you."

"What exactly do you mean when you say that?"

"Well, your emotional pain levels have been very high this lifetime, and the bigger they get, the more difficult it is for you to stay in your body."

"So then it's easier for beings to channel through me?"

"Exactly. But that's only part of it. The other part, which is very critical that you understand, is that so many of the thoughts, opinions, and beliefs that you've thought are yours are really just programming that you've accepted from your family, friends, teachers, which they accepted from their family, friends, teachers, and so on back down the line."

"Aye, ye, ye..." I feel my head swelling from all this information.

"Aye, ye, ye is right."

"James?"

"Is this too much?"

"Can we save this for another day?" I ask, feeling my head swell from all of this information.

He laughs. "Of course," he answers, pressing his thumbs into the palms of my hands again, raising his eyebrows in a way that lets me know they are too cold.

"James?" I ask tentatively. "What did you mean when you said that running male energy can be disastrous for a female body?" I ask, trying to get up the nerve to tell him about my battle with transient yeast infections.

"I've kinda had this issue well, for a lot of my life." I can feel my face heating up.

"What kind of issue?"

"Like a transient yeast infection."

"*Like* a transient yeast infection?" he repeats, confused.

"Well, it comes and goes. Doctors have prescribed me countless treatments and pills, which work temporarily, but they make it worse in the long run. I know something is off balance."

"It's too much male energy, where it doesn't belong," he says matter-of-factly. His eyes speed read the air in front of me, left to right.

"Too much male energy in a female body is toxic and will wreak all kinds of havoc because it carries a much denser vibration. It can manifest into infections like you just described or cysts, endometriosis, cramping, pain associated with your cycle, and any number of things."

"The thing is, this issue has been around before I was ever with a guy."

"That has very little to do with it. It's about the energetic information you are choosing to use to power your thoughts and your life.

"I don't get it," I admit, confused.

"Well... would you say that you are a serious person?"

"Hmmmm... I have my moments, I suppose. Maybe more than a few."

"Do you have to put a lot of effort into getting what you want?"

"Presently, it would appear I put in a lot of effort and still *do not* get what I want," I say dryly.

"Problem mentality?"

"Problem mentality?" I repeat.

"Oh, I dunno," he says breezily, "we could go to the Hollywood bowl tonight, but the problem is there's so much traffic. I could ask Betty to come to the party, but then I have to invite Veronica, and she doesn't get along with Archie anymore."

"Sometimes," I guess.

"What about punishment?"

"Punishment?"

"You wouldn't have any I-need-to-be-so-perfect-I'm-at-war-with-myself thoughts, do you?"

"Hmph. I think you know my answer to that one."

"Exhaustion."

"Shit."

"Control?"

"Rut roh."

"Competition?"

I drop my face with my hands.

"You aren't bad or wrong," he assures me. "What if I told you that all of these qualities that you identify actually aren't you at all?"

"What?" I ask, confused.

"They're a consequence of an overarching patriarchal culture that says there can only be one king, one president, one Superman. This turns the human experience into a serious affair that takes great effort to be number one. Not to mention there's a boat load of problems on the ol' camino to bein' top dawg," he slips into Trucker James twang. Lots of unknowns, so you gotta control everything in sight, and people don't agree with you, just punish 'em with a smart bomb. When the goal of life is to be number one, everyone and everything is a competition. And the whole thing is totally and utterly exhausting."

"Yikes."

"What are the female qualities?"

"When the feminine doesn't agree to the patriarchal programming, she retains the essence of her spiritual nature. Which means vibrating in amusement instead of seriousness, ease over effort, passion instead of problems, trust instead of control, permission verses punishment, collaboration as opposed to competition, and rejuvenation instead of exhaustion."

"Those sound just a tad more appealing..." I remark dryly.

"Thing is... it isn't so easy to do because men are in charge, and naturally, women want approval and acceptance from the people running this place, so you drop your frequency to match where the men are."

"Hmmmm... so that's how it works?" I muse, fascinated. "Wait—why do we even want to be with men if they are like this?"

"Well, this is just so familiar, most people don't know anything different. And, of course, not every man is here. The man who goes inside to heal and expands his consciousness beyond the centuries-old patriarchal programing also vibrates with this lighter vibration because that's the essence of his spiritual nature as a well.

These characteristics aren't just female, but it's easier for the women to get there because you naturally vibrate five times higher as the life givers and sustainers of the planet. It will be the women that lead the change on the planet by transcending the patriarchal controls, and in doing so help men return to the essence who they really are."

Interesting...

"So what do I do about it? You know... my issue."

"Hmmmm..." He strokes his beard as he looks more closely at my pictures. After almost a minute of silence, he says, "It's very important for you to work on staying in-body, and not channeling in these dense energies from your entourage when you get fearful."

"The problem is," I say, totally clueless I'm in problem mentality, "it's so normal to me, I'm not even aware I'm doing it. How do I tell if I'm running this more masculine-patriarchal energy?"

"Well, generically anytime you have cold hands or feet, you know that you are channeling and your original spirit isn't in the body. But you specifically..." he stops to read, "you know you're channeling denser frequencies when you feel like you have something to prove."

I feel my cheeks turning pink.

"You wouldn't know what that feels like, would you?" he teases.

12.

*"I've been afraid of changing
Because I built my life around you"
—Stevie Nicks*

"You're letting out a tremendous amount of grief," James informs me as I lay face down on his healing table in the middle of my living room. "Are you aware of this?"

Three weeks have flown by since our last session, and although I've been diligent about running hot pink throughout my body, I'm not sure anything's actually changed.

"By grief do you mean old pain?" I ask as he gently pulls the skin away from my spine.

"'That's correct; grief that's a dark inky-purple color. Pain that goes far deeper than the abandonment you feel from Aidan or Courtney; it's connected to your family."

I'm a little surprised—I wasn't aware I'd been abandoned by my family, but my body shudders, and I know, instantly, he's hit on something.

"Your agreement in this lifetime is with your father, so it's his abandonment impacting you the most. But, I also see you are holding onto your mother leaving the family as an abandonment. And, your sister, who you idolized, whether she's conscious of it or not, has been rejecting you on an energy level from when you showed up and her life as the only child in the family ended."

I'm reminded of stories my mother told me about my sister dumping a plate of spaghetti on my head or throwing potatoes in my face. When I was old enough to join the big kids in the sandbox, Mom would find Sophie meticulously piling sand up around me in an attempt to bury me alive. And one of my clearest memories is of Sophie gathering my hair into pigtails before pulling a shiny pair of shears from behind her back and snipping them off. In what seemed like slow motion, I watched my tresses drift to the floor like a fistful of feathers.

James interrupts me. "As long as you hold this abandonment in your heart, you will continue to be attracted to people that will eventually abandon you."

I let out a little groan.

"Meanwhile, the guys who *are* interested in a sincere connection and long-term partnership? You'll want to send them straight to Timbuktu."

"Why?"

"Well, channeling aside, this abandonment is a core picture for you. We all have core pictures that we carry from lifetime to life, and if they're not neutralized energetically, they'll have us creating the same situations over and over again. Our forms will change, but the conflict will remain if no recognitions are made."

"So you're saying I've been abandoned in many lifetimes and that's why I continue to be abandoned?"

"Exactly right, because spirit is always looking for an opportunity to help you heal old wounds inside of you. So you attract people into your life so you have an opportunity to heal this picture."

"Hmmmm..."

"It's also important to understand that in many lifetimes you've also been the abandoner. Something that's difficult for people to accept is many times when they're victims of terrible atrocities, in past lifetimes they were actually the ones that created those very atrocities," he says neutrally.

"The cosmic joke is, here I am in this lifetime trying to help people tear down the walls of illusion they've imprisoned themselves with, but I've had lifetimes creating these very structures that keep people imprisoned," he adds.

"Wait... I'm confused. I was under the impression that if you are bad in one life, you will be handed a worse fate in the next life, and if you do good things in this life, you will have a good life in the next."

Whatever happened to good Karma?

"Well, first of all, you want to just monitor how often you think of things in labels, like good and bad, right and wrong," he cautions lightly. Once you get past those judgments and can just be in acceptance of everything as it is, you will come into your clairvoyance."

I shift my body in an attempt to relieve some of the pressure in the face cradle.

"Often times people wonder how they raised two children the exact same way, with the exact same resources, experiences, and so on, but have dramatically different children from the day they are born. This is because we all have pictures from previous lives and things that we're working on that have yet to be neutralized."

"Can you give me an example?"

He pauses for a moment before saying, "OK, an extreme example is: someone commits a murder in this lifetime—that person was likely murdered in many past lifetimes, and then flipped to the other side. What happens on an energy level is when a person is murdered, he's ensnared by the hate-filled energy of the person who murdered him. And he's mad because he lost his life, his precious human body—his *human* experience. If this happens lifetime over lifetime over lifetime, the rage vibration compounds until that spirit is so full of hate that he flips to the other side of the dichotomy and commits a murder."

"Whoa." For some reason the image of Patrick Swayze getting murdered in that movie *Ghost* pops into my head.

"On the other hand, let's say someone has been a murderer for many lifetimes. They also accumulate the energy of their victims and carry a victim energy that also compounds, so then after many lifetimes of being a murderer, they may assimilate a piece of information they've picked up from an outside source and flip to being the victim of a murder."

"Can they ever be free of this destiny?" I ask, alarmed.

"Yesssss," he says slowly, "but because the lines of communication are literally shut down to them and the density of the energy blocks new information from getting to them, people do get stuck in this matrix for many lifetimes. However, the power of spiritual will always amazes me. After lifetimes of doing the same thing over and over, a person may gather a tiny piece of information that manages to squeeze through the bundle of energy, and suddenly, it's like they found the lost piece of the puzzle that allows a new different destiny path to unfold before them."

I listen as he reaches into the jar and scoops more coconut oil into his hands then rubs a cool lump into the arch of my right foot.

"Anyway, this is what *you* are doing in this lifetime! You are literally altering your course in this lifetime and for many lifetimes to come by healing your pictures."

"You mean, healing my pictures of abandonment?"

"Yes, and a few others as well." I can hear him smiling.

I go unnaturally still, stalled in my skin as a chill curls down my body, stunned by the enormity of this understanding. For years I've suffered heartbreak from abandonment, wondering why this has happened to me again and again. And if I'm honest with myself, I know I inflicted this same hurt on others—sometimes, not even sure why I'd cast them aside and feeling terrible about it afterward. A dull pain thuds in my heart, thinking about how hurtful I've been.

Hearing me telepathically, James reminds me, "You must validate your path. Everything that you've done has brought you to this moment. You are very brave to face your pictures. Most people just want to order another martini and book another trip to Cabo. The last thing people want to do is face their pictures. People would rather have tea with the biggest, baddest boogieman you can imagine before facing their pictures. The work you are doing in this lifetime is healing many, many lifetimes, and you are changing the course of your epic for this lifetime and many to come."

Everything is right, right now. Everything is right, right now.

"Your immune is low," he declares.

"How can you tell?"

He chuckles lightly. "I think I may have mentioned before

that traditional medicine knows very little about *why* our bodies break down and get sick. As I've told you before, they are good at labeling and even stabilizing conditions, but there's just so much about how these bodies function that most people don't know. When I'm in a healing space, I have access to your entire universe.

"I see inside your aura and have access to your energy centers. I can see where things are impacting you on a very deep level. I have the ability to actually go inside your body and repair things that are broken, destroy the molecules of negative energies that are on their way to manifesting into illness, remove blocks, and spiritually glue things back together that have been disconnected."

I yawn deeply, one-two-three times in a row.

"Thank you."

"For what?"

"Yawning is an energy release that occurs for various reasons—one being the validation of spiritual truth."

I yawn again.

My mind drifts back to what he said about my dad. I'd heard about this whole "daddy issue thing," where girls with absentee or abusive dads are forever doomed to pick men just like their fathers. Let's face it; I clearly have some issues, but Dad—my funny, sweet, dear dad?

∽

When I was four, our family moved from Berkeley to Lafayette, just over the hills to the east for the good public schools. We moved into a large, one-story house, the entire eastern side of which was floor to ceiling windows with an unobstructed view of

Mt. Diablo's commanding crest. With its clean lines and blurred indoor and outdoor living spaces, the house was reminiscent of one of Frank Lloyd Wright's designs. The yard surrounded the house like a crescent moon. In the driveway a 1950's gas pump, now purely decorative, added to the mid-century charm, and out back an S-shaped waterslide arched into the rectangular pool.

We took swimming lessons from an old lady named Ms. Howl, got a dog and named him Winston, and started elementary school down the street, filling our pockets with sugar cubes in hope that the horses would be hungry along the way. I began ballet classes, while Sophie's beautiful soprano voice earned her a spot in the prestigious San Francisco Girls Chorus. Everything seemed rosy until less than a year after we moved, Mommy told us she was moving to another house on the other side of town and Daddy wasn't coming.

"Sometimes mommies and daddies love each other but they don't want to live together anymore," they explained. Of course, even at age four I could tell something was wrong, especially when Sophie started wailing. From that point on, we split our time between two houses.

Our schedule was school weeks with Mom and the weekends with Dad—an arrangement benefiting everybody because Dad worked full time during the weekdays and Mom was always jetting off somewhere fabulous on the weekends. Dad would pick us up at Mom's house on Friday on his way home from the office, and we'd head straight for Roundtable Pizza, where he'd pull a wad of cash out of his pocket, plucking off a couple twenties for each of us to indulge in as many Cindy Lauper songs and games of Ms. Pac Man as we could stomach, while he drank a pitcher of draft beer and read the *San Francisco Chronicle*.

Back at the house, we'd all pile in Dad's king size waterbed for a slumber party along with our matching stuffed bears. Dad's was the biggest, Sophie's was medium size, and mine was the baby. We'd stay up late watching one of the three movies we owned: *Sixteen Candles*, *The Sound of Music*, or, my all-time favorite, a made-for-TV movie about the gold medalist Nadia Comaneci we'd recorded on our trusty Beta.

Morning's breakfast wasn't complete without Daddy's special drink: freshly squeezed orange juice blended with vanilla extract, sugar, heavy whipping cream, an egg, and some ice. Dad was raised by Portuguese parents, who believed adding heavy whipping cream, an egg, and some butter and sugar to just about everything was nutritious.

We'd gather in his makeshift art studio, donning his old tees as smocks. He'd set each of us up with our own easels, a bucketful of brushes, and a plastic plate for a pallet, but after that, he let us just do our thing.

"Just let it all out," he'd encourage. "There are no rules."

Not believing ourselves to have our father's innate talent, we usually gave into the lure of playing outside. Sophie made clear that she was the boss, for the following reasons: she was older, taller, and left handed, which clearly meant she got to go first, have whatever side she wanted, any color she chose, and no, I could not touch her stuff under any circumstances. If I didn't comply, she wouldn't play with me. And if she had a friend over, I wasn't to bother them.

If I did comply, which I always did because I was sure she was the coolest girl I'd ever met, I got to be her accomplice in lemonade-stand pursuits, stealing eggs from the neighbor's chicken coop that we'd attempt to hatch in our slippers, or playing Marco Polo in the swimming pool for hours on end. Pruned and waterlogged and with eyes like vampires from the chlorine, we'd refuse to leave the water, forcing Dad to bring our hotdogs to the pool's edge if he wanted us to eat.

Sophie was my hero, and I could never understand why she was so nice to her friends but not to me. If Dad noticed the hierarchy between us, he never mentioned anything. If he caught us fighting, he'd dismiss it as nothing more than a sisterly squabble. I just tried to be as agreeable as possible with the hopes that maybe Sophie would recognize me as a friend. That finally happened years later when I went to boarding school. Home for summers, Sophie and I never got along better. I guess I finally transitioned from annoying kid sister to friend, and when I returned home to discover that I was no longer welcome in the cliquey circle of hometown girlfriends, Sophie and her friends embraced me! My dream come true. We'd cruise around in her silver Cabriolet, lay out by the pool, shop, hit up parties together, and take trips up to Lake Tahoe without our parents. We thought we were *so* mature!

But back when we were little, when I was still her chief annoyance, most winter weekends we'd go up to the snow, where Dad insisted we learn the sport he loved so much. The three of us would cram onto the single bench cushion that was the front seat of his suburban and sing along to Laura Brannigan and Paul Simon as we headed into the mountains.

Once at our cabin—a cozy little place, with bright orange 1970's red and orange shag carpet, that Dad and his best friend had scraped enough money to buy when they were twenty-five years old—Dad would crawl into the downstairs closet to turn the water back on. Then, as the water began hissing and spouting up out of all of the faucets, we'd all scramble around, trying to turn them off as fast as possible.

Decked out in navy-blue bellbottom ski pants with rainbow suspenders, he taught me to ski by guiding me down the mountain wedged inside his legs. He started out by finding "the easy way" down, building up my confidence, and by age nine there wasn't a run on the mountain I hadn't been down.

The place for après ski was Le Chamoix, a loft bar that was famous for its hot sausages called squealers. Dad was friends with the bartenders, so they let Sophie and me in. Dad would amble around, chatting with other locals with a pitcher of beer in one hand and a squealer in the other, while Sophie and I wrapped ourselves around his legs, using his ski boots for seats. "No reason to fight the traffic," Dad rationalized as he ordered another pitcher of beer. Later, at the cabin, Dad's hard no-TV rule forced us to read books and play endless games of chess, Connect Four, and Monopoly. "Oh, let's talk to each other and remember why we're a family," he'd say when we begged for a television.

At bedtime, burrowed into our sleeping bags in the bunk-bed room, we'd beg Daddy to tell us one of his stories. He'd lie back with his eyes closed, rubbing his temples and murmuring slowly, "Let me dig through my files and see if I can find a good one." If we were lucky, it became a two-part story, as was the case with *The Magic Rocking Chair*. The story began with a young girl's adventures traveling back in time merely by rocking backwards, only to be left with the cliff hanger—to be continued the next night—when she sat down on the magic rocking chair for a second time, this time rocking forward first; an action that sent her reeling into the future. He entertained us with vivid descriptions of her escaping the castle to be with her true love—an artist boy, and then the next night she skipped around along the Milky Way. Looking back at these stories now, the fact that he was able to bring them around, leaving us a little lesson at the end, when he was likely stoned out of his mind, was rather remarkable.

"Just packin' around... three bugs in a rug," he'd say, shaking his head. The tinge of sadness dimming his smile didn't escape my young self; it was obvious he still wondered why my mother hadn't wanted this life.

Despite all of these wonderful things, Sophie desperately missed our mother and would often wake up in the middle of the night crying, "I want my mommy," and asking over and over again, "Where's my mommy?"

My dad looked so helpless then.

Wedged between my parents' contention and the prickly angst of my sister, I aimed to be the perfect daughter. Like a bald guy overcompensating with a goatee, I tried to balance my sister's unease with being as easygoing as possible. The last thing I wanted was for him to feel like we didn't love or appreciate him, or the worst scenario possible—to not be able to spend our weekends with him because we were too much of a problem.

I soon discovered that by doing everything in my power to be the most relaxed and non-complaining kid, I was rewarded. Not with more clothes or toys, but with the many gifts that came with my dad's friendship: more laughter, a closer bond, and grateful sidelong glances acknowledging we were in cahoots against everything life was throwing our way.

Stella, our British au pair, was the only woman we ever saw around him for the first few years after our mother moved out.

She was hired when my parents were still married, and then stayed on to help for a few years. She had a thick mane of wildly curly hair and liked to drink, laugh, and lay out topless by our pool. It was the 80's, and nobody batted an eye. Her room was on the opposite side of the house, and she only joined us sporadically on our adventures, but years later, when Sophie and I were eavesdropping on a phone call between our parents, we discovered that soon after the divorce, our father began properly shagging the nanny.

We liked having her around, but it's the memories of when just Dad and I were together that are etched in my heart, so simple and sweet at the same time. Crisp fall mornings at my soccer games, followed by salami sandwiches on the patio at Daniels' Deli. Afterwards we'd venture across the street to the Lafayette Bookstore where I had free reign to stack as many books about the magical and mystical, or portals to other realms of reality on the checkout counter as I could muster. Back at the house, he'd build me a nest with down comforters, blankets, and pillows in front of the fire, leaving me happily engrossed in other worlds. Little did I know these peaceful afternoons, when I was left to the expansiveness of my own imagination, were a resource that would carry me throughout my entire life.

Come Monday morning, Dad would pull my hair into a ponytail on the top of my head and send me off with two identical brown bag lunches packed to the brim.

"For trading purposes," he explained with a wink.

Then, after almost seven years of this reliable routine, things changed almost overnight. Dad had "met someone, and she's coming to Tahoe with us," he explained as we pulled into the Sacramento Airport to pick up a slender woman eleven years his junior who could've easily been Annette Benning's stand in. They'd met when she led a sales workshop for his company.

Arah seemed as surprised as we were that this was how our first introduction was going down. And what started with one weekend in Tahoe led to her leaving her Minneapolis home to come to live with us. Six years later, they got married in the backyard, shoving cake in each other's faces in front of sixty of their closest family and friends.

My ten-year-old self knew Dad deserved to be happy, and I did actually like Arah. She was smart, with a quick and sometimes sarcastic sense of humor, and from day one she treated me like a person, not a kid.

But, inevitably, the magical world of the three bugs and a rug died the day she arrived. Naturally, she slept in his bed, so there wasn't room for us, or the bears, anymore. And she wasn't a skier, so our trips to the mountains together became sparse, and our long-standing schedule of weekends with Dad and weeks with Mom was modified to three weeks on, three weeks off. Most likely they wanted some weekends to themselves; or, as it was communicated to us, they wanted more "real time" with us.

The most obvious change I witnessed was a difference in the vibe of the house. It still felt like "home," but now Dad needed more from us, and in return, we got less of him.

"It could be worse," everyone told us. "At least she doesn't have kids."

With his goofy sense of humor and offbeat genius, I never stopped adoring my dad, even if from a greater distance. As the roads of our lives continued to take us down separate paths,

I missed him terribly, and the special memories of my enchanting childhood with him were never far from my mind.

~

So now, as I lay on the healing table, listening to James talk about this abandonment I'm holding inside of my heart related to my father, tears pool in the corners of my eyes. Even though he didn't physically leave me, he abruptly abandoned the enchanting world he'd worked so hard to create for us.

"What you have to understand is that you and your father have a very long epic connection," he pauses, "and you came in for your dad."

"Came in where for my dad?" Sometimes it's like James is speaking an entirely different language.

"You came into your human body; remember, this is just the container," he explains with a smile, pinching the skin on my forearm.

"So you are saying I chose to be in my family because of the past lives I had with my father?"

"You got it," he says, enthused. "As spirit we choose our physical bodies based on past lifetimes and the promises and agreements we made in that lifetime. But the thing is, your dad wasn't your dad in those lifetimes." And then, as casually as if he were informing me that my root beer float is ready on the counter, he says, "You were lovers." A tingle shoots through my heart.

Weird!

"In one of your lives it looks like you were salsa dancers or something." His eyes move very quickly left to right. "I see you twirling all around to different competitions." Then, casually, "fun outfits."

Suddenly, I'm on the back patio where my dad twirled me around as a young girl to Elton John's "I Guess That's Why They Call It the Blues."

"When you tell someone you are going to love him or her forever and never be apart, you are literally agreeing to be with that person lifetime after lifetime. Remember, forms change; agreements remain."

Holy shit.

"Many women are never able to disconnect from Daddy—which makes genuine intimate connection with a man very difficult—because the epic connections are so strong."

He's silent for a minute, then asks, "Are you aware of making your dad senior to you?"

"You mean like wanting his approval?"

"Exact-a-mundo, Sweet Pea."

"But isn't that normal?" I can feel myself heating up in defense. "You know, wanting your parents to be proud of you?"

"Normalcy is a lot of things: competition, pain, performance..." he says neutrally.

"*Riiiiight...*" I mumble sheepishly.

Suddenly it hits me like a Mack Truck meeting a deer at 70mph on a moonless night. Between trying to be perfect for my dad to gain his approval and performing so my mom would loosen her reigns on me, I've never once really explored what it means to be me.

"Just as you did with Aidan, when someone else is senior to you, you lose affinity for yourself because, in essence, you are saying that you are not good enough just as you are, so you have to perform, which means you are inauthentic, to receive love."

"Way to bring it all around to present time," I say sarcastically.

"This is very common because women have been second-class citizens for so long. Of course, there are exceptions, but generally, women will change everything for a man, taking on his vocabulary, his interests, his group of friends in return for acceptance. But the cosmic joke is you never really feel accepted because it isn't the real you that is being accepted. It is the performance that is accepted. Which is a deep contrast to real love."

Amber immediately pops into my mind. Whenever she wanted to prove a point, she'd say, *"Robert will tell you"* or *"Robert says,"* as if his word held some greater importance.

"You've essentially springboarded yourself into a lifetime of performance because you've believed that there is a *right* and *wrong* way to be, to live, and to create in order to be accepted. This ends up limiting not just what you create but also how you are able to create for yourself, which are both very different than creating from a place where you have belief in yourself."

"Aye, ye, ye... OK, I'm officially hard times-a-roo," I declare, slightly defeated. "Now what?"

"That's really up to you. If you don't remove your father from your heart, you will have difficulty really connecting to a male partner and creating authentically for yourself. Not to mention you're holding this energy of abandonment here." He points to the center of my chest.

"But I love my dad! What does that *mean*, to remove him from my heart?"

"You have an incredible amount of affinity for your dad, and he for you. He didn't intentionally abandon you. That's just how your young mind processed it. To remove his energy doesn't mean that you don't love him," he explains calmly. "In fact, as you are able to remove him from your heart, your love will most likely grow stronger because you will rid yourself of this abandonment vibration, allowing yourself more compassion for him and everyone around you."

Looking back now, I did feel abandoned when Arah came into our lives, and it's definitely how I felt back in ninth grade when I went off to boarding school and returned home for Christmas break to find all of my friends had decided I was no longer welcome in their group. And never had I felt more abandoned than when Aidan started pushing me out of his life after all of the promises we made to each other, coupled with the rejection from Courtney."

"Knowing that you are creating everyone and everything for your personal benefit and evolution means no blame or shame to anyone in your life for any of your circumstances," he reminds me kindly. "You must remember your mother leaving your father had nothing to do with you. She, like everyone else, is on her own path, working out agreements from the past."

I stare back at him unconvinced.

"You might want to look at letting go of this blame you have for her in your heart. It had a dense vibration that isn't serving you."

"Hmph."

"Now I know I'm making sense! When you understand spiritual law, you see that you are indeed creating everything in your life for your personal growth and benefit. *Everything.* And it's your responsibility to release energy that's been in your heart; otherwise, you'll continue to create this cycle of abandonment again and again."

"Well, if that isn't motivation to change, I don't know what is!" I lift up my head and flash him a crooked smile, trying to lighten up the heaviness I feel settling in around me."

"When I look at your heart on an energy level, it has a very dark energy in it, but you are starting to bring some green in as well, which is a power color for you, but we do need to do a some heart healings; otherwise, down the road, this will eventually lead to a heart attack."

"It will?" I ask, startled.

"No, I just made that up," he jokes, kneading his hand into my calf. "Why do you think heart disease is the number one killer in the US?"

"Mickey D's and a sedentary lifestyle?"

"Haven't you ever heard someone say, 'he was a marathon runner, and a vegetarian, *never ate a piece of bacon in his life!* Then he just dropped dead from a heart attack'?"

"That's from feeling abandoned?" I exclaim in disbelief.

"Or any type of heartbreak really... True or false, when you have felt rejected, ridiculed, or betrayed, you have physically felt pain in your heart?"

"Truuuue..." I say, recalling that piercing feeling.

"Thank you very much," he says with a friendly smirk. "Now it's not that you're going to have a heart attack right away, but if that dark energy stays in your heart, you will continue to attract more of it, and that density will compound upon itself, eventually hardening into plaque and calcification until the heart can no longer function properly and shuts down."

I imagine a little charred briquette pulsing rhythmically in my chest cavity.

"You know you are doing really well?"

"I don't know. Little ol' dark heart over here has a long way to go."

"Yes," he says slowly. "But you are doing it. And you are already changing just by looking at the ways you have been creating in this lifetime."

"But how do I remove the dark energy out from my heart?"

"By doing the healings I can help you to move that out, but it's up to you to replace that energy with a consistent female vibration."

"By filling in?"

"And by *transmuting*," he reminds me in a way that says he knows I've not been transmuting as much as I should. But one of the fastest ways to shift and increase your vibration is to engage in a creative passion."

Not this creative passion stuff again.

"Writing, painting, playing piano or ukulele, writing a poem—all of these things are big power levels for you because it's a very different way of creating. These are all authentic creations that will expand your vision of self, deepen your self-worth, and dramatically increase your energy vibration."

I get what he's saying—sort of—but this likelihood of me actually breaking through to partake in a creative activity after decades of not is pretty slim.

"I'll try."

"OK, completely relax, let your head and neck go, and I'm going to help you extend," he informs me as he cradles my head in his warm hands. "Ready, one, two, three, extend," he commands as he pulls my head gently away from my body. I visualize the arch in my spine and the space increasing between my vertebrae.

"Extend, extend, extend," he coaches me until finally he returns my head to the table.

"We are going to do a few more of these; is that OK?"

"OK... aside from this being the best massage I've ever received, what exactly are you doing?"

"As I told you before... I'm entering your body through your aura and have access to your energy centers, where I can see where things are impacting you on a very deep level. I'm inside your body, literally repairing things, removing blocks, and spiritually stitching things back together that have come unhinged. I'm also destroying the molecules of dense energies that are on their way to manifesting into illness.

"Um, hmm. Feels good." Nearly sedated at this point, I ask, "What is it specifically that the extensions are doing?"

"We are trying to increase the flow of energy—which is your life force—up from your first energy center and into your heart and all the way to your head so you can reduce the analytic mind."

I stay quiet for a second, processing what he just said.

"Just like a car needs the fuel to run properly through the carburetor for the best performance, you need energy to run through all the centers to operate at your optimal level."

I run my fingers through my hair, feeling grooves on the side of my head.

Picking up on my cue, he rubs the grooves and explains, "These grooves indicate that your analyzer is swollen right now. You've been attaching meaning to these repetitive levels of good, bad, right, and wrong of how you think you are *supposed* to be."

"That feels so good," I murmur. "Head rub is my favorite."

"You like your head being rubbed because it reduces your analytic mind, which is your biggest obstacle to feeling good about yourself. As you diminish the analytic, you won't have looping thoughts that you aren't good enough or capable enough to do something because this fearful programming has no way to live."

His words blur together as I begin to drift in and out of consciousness. The last thing I remember is him saying something like, "soon... creating... fearlessly... passion." Or maybe it was part of my dream. I guess it really doesn't make a difference because apparently, the events that take place in our dream space on the astral dimension are just as real and true as this physical plane reality anyway.

13.

*"Heaven knows it wasn't you
who held me down
Heaven knows it wasn't you
who set me free
So often times it happens that we
live our lives in chains
and we never even know
we have the key"*

—Eagles

The first few weeks after my first body healing, it's like I'm surfing on an endless eighty-degree wave as dolphins frolic beside me. I can't remember the last time I felt so energized and alive. People ask: Have I changed my hair? Am I doing something different with my skin? Did I lose weight? No, it must be that I've gained weight, and because of that I'm more youthful.

Of course, nothing's changed, but just like when your new favorite song comes on the car radio, and *voilà*, life is instantly better than it was a moment before. Whatever issues I'd been stressing about—Courtney, Amber, my finances, my boss—seem to slide off my skin like a water droplet off a mallard's waxy feathers.

I begin spending time with my college housemate, Samantha, who recently moved to town from San Francisco. Suddenly, my world widens beyond Amber and the jam-band scene, as Samantha introduces me to a reality unfamiliar to me—the artistic side of Los Angeles. She has a regular singing gig at an underground speakeasy in Venice that attracts a mix of artists, writers, and fellow musicians. This secret language of artistic expression captivates me, and I have to push away a prickly tinge of jealously that I wasn't born with the creative gene. A cute screenwriter with wire rim glasses asks me out. As temping as his invitation is, I remember James' words that if I want to attract a partner with more significance than a palm frond, I need to cool it on dating and work on myself for a while. Instead, I pull a pretty piece of stationary out of my desk drawer begin to make a list (in no particular order) of all of the things I want in a partner beginning with, "My love, I can't wait to meet you."

You Are:

1. Someone I can talk to about everything
2. Spiritual
3. Open-minded
4. Someone who cares about other people
5. Affectionate
6. Passionate about what you do
7. Funny and think I'm funny
8. Courageous

9. Healthy
10. A music lover
11. Curious
12. Attractive to me and have pleasing hair, lips, expressive eyes, and a tan
13. A skier/snowboarder
14. Surfer
15. Someone who loves to travel
16. Romantic
17. Patient
18. Adventurous
19. Honest
20. A family man
21. An entrepreneur

Then I fold it in two, give it a kiss, and stick it in between the pages of a book about the history of Yosemite. I slide it back into my bookshelf as I push aside embarrassing thoughts that it might be the cheesiest thing I've ever done in my entire life.

A few weeks later, on one especially balmy fall evening, I make my way out to my little patio with a glass of pinot noir. Tucking my legs up under my thin gauzy dress, I inhale the hay-like sweetness of the fresh lavender as the thick Italian light bulbs cast an inviting glow across the garden.

Céu's sultry Brazilian beats waft into the air as I feel a Cheshire Catlike smile spread across my face. Sitting by myself, wrapped up in my aloneness, I can't help but to wonder...

If nothing is actually different, is life really just in our minds?

Even though the night is warm, I feel a slight chill, remembering how helpless I'd felt just a couple of years ago, when I was confronted with the email exchange between Aidan and the unsuspecting cell phone store mother he'd slept with. Of course, he told me he didn't actually sleep with her, and rationalized it as nothing more than the natural thing to do before getting ready to propose to the love of your life, and, of course, he would never do it again.

Right.

I was so terrified of losing my life with Aidan; I let myself believe his excuses and buried the incident under a string of events. Even though a patchy orange rash erupted all over my body no doctor could explain, I pushed on, busying myself with work, exercise, and partying, and when it was time for bed, I let Xanax numb me from the deep rejection I felt as Aidan turned his back unapologetically to me once again.

~

A few months later, on a chilly night in early November, I came home one day to find Aidan depressed on the couch, staring blankly at the muted TV. I begged him to let me in and tell me what was going on, but he wouldn't respond.

"You have your health, family, and friends who love you, you have enough money to travel the world and never work again, what could possibly be so wrong?" I implored.

For the first time in months, he was honest with me when he said, "I really don't know."

We decided to take a break. For three months he would live at the house he bought down the street that we'd been planning on moving into while I'd stay in our place. With a boldness I didn't really feel, I suggested we date other people and see if we're right for each other after all. I could tell he was shocked, but he agreed. At the end of month two and after thinking about it for nearly six years, I called James.

~

I take another sip, rolling the wine around my tongue, remembering how stuck I felt in my narrow little world, and vow to never lose myself in a relationship like that again. An odd feeling I can only describe as peacefulness settles in around me. Peace for being alone and being OK with it—for living an independent life. I'd been under the illusion I'd always been an independent girl—easy to do with a man constantly by my side.

I tilt my head back and let the warm breeze tickle my skin as I relish in the sweetness of being by myself. A motorcycle roars by, a crow caws from up in the canyon, and I hear a door creek open and shut. I feel safe and cozy in my bungalow and proud of myself for creating such a lovely sanctuary for a home. Time seems to stand still in my little canyon as I sink deeper into contentment.

But just as the most wonderful things in life seem to be fleeting, before I can get too comfy in my calmness, the exact opposite feelings come crowding in, like a hoard of unruly Raiders fans storming the stadium after a beautiful play by the opposing team.

"*You are alone!*" they hiss venomously. "*All alone.* "*Being alone sucks... You're thirty now. Over the hill. Good luck ever finding someone who will ever love you for you. You are forever doomed to a lifetime of palm fronds!*"

I fight off the urge to down my wine in a single gulp, to go inside and call someone, turn on the TV, or slink away in the never-ending abyss of the internet. Instead, grounding myself into the planet with golden chords, I begin running bright colors through my body, which curbs the anxiety slightly, but just as easily as it came, my happiness contentment slinks away into the night.

Trying to sleep that night, I wonder if I had actually been that happy at all, or if it was just a figment of my imagination. My mind drifts to my mother. Mom has always had two speeds: fast and faster. After my parents got divorced, when we were with her during the school week, things usually felt rushed, as if we were just doing the current activity to get to the next. She'd work herself into an anxious shape over anything at all, and then, like pulling the plug on a puffed up inner tube, she'd sit at the kitchen table reading the *New York Times, clinking the cubes of ice around in her glass of Dr. Pepper while smoking one Salem Light after the next until she deflated herself into a state of calm.*

◇

Mom was born Mary Martha Smith, which anyone within spitting distance could see was a name for another woman. So one day she marched down to the social security office and changed her name to Mari (Mar-ee). In our blink-and-you'd-miss-it town, Mari stood out like a checker on a chess set. She was always embarking on some new career, and while none of them really lit her up inside—she always looked the part. At one point she toyed with the idea of buying into an exercise studio and would show up clad, in, say, a lavender leotard and matching leggings, her tiny waist accentuated with a thin yellow belt, which, of course, matched a bright yellow ribbon swathed around her blonde side ponytail.

Chugging up to the school round-a-bout in her silver diesel Mercedes a good forty-five minutes after the other kids had been scooped into station wagons and mini-vans, she'd stamp her cigarette into the ashtray before leaning over to fling open the passenger side door, calling out effusively, "Hello, darlings!"

By that time, the school principal, with her perfectly coiffed silver bob and monochromatic suit, would be outside to make sure that we had a ride home. My mother would get out of the car and chat with her for another half an hour, while we tugged on her leg, or shouted from the car, "Let's GO, *MOM*."

In the car we'd beg her to not be so weird. To this she would retort, "Oh, you want me to be like those *Lafayette Mothers?* They're so... pedestrian." Clinging to her hip city persona like a former beauty queen still wearing her crown years past the pageant, she refused to adopt any obvious signs of suburbia. She'd wiggle into tight black leather pants, slip into a pair of stilettos, and slip out to a "meeting" at 7:00 p.m., promising to be home soon but not before giving our babysitter a quick chicken paillard cooking tutorial.

However, in the privacy of our own home, she took her mom duties seriously. Homework, chores, and orders to eat everything on our plates. Never once did we miss a dental cleaning or a doctor check-up, and we had our hair trimmed every six weeks at the nicest salon in town. There was never a shortage of hugs, kisses, I love you's, and enough clothes to wear something different nearly every day of the month, but with no weekend playtime, it was difficult to cultivate that same bond with her that we had with our dad.

Mom's razor-sharp mind didn't miss a thing; politics, football, and fashion were her great loves. She could name all the members of The Cabinet just as easily as she could tell you how much each football player was drafted for across the entire NFL.

Sometimes I would feel the structure of the house trembling, sure the San Andreas fault line was quaking, until I'd hear Mom's deep, breathy voice ricocheting down the hall, "Touchdown Niiiiiiiners!!!" I'd scamper into the den to see what the fuss was about to find her shouting and stomping with glee, Heineken in one hand, Joe Montana signed football in the other.

"How did I get these wuss daughters that don't care about football?" She'd shake her head in disbelief that such a thing was even possible.

A natural leader, I can think of a dozen careers my mother would be amazing at: real estate tycoon, fashion designer, restaurateur, general contractor, drill sergeant, interior designer—really anything that involves being very assertive and directing people. One career we're all very fortunate she never embarked on is poker player. She may think herself to have a good poker face, but her every thought flecked across her pretty face like chocolate sprinkles on a vanilla cone.

She was a master of the brave front, but her electric blue eyeliner did little to hide the fear in her aquamarine eyes. Fear that we weren't going to turn out "right," being that we were children of divorce and all in a time when it was still considered taboo. In an effort to manage her fear, she did her best to orchestrate the elements around her. Not one to invite confrontation, if I looked like I was doing the things her way, I could earn myself a little more freedom.

As the wheels of her car crunched into the driveway, I'd leap off the black and white striped couch in the den, switching off the television in one stride, then scrape like a tadpole across the hardwood floor so not to expose myself through the row of windows facing the front walkway. I'd hear her key slide into the lock just as I'd hurl myself into the wingback chair, kitty-corner from my bedroom door, snatching up a book, or some homework, or anything that said, *Nope. I haven't been playing Nintendo for the past five hours straight. Not me.*

As we got older, she made her parenting strategy clear: *I am your mother, not your friend.* She was trying to keep us safe and so worked to influence everything I did, which could feel like she was analyzing my every move with the precision of a scientist scrutinizing her colony of fruit flies. If we asked why all of these activities, lessons, and rules were necessary, she'd retort, "I don't care if I'm popular like your *Disneyland Dad*," while usually tacking on some variation of "you'll thank me when you're older."

My mother prided herself on having no filter. Usually after a displeasing call with my father, she'd declare defiantly, "You girls must absolutely always make your own money! Otherwise you'll be a kept woman." And then at some other odd moment, usually after a run in with some calm, poised woman dressed in couture, she'd murmur under her breath, "Well, of course she looks like that. She doesn't have to work... *must be nice.*"

Occasionally, her idea of what was best for us sparked a shouting match. These didn't last very long, and usually ended with her brokering peace with some biblical reference (even though she was only a Christmas Eve and Easter church goer) like, "The Bible says it's important to turn the other cheek." Then she'd rebrand our argument as a positive thing, saying, "At least we're not all going to end up in mental institutions for holding our emotions inside."

Blessed with the gift of gab, and a sparkling curiosity, people fell in love with her everywhere she went. With more questions than an investigative reporter, she gathered more information about the cashier at the dry cleaner than I have about some of my own cousins. "People are my passion," she'd often say in response to why we'd just spent an extra twenty minutes in the hot car, while she caught up with the station attendant. "There are just so many different types of people to know."

Hers was the house that took in her "orphan" friends with no family to speak of on Christmas Eve, making sure everyone had something special with their name on it under the huge tree, carefully decorated with a slew of eclectic ornaments she'd been collecting for decades. Let's just say she's never been known for her cooking, but Christmas Eve she pulled out all the stops. The menu was always the same: duck pâté and cheese plate, jumbo shrimp with cocktail sauce, and baked brie in a pastry shell were passed on her grandmother's sterling silver. Dinner was a standing rib roast cooked medium rare, with a side of horseradish, I could never stomach. I'd fill up on butter-soaked green beans with tarragon, fingerling potatoes, and fresh warm rolls from the local bakery. Champagne flutes were topped off frequently and generously. After dinner, everyone would gather by the fire for a ruthless game of Monopoly, where "as a banker" she shamelessly passed me hundreds under the table.

A couple years after my dad met Arah, Mom was set up on a blind date with a Jewish law school professor named Jacob, who apparently was a big deal in the world of academia, even though with his humble demeanor and simple tastes you'd never know it.

Having transitioned some years earlier into a role as a professional stylist, she simply wouldn't tolerate his wardrobe, which looked like it escaped from a 1970's time capsule, so she promptly initiated a man-over on him, and underneath all that polyester happened to be a handsome man.

Being an acclaimed scholar, he had invitations to cocktail parties aplenty and speaking engagements all over the planet—opportunities that allowed him and my mom to enjoy extended stints in Amsterdam, Portugal, Barcelona, Italy, Israel, Turkey, Greece, Australia, and New Zealand while he served as a visiting professor.

It wasn't long before high school was on the horizon and Mom's almost predatory instincts picked up on my waning interest in my studies, declaring, "It's paramount Emily go to a preparatory boarding school." My chief priority at the time was my latest crush, so this did not sound even slightly appealing, and I actually thought I had a shot at staying, with Dad in my corner, vehemently opposing the idea.

But Dad's logic, "What fire would I lay by when I need to stay home sick from school? And more importantly, what about football games and cheerleaders?" stood no chance to Mom, who makes Alexander the Great look like a pansy blowing in the breeze. It would be decades before I could appreciate how my mother's tiger-like intuition was responsible for one of the pivotal moments of my life.

Boarding school was a confusing experience, or maybe that's just adolescence. On occasion, I felt very free and independent, while other times I felt like the walls had eyes and ears and every move I made was being monitored, even though it was a pretty spectacular place.

In an instant, my days of passing notes and flirting in the back of the class were over. I was propelled into an entirely new reality where eight or so kids from around the world sat around a mahogany table in spirited discussion.

Set high upon a bluff, overlooking Santa Barbara's jagged coastline, stood individual white Spanish style houses with uniform, red tile roofs. Weekends we were invited on kayak trips down the Kern River or rock climbing in Yosemite. We were encouraged to volunteer off-campus with elderly and marginalized communities. Drama, pottery, photography, and painting and drawing classes were part of the regular curriculum. Students put on plays, mock trials, and attended study abroad trips. Not one person failed to attend college. There were only 200 people in the whole school, and 30 percent of them were on scholarship. My eyes were being opened to the international world that I would soon explore.

I wish I could say I took part wholeheartedly in all this exceptional school had to offer, but I was in the throes of teen angst, more concerned about what was going on with my boyfriend and, as I'm beginning to find out, looking for approval and social acceptance rather than partaking in the school play or serving my community.

Being away improved my relationship with my mom significantly. Under the close supervision of professionals, she felt a little more at ease just being my ally. She was equally supportive if I called to complain that I was in trouble for some shenanigan I'd gotten myself into, or if she received the bill for my "emergency" credit card and the *emergency* happened to be more than a few cashmere sweaters from the J. Crew catalogue. After all, from her experience as a woman in the world, she believed that my physical appearance was my greatest currency. And, fresh off many international adventures of her own, she encouraged me to do an exchange program in Spain the summer before my junior year.

In my absence, Sophie had to shuttle between the two house-holds by herself. Whenever I asked her how it was, she'd say, "You're *soooo* lucky you don't live here."

In college, when I was debating over possible majors my mother said, "You know you really have a gift for writing," but I brushed her off. "You take after Nanny," she insisted, comparing me to her mother who earned a graduate degree in English from Northwestern in the 1930's.

"Hardly," I scoffed.

My mother always said I could do anything. She said I could be President. She said it because she wanted it to be true, but my little girl eyes saw a beautiful, intelligent woman—who had as much style, swagger, and, creativity in her eyelashes as Mick Jagger had in his tight leather pants—scrap her childhood dream of being a fashion designer because an art teacher told her that she couldn't draw. Instead, she became a fashion stylist, while somewhere in the whitespace breathed the belief: *You're only allowed to do it if you're born with extraordinary natural talent.*

So, I ignored her ample encouragement and picked a major I could do with my eyes stapled shut—communications. Somehow, between skiing and partying, I still managed to graduate in four years, without ever seriously considering what I'd do with my life. Something, or *someone*, would work out.

~

Lying in my bed, with my own mind struggling for contentment, I feel compassion rather than annoyance that my mom never sits still, stops asking questions, or lets her busy mind stop churning. The world is not the most hospitable place for a woman.

I can't even imagine what it must've been like for her generation.

As I drift off to sleep, I can't help but wonder if my mother and I are far more similar than I've been willing to see.

~

"Jaaaames," I half whimper into the phone the following day.

"Yes, Sweet Pea? What can I do for you today?" I can hear him smiling on the other end of the phone.

"I just don't understand," I launch right into it. I really felt like things were finally getting better. I can't pinpoint anything specific, but I just felt—well, happier."

"You're doing well," he validates me as usual. "Even better than you know. Now that you aren't numbing yourself out with drugs, you are more sensitive to the changing cycles of the planet. We just entered a very dense cycle. So if you are aware of a much heavier energy, you are coming into your abilities."

"All of a sudden I feel like everything is just..." I pause, looking for the right words. "I mean, I'm thirty-one years old now and I always just thought..." I trail off.

"Yesssss?"

Great, he's going to make me say it.

I take a deep breath.

"I just had a very different vision for myself by the time I got into this decade," I admit, feeling defeated. "I mean, I went to a good college; sure, I partied most of the time, but still managed to get straight A's in my major. Then again, there's a reason all of the football players were in my classes," I concede. "I have a family that loves me, I've never physically harmed anyone... I *recycle*!" I feel myself unraveling into the depths of self-pity.

"Good thing someone is getting a healing tomorrow!" he exclaims cheerily. "You must remember that spiritual growth is not linear, and everything that you've been doing actually *is* shifting things, whether you are seeing manifestations on the physical plane yet or not. In the healing we did, we cleared away a lot of energies you'd accepted that weren't you; that's why you felt so much better. With a denser cycle it's easier for you to accept denser beings into your entourage."

"Hmph."

"I love it when I get a *hmph!* Keep in mind, our planet is spinning through energies and we travel through an expanding universe. As we pass through these dense dimensions, that's going to impact folks immensely."

"Well, when you put it like that..."

"I know things aren't really what you envisioned for your life, but if you can remain in gratitude for all of the things that you do have, you might create a life that actually *exceeds* your expectations."

"Really?" I sigh, wanting so badly to believe him.

"No, I just made that up," he says, feigning exasperation. "But we are also going to do something new tomorrow in addition to a healing. It's called the Archival Equation of Life Chart, and it will really help you see what is holding you back from being a passionate creator."

"Okaaaay..."

"Oh, c'mon, Sweet Pea! It's going to be a blast!"

I try to muster up some enthusiasm. "If you think it will help, I'm in!" I say brightly.

~

The next day, James shows up with a thick roll of white drafting paper and a plastic briefcase.

"Isn't this great?" he asks, giving me a hug.

"Yeah," I smile, wishing I could just get on the healing table.

Being an artist, James loves anything that involves putting pen to paper. I, on the other hand, am not even a fan of my own handwriting. I stall, showing my new drapes and a lamp I got for my bedside table.

"So, do you want to get to it?" he asks with a twinkle in his eye.

"Let's do it," I say, trying to pump myself up.

We shuffle around my furniture and spread a five-foot-by-four-foot piece of paper on the carpet.

James opens his little plastic briefcase, and dozens of markers of all shapes and sizes spill out. Then he holds out a stack of about thirty index cards and tells me to shuffle them, and then pick one. I shuffle them carefully, curious as to what they are. The first one I turn over is REJECTION.

This is gonna be a barrel of fun.

"Without looking, pick a color and write it down," he instructs.

I reach over to the briefcase and slide my fingers over a handful of pens before committing to one. Puke yellow.

"My favorite color," I say sarcastically.

"*Very* amusing," James says, the little corners of his mouth curling into a smile. "This is going to be *so* good for you."

"Rejection. Yes, I am familiar with it, maybe a little too familiar..."

"Take your pen and write underneath rejection the three people that you feel most rejected by."

Printing in all capital letters, I write AIDAN and COURTNEY. "Those are the main two."

"You are omitting someone very important."

I rack my brain, trying to think of who it is.

"*D-a-d-d-y*," he spells it out for me—literally.

Oh, riiiiiight...

I reluctantly write the word "Dad" under the other two.

"Good job," James says very slowly, as if I just did something really complicated like bending my body into a human pretzel. "Pick another card."

I close my eyes and pluck one from the deck.

REWARDS.

"I like this one."

"Pick a new color and write down three rewards that you want."

I rummage around in the briefcase for so long that James finally jokes, "Let the court record show that the witness is stalling..."

"OK, OK." I brandish my selection. Aquamarine—my very favorite; now this *is* amusing.

I flick the card back and forth, considering, *What do I really want?*

I write:

1. The opportunity to do something that genuinely inspires me each and every day.
2. A loving and healthy family of my own who genuinely enjoys spending time together.
3. Vibrant health.

"Wow, those are some good ones, Sweet Pea! You really are growing," he exclaims, enthused. Then his voice drops a few notches and he orders, "Pick another card."

When I pull the next card, PASSION...

I'm passionate about a lot of things... fashion, traveling, skiing, I love cooking... Does listening to music and dancing count?

I end up with a red pen that barely has any ink left in it and write down "traveling," "skiing," and "music/dancing."

"OK," he says neutrally, but I know that he is holding something back.

"What?"

"Nothing. We will interpret it all at the end."

I end up writing thirty words on the chart, with three additional words to accompany them. It turns out there are fifteen positive cards, and fifteen, I guess you could say, not-so-positive cards. I'm absolutely exhausted and practically begging (telepathically, of course) to get on the healing table, but James insists on interpreting the chart.

To my amazement he weaves through my responses, showing me how specific relationships I have with people and events and beliefs associated with words such as rejection, fear/survival, resentment, competition, meaning, seniority, controls, agenda, apathy, blame/displacement, dependency, negative individual, disappointments, resistance, and judgment are directly impacting my happiness, health, and prosperity levels and ability to get closer to concepts like celebration, rewards, destination, creativity, passion, joy, knowing, relationship, path of action, resources, valuable, recognition, priorities, positive individual, and worth.

Seeing as we've spent the past two years working towards pulling down the illusions I've so carefully constructed in my mind over the past thirty years, many of the correlations are not a complete surprise. Until we get to apathy, that is.

Good ol' "I'll just do it tomorrow" apathy; my familiar pal, "I just can't seem to find the time" apathy; annoying "Why don't I have more energy?" apathy.

"So what is apathy?" James asks.

"Laziness," I respond certainly.

"Yeaaaaah... but what is laziness?"

"Lack of motivation?"

"Apathy is a condition stemming from the desire to be perfect."

I feel my face flush, and beads of sweat prick the back of my neck.

Of course, I want to be perfect. I just don't want anyone to know I want to be perfect. It's all very complicated, you see.

"Being the competitor that you are, you have to be perfect in order to participate. But you can't ever reach that vision of perfection because it doesn't exist. You believe that since you're not perfect, you're not worthy or valuable enough to participate because you don't want to look stupid or, well, not perfect. The definition of perfect may as well be hatred. Because not being perfect is failing, it's that fear of failure that keeps you from sharing in the true joy of life."

I sit quietly, digesting his words.

"And all this business about you not wanting people to pity you is just competition and performance. You don't want people to see the cracks in your armor of perfection. This goes back many, many lifetimes."

"So, basically, you're saying back when I was a concubine in 45BC, I had the tiniest feet and whitest face?"

"Most likely..." he says with a little smirk. "Do you know what the true joy of life is?" he asks excitedly.

I raise an expectant eyebrow, indicating that question and answer time is over.

"The true joy and foreplay of life is being a passionate creator. It's great that you have *interests* like skiing, traveling, and going to the gazillion concerts you go to, but being a passionate creator is something *very* different. Passion makes you feel connected to who you are and why you're here. It's when everything falls away and all feels right in your world."

"Hmph."

"I don't care what you do, but when you are passionately writing, painting, making your own music, performing, whatever, you are vibrating with a fearless energy because your passion to create is so strong and feels so good, it overrides your analyzer that's telling you the fear of failing or being judged is so great that it is better to do nothing all."

"What's happening on an energy level," he continues patiently and without a trace of judgment, "is that this perfection energy is very dense and causes the analyzer to swell. Then your entourage starts feasting on it, like it's Thanksgiving dinner," he says dramatically. "When your analyzer and entourage are steering the ship, you find yourself filled with an excess of negative energy that leaves you with no choice but to shed yourself into immense overwhelm and apathy, unable to find the passion or motivation to do much of anything. Stuck in the muck of the energy control loops in your mind."

Whoa... here I thought you're either born with the creative gene and the urge to partake in artistic activities like that or you aren't. I'm aware enough to admit I'm fearful about things, but I'd never even considered for a moment that my laziness was a direct descendant of fear of failure.

I nod.

"And, I told you that first time we met that you are an extremely creative person; do you remember that?"

Am I really creative? And have I just been blocking it all this time?

"That is why we do the Equation of Life chart, to bring all of these things to the surface so you can see what things from your past you are holding onto; events you give meaning to that are preventing you from being the passionate creator that you are and keeping you stuck in a pastime vision of yourself. After you identify it, you can heal it."

I let out a long sigh.

"What do you think?" he asks.

"It's pretty right on," I admit.

"Once we realize that every single, person, event, job, illness, whatever that we encounter in our lives, *we* create so that we can learn about ourselves, the faster we vibrate out of victim nature and into gratitude. Which is the foundation of all effortless manifestation. And yes," James says in a mockingly exasperated tone, "you can get on the healing table now."

14.

"You were better for me
than I was for myself
For me, there's you
and there ain't nobody else..."
—Marvin Gaye

November shows up with heavy clouds rolling in off the ocean, creating a sullen sky. Summer is officially over. Even though it's only four thirty in the afternoon, it's already getting dark. I light a fire for the first time in my fireplace, dig my fluffy blanket that my mother brought me home from New Zealand off the top shelf, and mummify myself on my red couch, watching the orange flames flicker until my eyelids grow too heavy to keep open.

I must've dozed off because I wake up with a startle to discover it's pitch dark out and my phone is vibrating softly on the carpet.

"Kor?" I answer softly after I recognize my friend Korri's name light up on the screen.

"Hey, mate, I'm gonna have to meet you there." We're going to see *Galactic* play at the House of Blues tonight.

"Hmmmmm..." I moan lazily into the phone. "I don't know if I should even go. I'm so comfy!"

"Maaaaaaaaaaaaaaate, you're coming," she orders sternly. "And I'll see you there."

Click.

I stall for a few more minutes, staring at the orange, glowing coals in the pitch-black room.

I mean, what will I really be missing if I just stay here?

Then, as if she can hear my thoughts, Amber texts: **Do you want to share a cab with us to the show?**

Even though Amber and I have spoken very little since our party, and the likelihood of us ever being peas and carrots again is slim, the resentment I've been hauling around all summer has vanished like a ten-piece set of Louis Vuitton luggage left unattended to outside the train station in Rome.

Sure, I text back.

Right as Amber, Chad, and I are climbing out at the venue, I'm surprised to get a text from the sexy Texan, Walker. It just says: **Galactic?**

Me: **Yes, please!**

The band is running late, so we hit up a bar across the street where some of our other friends have gathered. By the time Walker comes in, I've knocked back two Crown and gingers. Since drugs are no longer in my picture, I can't drink like the shipwrecked sailor I clearly once thought I was; after two drinks, I'm good and buzzed.

"Hello, Emily," he says, leans down to give me a warm hug.

"Hi," I respond, the surprise apparent in my voice. "You came all the way up here for the show?"

"Well, not *just* for the show." His blue eyes twinkle flirtatiously as he pulls up a stool next to mine.

~

When I wake up the next morning, I begin to retrace events of the night in my mind. I remember stopping by Amber's impromptu party after the show, getting a ride home with Walker, and unfortunately—or *fortunately*, depending on how you look at it—drunkenly rustling around in my bathroom cabinet, looking for condoms.

My phone rings in my purse, interrupting my reminiscing.

Has that ring always been so abrasive?

Stretching to reach it without getting out of bed, I lose my balance and topple on the floor, bringing my pillows and comforter with me. As I open my purse, I see that the teeth of the zipper are slightly off track because the purse is so full. I'm relieved when it finally opens, then horrified to see a big lavender-colored vibrator staring back at me. Then the incident at the sex shop comes rushing back to me, and I burst out laughing. I press answer on my phone and say dramatically, "You are never going to believe this."

"Mate, what the hell happened to you?" Korri asks, probably referring to the fact my voice sounds like I'm a four-hundred-pound phone sex operator who has been chain smoking for no less than thirty-five years.

"Well, I'll put it to you like this..." I pause for suspense. "I brought Hugs not Drugs home with me, and remember about five minutes of the entire night, and woke up to find a lavender vibrator in my purse."

Silence.

"What's the vibrator doing in your purse, mate?"

I get it. It takes more than this to get a reaction out of an Aussie, especially Korri, who in her day was one of Australia's top fashion models.

"The worst part is, he is completely SOBER, and I, *obviously*, am not."

"*Mate! You're fucking kidding me!*" She starts laughing and then choking on her laughter. This, apparently, was enough to have an effect on her.

"*See what I'm dealing with now?* He probably thinks I'm a nutcase."

"I doubt it."

I have to leave for a meeting in thirty minutes, but I lay on the floor for a few moments longer. My phone vibrates—it's a text from Walker: **Good morning, beautiful. I am sorry I had to leave, but my friend needed me to pick him up. I had lots of fun last night.**

I text back: I just found a lavender vibrator inside my purse :/.

Walker: **Lol! That was funny! That guy wasn't letting you out of the store without one! I wish I were still in your bed... W**

Now I remember our foray into the sex shop on a mission for batteries for Amber's rooftop stereo. And the pervy, gold-toothed man who insisted I take home the lavender vibrator as a "gift."

It's official—I'm hungover in a way that can't be fixed with a shower, a green juice, and a vitamin C packet. Based on my theory that nobody ever suspects the hungover person to be the best-dressed person there, I get dolled up in one of my most formal suits, and matching heels, blow-out my hair, and carefully apply extra undereye concealer and mascara.

Sure enough, nobody at work notices my bloodshot eyes, sallow skin, and whiskey scent because they're all so surprised by how together I look.

My phone buzzes with sweet texts from Walker, which helps jog my memory about how much fun we had, and just as I start to get really excited about him, I start to wonder if there might be something wrong with him.

Can there really be a guy in LA (OK, Orange County) who is actually interested in a sincere connection?

Throughout the day, I do my best to push aside my concerns that he might be a serial dater, or stalker, or straight-up weirdo.

Later that night, he texts: **Should I check out Blues Traveler HOB or Galactic @ Belly UP?**

Another show tonight?

All I can I think about is getting back into bed with some Thai takeout.

I text back: **Wow, you have the energy for that?**

Walker: **I always have energy to boogie!**

Oh yeah, he's *sober.*

This is officially new territory.

The following Saturday, fires are ravaging the foothills east of Los Angeles, and thick grey smoke chokes the sky. I'm getting into my car when Walker calls.

"Whatcha doin?" His low Southern drawl is undeniably sexy.

"About to head to the beach in search of cleaner air."

"I have a better idea. Why don't you go the other way and come meet me out in the desert?"

Right now?"

"Sure, why not?" I can hear him smiling on the other end of the line.

"Well, maaaaaybe..."

"If not for me, then to get out of the smoke and for the amazing dinner I am going to cook you." His voice is calm and deep.

"Where are you?"

"In Palm Desert at a buddy's place."

"And you're just out there by yourself..."

"Yeah, I wanted to play some golf and I came in search of more breathable air. Which is what you should do too."

"Let me think about it for a minute." I stall, trying to decide if his being out there alone is weird or cool.

"OK, give it some thought and let me know," he says easily.

I dial Korri. "Hugs not Drugs just invited me to Palm Desert with him."

"That's great!"

"Yeahhh..."

"What do you mean, yeahhhhh?"

"I'm not sure if I want to go."

"Why the hell not, *mate*? What else do you have to do?"

"True. I don't know; something is holding me back."

"What?"

Maybe that there might be more to his addiction thing than I can see? The chance of getting hurt? My entourage?

"Just go."

When I call Walker back to say I'm coming, he says earnestly, "I'm really excited to see you."

During the two-hour drive, I'm unable to settle on an opinion about him. My mind does more flip-flops than a gymnast mid floor routine.

I've narrowed it down to one of three things: He's either: A, a total player with the significance of a palm frond; B, a codependent serial dater; or C, he actually is a sweetheart who is looking for a sincere connection, and making a girl dinner is something he thinks is fun.

Walking up to the gravel path lined with little cactuses, I take a long deep breath of the relatively clean oxygen. My heart skips a little beat as I knock lightly on the door.

"Well, hello there. You're beautiful!" he exclaims, lifting me into a bear hug, brushing his lips softly on mine on the way down.

Okaaaay... so we're on this level.

He leads me out back where I smell the steaks grilling on the BBQ, and I am pleasantly surprised to see him uncork a bottle of La Crema cabernet and hand me a glass.

With the Santa Ana winds swirling lightly around us, we slip in easy conversation, and we discover that although we've taken different paths to get here, we both understand ourselves to be on a spiritual path, and we are both double Aquarians, born three years and three days apart—I'm older.

He tells me he's been sober for three years. I listen intently as he tells me how he was forced to confront it at such a young age. I know very little about addiction, despite the fact that I, and most of my friends, abuse alcohol on a regular basis.

"I grew up believing that if I wasn't number one, my father wouldn't love me. There was so much pressure on me to be the best—especially from myself..." he trails off. "I believed this would win his affection. Not to mention, my house was not a happy place to grow up, and none of my friends wanted to come over to my house because my dad was always yelling at my mom. Then, at age fifteen, I had my first drink at my sister's wedding, and all of the stress I'd been carrying around my entire life disappeared, and I decided that I *really* liked the way it felt. So from then on, I was getting wasted and checking out as much as possible."

I think of my own desire to win my father's approval. Thankfully, he didn't believe that the road to success was paved with good grades. *C students rule the world* is one of his core beliefs.

"Then it also became a bit of a 'fuck you' to my dad, who I believed would only love me if I was successful. I went from being valedictorian of my class in eighth grade and a star baseball player to quitting the team and getting kicked out of school. Then in college it was more of the same... getting wasted, in fights, arrested. But I do have to give my dad credit, too, because he never gave up on me, and three stints in rehab later, I've healed enough to know that I want a very different life—one where I'm a positive contribution... you know, being part of a higher frequency on the planet."

Now you're speaking my language. OK, probably not a total player, but he's not out of the woods on the whole codependent serial dater thing yet.

Sitting under the startlingly clear sky, the warm wind whistles through the palm trees; their methodical cha, cha, cha sounds filling the otherwise quiet night. My heart isn't trying to leap out of my chest, and I don't feel like I'm falling off a cliff. Actually, this is the most relaxed I can remember feeling in a long time. It's like we're dear friends that have been reunited after years of being apart.

I decide to open up to him about my work with James and my own journey inward. This doesn't faze him at all and, much to my surprise, he's done some energy work too.

Mid-sentence, he pulls me onto his lap and plants his full pink lips on mine. Seeing as our first romantic encounter is a bit of a fog for me, I feel like this is our first real kiss. It's slow and gentle, and I don't want it to end.

"You know what they say... third time's the charm," he says, his low voice taking on a sweetness. "It's like the universe is trying to tell us that we need to know each other..."

"I like that," I say, leaning my head back—a not-so-subtle message for him to kiss me again. He presses his lips to mine, then lifts me up and carries me in my long white dress, like a bride, to the bedroom.

The next morning, I wake up covered in goose bumps alone in a cool, dark room. Sunlight filters through the slats in the blinds, and I listen hard for a moment to see if I can hear Walker, but all I can hear is the *whoosh, whoosh, whoosh* of the fan circling above. Pulling on some clothes, I wander barefoot out into the main room to find him slicing strawberries into a bowl of granola.

"Damn, I wanted to bring this to you in bed," he says, obviously disappointed.

Who is this guy?

"Thank you," I say politely as he places a bowl in front of me.

"Let's eat breakfast on the patio," he suggests.

We take our bowls outside, he puts on Bob Marley, and we lounge around by the pool, sharing stories, playing backgammon, and splashing around. It's unusual hanging by the pool all day and not cocktailing, like every other time I've been to Palm Desert—*unusually nice.*

What I'd intended to be just a one-night visit flowed easily into two, and from that point forward, Hugs not Drugs and

I can't get enough of each other. I never thought a Texan, blazer-wearing, country-club, *sober* guy would be my guy.

Maybe a sober guy is exactly what I need?

I'd always been under the impression that drinking equaled fun and sober equaled boring. But Walker is usually the first person on the dance floor, never afraid to wear some crazy get-up to a party not even calling for costumes, and, many nights, happy to stay out later than I do—especially if live music is involved.

He makes no attempt to play it cool and pursues me with such intensity; I teeter between wondering if this is just an extension of his extremist DNA, or if I've actually just become a woman worthy of being pursued in a proper way.

When I find out his last serious girlfriend was over a year ago, I decide he's clear on the serial dater bit. He *might* actually be a really good guy. He certainly listens when I talk. I once casually mentioned liking calla lilies, and the following day a big bouquet arrives on my doorstep. And soon bouquets are arriving every week with cards that say ridiculous things like, *"You are the most beautiful woman on the planet, and I'm so grateful to have you in my life!"*

Ridiculous things I can't get enough of. Despite the fact, we are undeniably falling for each other, Korri and I have been planning a three-week-long trip to Brazil, Argentina, and Uruguay, and frankly, a boyfriend is the last thing this trip calls for.

As Walker and I snuggle deep under the covers on the very rainy, dark, and unusually cold Los Angeles afternoon the day before my departure, our arms and legs and heads and hearts as close as they can be, I find myself thinking I've never felt so safe in my entire life, and there's no place I'd rather be. Even Brazil.

"I'm really going to miss you," he admits, brushing my hair out of my face and looking me square in the eyes.

"I know. Me too."

I can sense that he is building up to the conversation about "us." I'm not ready for it.

"I know you're going on your trip," he starts out slowly.

No! Don't say it!

"And I want you to have fun and do whatever feels right, but I just want you to know I'm not going to be seeing anyone else."

Wait. I wasn't expecting that.

Unsure of how to respond, I tip my chin up and give him a kiss.

Finally, I decide on, "I like that."

It's not that I'm planning on running down to South America and making out with every guy I see, but I'd planned on being a single gal, fancy free amongst hot Brazilian surfers and Argentinean polo players.

Wait! Maybe he's two steps ahead and knows that just by not trying to control me, I will control myself?

Whatever the reason, his confidence is off-the-charts attractive and I can feel myself fall a little deeper.

"You know you can call me anytime... The bill's on me," he offers with a smile.

"Really?"

"*Anytime.*"

My body buzzes with happiness as I nuzzle his chest.

Am I in love?

It's been so long, the feeling is almost unrecognizable.

The morning comes too quickly, and soon we are hugging and kissing on the curb of the airport with the fervor of people only newly in love.

As Korri and I wheel our bags up to security, she shakes her pretty blonde head. "*Jeeeez, mate.* This might be it for you."

I don't say a word but wonder if she might be right.

Could Hugs not Drugs be the one? It's obviously way too early to tell, but there is something different about this one.

Down in Brazil, I'm baffled that amid the thick, sultry air, hot surfer bodies, sexy accents, and caipirinhas, I find myself wondering what Walker is doing. Turns out he's wondering about me, too, because over the next three weeks of surfing, exploring, and dancing my way through South America, I find enough time to ring up a thousand-dollar phone bill talking to him.

When I touch down at LAX, Walker is patiently waiting to welcome me home. My bungalow is full of little gifts, carefully wrapped, each with a little card.

This guy is no palm frond!

We fall right back into step with each other, doing couple-y things like dinners, hikes, concerts, and weekend trips. I'm amazed at how easily it is to connect. It's partly because he doesn't drink: With no drunken promises that won't be honored, there's not a shred of drama, disappointment, or distrust. After only three months, I feel like I've known him my whole life.

15.

"Ooh-ooh child, things are gonna get easier
"Ooh-ooh child things'll get brighter"
— The Five Stairsteps

Over the next couple of months—despite the fact that we live in different cities—Walker and I begin spending nearly every night together. Most of the time he makes the hour and fifteen minute drive up to my little bungalow, but at least a couple days a week I head south, down to the quaint town of Newport Beach where he lives just two blocks from the beach, in an airy garage apartment with light maple vaulted ceilings and a little thing I like to call a *washer and dryer!*

Maybe it's because we're both February babies; maybe it's simply because we have the same taste on music; or because we've both started to peel back the layers of the all-pervading unconscious; but I can't remember a time when I've felt more compatible with anyone. We stroll hand in hand along the shore at sunset, pack picnics, and spread out for hours under the Southern California sun, leisure over yummy dinners, zig-zag through the streets on beach cruisers, watch films and documentaries, spend hours in bed roaring with the sensuality of new love, all the while, gabbing, gabbing, giggling, and gabbing about every little thing trotting through on our minds.

Was Jody ever right! I guess I didn't know what I didn't have until I found it—how different it is to be with a man I can really talk to and one who shares his thoughts and feelings so easily to me.

With Walker in my life, everything seems to take on a more even pace, and it becomes easier for me to identify when I'm in body or bringing in my entourage. The signs are undeniable: my body begins to feel like a human Popsicle; my patience resembles something like a third grader waiting in a very long line on hotdog day; and if I didn't know better, I would think I'm a ditz—leaving my keys in the door, or the refrigerator door open, or forgetting my purse. If I catch myself in this state, I take a few minutes to close my eyes, breathe deeply, ground myself to the planet, and call my spirit back into my body. Usually, within a few moments, I return to my body and I feel warmer and I recognize the peaceful me—hopeful, playful, less critical, and less agitated. I laugh easily and accept more.

When I share my joy with James, I'm surprised that he doesn't seem happy for me.

"I don't understand. I thought you told me that he was a loving and sensitive spirit?"

"The original spirit is loving and sensitive, but when I look closer, I see he doesn't have a very strong spirit-to-body connection. Which means he doesn't have a lot of control over the spirits that come through him. Which accounts for his addiction issues."

"But he's so sweet and loving to me," I protest.

"Well, that's a good thing," James says warily. "It's just that his spirit-to-body connection isn't the strongest, which makes him more prone to entourage controls. And when I look at your past lives together, I see they weren't the best. When we have a past life that's still energized in our spiritual universe, we recreate that situation over and over again until it's neutralized. I see Walker has an energized picture to run away when things get hard." He pauses for a second. "Oooh, he ran from his platoon," as if that explains everything.

I don't say anything.

"My main concern is that you're safe."

But I haven't felt this safe in years.

Annoyed, I begin looping on things he's told me, trying to poke holes in his teachings.

I mean if competition is bad, why are the most successful people typically extremely competitive? What about survival of the fittest? And he says we create our own illnesses and have the power to heal our own bodies without surgery or drugs? Why doesn't anyone speak of this? And possibly most crazy of all, that I am a healer in my own right, not to mention a wildly creative person?

James continues to insist that I'm a tremendously creative person, which makes it even more frustrating that I don't feel like I have one creative cell in my entire body.

For several weeks, I pull away and avoid his calls, convinced that his teachings make no sense and that he's wrong about Walker.

I mean, he can't be right all the time.

Then, I boomerang back in the opposite direction.

Or is it so crazy? Maybe the addiction stuff with Walker is a bigger deal than I can comprehend? And James did heal my sore throat over the phone in less than ten minutes.

And for all my doubts, I've undeniably made countless positive changes since we've reconnected. I've had physical, visceral reactions in our sessions; the thoughts in my head are more accepting than ever before.

Maybe it's just my entourage not wanting me to grow and change?

Whatever the reason, when my laser hair removal lady tells me she just had a reading with Jennifer Aniston's psychic, I can't help but to think this is a sign—a perfect opportunity to ask about James and Walker.

She doesn't have an opening for three weeks, and by the time I'm actually driving over to my appointment, I'm nervous and clammy and feel like I'm on my way to an illicit affair. I catch my guilty gaze in the rearview mirror.

Has it really come to this, Emily? Going behind my resident psychic's back to check up on him with another psychic? Apparently, yes.

I haven't told Walker what I'm up to. I don't want him to think I'm some crazy lady going around to different psychics.

When Ava greets me at the door of her office—a ten-foot-by-twelve-foot room with a large window looking out over the lush greenery of Beverly Hills—I like her instantly. Her long shiny black hair hangs down to the middle of her back, and her big onyx-colored eyes are lined with thick kohl-colored pencil. I estimate her to be in her early fifties, and her words roll off her tongue in accented English that I can't quite identify—maybe Persian? Her energy calms me at once, and before I can even sit down, she says, "I see love, I see soulmate; I see marriage next year."

I feel my heart pounding inside my chest as I sit down in one of the four chairs she has gathered around a wooden table. She takes the seat next to me and asks, "Whose name starts with W?"

"Walker?" I ask.

"Yes, that's it. You are soulmates," she says with absolute certainty.

Hey now! Such bold claims, right out of the gates!

"I see that you are both Aquarians. This is very good for both of you because you understand each other."

She pauses for a moment and seems to be staring off, and up, and inside somehow all at the same time. Different from James, but I can tell that she, too, is reading something.

"He is a very good person; a kind man," she says, her voice softening.

Seeeeee, James!

Then she hands me a few decks of regular old playing cards and tells me to spread my energy all over the cards. I close my eyes and try not to think about anything specific as I shuffle the cards around in my hands.

Ava begins laying them out in a pattern on the table and explains that there are angels who talk to her, to help her to interpret the cards.

Fascinated by seeing how another psychic works, I hand her the cards.

After feeling nervous all day, I'm eerily calm now. She lays the cards out before her: rows of hearts and diamonds of varying numbers and queens, kings, and jacks aplenty.

"Wow," she says under her breath. "Your life will be filled with much love, prosperity, and happiness."

I like her. A lot.

She reshuffles and lays down more rows of hearts and diamonds.

"And you guys are going to have plenty of money," she says matter-of-factly before flipping another card. Her onyx eyes open very wide with surprise before she says, "A LOT of money."

For a girl carting her clothes back and forth to the laundromat with hands that look a good ten years older than they should from washing many a dish, this news is *mighty* encouraging.

Then again, when I ask her how I'm going to make my millions, she isn't able to see that. She flips a few more cards and then pauses for what seems like a long time and says, "There is a man, from a past relationship, who is really focusing to you right now. It looks like someone you spent many years with."

I open my mouth to speak and choke on a little sob.

Where the hell did that come from? It's been over two years! Why is this still affecting me? Let me be free from the past!

"There was someone I was with for nearly six years," I admit quietly.

"We need to do a reading on this person," she decides and passes the cards back to me. "Close your eyes and just say his name over and over in your head."

I do as I'm told and pass them back to her. She turns them over the same way that she flipped over the cards for me, except this time the space in front of her is nearly all black, covered with an assortment of spades and clubs ranging from ace to king.

"My goodness," she says her eyes cloud over. "I see this was a very unhappy relationship for you."

I nod quietly. She lets out a very heavy sigh, almost as it something is causing her a bit of pain. "This would have been a terrible life for you."

I sigh, thinking about how we unraveled into darkness.

"I see he has a lot of money," as she points to the only red cards on the table, a king, queen, and ace of diamonds somewhere on the right side of her assortment of maybe fifteen or so cards. "These are the prosperity cards."

"He does," I confirm.

Ava considers the cards for a few moments and says, "He won't find true love unless he makes some big changes."

What she says doesn't really surprise me, but just knowing that I, personally, couldn't have done anything different lightens a bit of this heaviness I've been hauling around in my heart.

"Your angels actually kept you there longer than you wanted because Walker wasn't ready yet."

I remember lying in bed, crying and begging myself for the courage to leave a full year before we actually broke up.

"I see if you had left your last relationship earlier, you would've met somebody else, and succumbed to feeling like you are supposed to get married, and would've missed out on being with Walker."

Interesting strategy, angels!

Before my mind has the opportunity to think about having angels who are looking out for me, she looks back at her cards and continues, "Has he asked you to move in with him yet?"

"No! We've only been dating for a few months!"

"He will, soon."

Her words are so far from what I've allowed myself to entertain, but I want to believe it all. Even though I'm genuinely happy with Walker, to actually hear our future laid out in such a wonderful way makes me almost giddy.

"Are you getting a new car?" she asks.

"No."

"Hmmm... I see something with a car," she says. "Do you work on commission?"

"I do."

"In July you are going to have a big chunk of money coming to you."

"I like the sound of that!"

"I'm seeing something really strong in a car. Just be careful. It could be as simple as a ticket or something, but it might be an accident."

"I will."

"Have you ever considered acting or writing?"

"Yeah," I admit sheepishly, "but I have absolutely zero training in either area."

"I see these to be high levels for you, especially writing."

I think about how James also told me this on my first reading with him.

"I just wouldn't even know where to start."

"I see that you don't need to worry about it. Just write what is close to your heart—what matters to you. I see writing or heading an organization that helps others will bring you great happiness."

My heart does a double beat.

"Do you know a Mike?" she asks.

Mike... I rack my brain.

"He's very strong around you."

I shrug unable to place a Mike and far more excited about all of the other things she revealed.

"Do you have any other questions before we finish up?" she asks kindly.

"I think that pretty much covers it, unless you have anything else you think is important," I say slowly, still reeling from her predictions.

"Just be careful in your car," she warns again.

"Oh, one last thing," I stall, laying two hundred dollars on the table. "What do you see about someone named James?"

She pauses for a second, shifting her gaze away from mine.

"He is someone that has helped you very much."

"Oh, he has so much," I confirm, my heart filling with emotion over the thought of doubting him. "Thank you!" I give her an impulsive hug.

As I get up to leave, Ava says, "Emily?"

"Yes?" I face her.

"You can trust him."

I must look at her a little dazed because she clarifies, "James."

More confused than ever, I say, "Thanks," and head for the door.

16.

"Imagine there's no countries,
It isn't hard to do
Nothing to kill or die for
And no religion too
Imagine all of the people
living life in peace"
                    —John Lennon

After a few uneasy nights' rest, I settle on the conclusion that James undoubtedly has my best interest at heart. He's patiently guided me away from destructive thoughts and behaviors and helped me identify the difference between truth and illusion. The simple answer is he must be wrong.

I mean, he can't be right one hundred percent of the time, can he?

If he knows about my trip to see Ava, he doesn't say anything.

When I tell him Walker wants to do a session with him, he concedes, "Well, if he's willing to look at truth and heal, that's a positive thing. And just remember, whatever happens, you created Walker to learn about you."

≈

"Hello?" I peek my head inside as I tap the back of my hand lightly on the open door.

"*Hell-llo*," James calls out.

"How'd it go?" I ask softly as I walk into my bungalow.

Walker just nods and gives me a small smile.

"He did really well," James says, giving Walker a friendly pat on the back. "Does he look any different?"

I scan his face as I cross the room to give him a kiss.

As I get up closer, I see that his eyes, normally a grayish blue, are brighter and his expression seems softer.

"A little bit," I agree, nodding.

"Oh, c'mon! He looks more than *a little* different! James implores. "He does need to get some food and get to bed early," he says, turning to Walker.

"That's the plan," Walker says with a smile. "Oh! We have pizza in the fridge," Walker remembers, heading into the kitchen.

"And absolutely no electronics tonight," James insists sternly.

"Yessir!" Walker calls back from the kitchen.

"You know, he did very well, for his first time," James says to me. "His parents are pretty conflictive in his universe, so we had to move them out."

Walker returns with a platter of reheated pizza, a stack of napkins, and a few plates.

"Do you want to tell Emily about your session?" James asks.

Walker nods with a full piece of pizza hanging out of his mouth.

Finally, all he says is, "Doug," and puts the pizza back in his mouth.

I nod.

"He's given up his seniority to his father and he needs to take it back. No matching pictures here!" James declares gaily, turning to me with a big grin.

Walker looks at me with amazement and says, "He took Doug out."

"What does that mean?"

"I've had this constant burning feeling right here," he presses just under his ribcage, "that rises up into my heart and esophagus since I was fourteen years old. I've taken Tums, Zantac, Prilosec, Prevecid, Nexium, and I even tried acupuncture and herbs, but nothing helped—until now," he pauses, taking a deep breath as if to assess how he's feeling. "It's crazy."

"It was his dad directing energy into his third and fourth to control Walker's energy system, the amount of energy he has available to create. We moved it out."

"Just like that, he's cured?"

"Well, I helped him move it out; now it's up to him to put up a protective bubble and not give up his seniority to his father anymore."

Walker and I exchange a quizzical look.

"You both must remember that nothing, no one, nowhere is greater than you *for* you," James says, sinking into the red couch, and letting out a long sigh. "This is something that is very difficult for people to understand because we live in a hierarchical society where the policeman is greater than you; the senator is greater than you; the president," in his best George W. twang, "well, he's surely greater than you; he's the *Pres-i-dent of the U-nited States!* When in reality, no president, no pope, no deity, shaman, no government, billionaire, nuthin' nowhere is greater than you *for* you!"

"But..." I stammer. "I mean... well, why does everyone act like that's just how it is?"

"Just because something is widely considered true, doesn't mean it is. Think of how long people believed that the world was flat."

"*Riiiight.*"

"People have been going along with this without giving it a second thought because for centuries, the religious programming on the planet has taught people that God and Jesus are *greater* than you, the pope is greater than you, the king is greater than you, your D-A-D-D-Y is greater than you. And now, we are an entire lopsided society full of *Daddy Worshippers.*" He shakes his head in disbelief. "Religion says that we've been granted this one life and we must try and be as perfect as possible to avoid everlasting damnation, meanwhile praying to an almighty God so we make it into the pearly gates of heaven where, *then,* we will be peaceful and happy. This, in actuality, is the exact *opposite* of what the true nature of our spirit is."

"What is our true spirit nature?" Walker asks curiously.

"We are infinite spirits that have conscious choice to take a physical form, and we will have that choice again based on our agreements from past lives. Who your dad is now may have been a lover, or a brother, your child, or your opponent before. You have vast amounts of knowledge that you've become unconscious to, but it's still inside of you—literally lifetimes of information that you can access as you increase your consciousness."

"You mean through meditation?" Walker asks.

"Deep meditation and the astral."

Walker and I raise our eyebrows at each other.

"The Bible says God is an all-powerful, perfect being that has a purpose for you—after all, he created you. Since God created you, and is responsible for you, he's obviously greater than you, so your belief is externalized, which results in no internal belief for yourself, which makes it very difficult for folks to understand innate human powers like clairvoyance and the ability to heal our own bodies. But religions say, as long as you believe in God and are perfect for God, he will take care of you. *After all, he's the ultimate daddy!*"

"Come to Texas; we'll teach you all about it," Walker says with a crooked smile.

"People take comfort in the idea that someone else is taking care of them and responsible for them, but the truth is, nobody is responsible for you except you, and nothing that is natural is perfect. A tree doesn't grow perfectly straight, a flower doesn't bloom with a perfectly equal number of petals, our human bodies are not perfectly symmetrical... science even has declared that the universe in all its beauty is one, NOT PERFECT, chaotic place. So why would God be perfect, and how could we be perfect for God? The answer is we can't. But in attempting to be perfect—as, Emily, you've recently learned—we stunt our growth and creativity because we're afraid to do anything that might expose us as not being perfect."

"But there's *something*," I push back, unwilling to accept there isn't some higher power that created the miracle of existence.

"Now let me be clear," he pauses, "I'm not saying that there aren't powerful energies coursing through the universe at a very high frequency that you can align with, because there are. The frequency of pure love is the highest, fastest, most potent healing energy I've seen. I'm just saying that there's not some man with a white beard in the sky keeping track of everyone's rights and wrongs, giving and taking away life and calling the shots."

"The thing is, I wouldn't really say I'm a religious person," I object, trying to remember the last time I was inside a church.

"Thank you," he says with hinting sarcasm. He stops, looking off but in front of him in the way he does when he's reading my pictures. "You've actually had many religious lifetimes," he says neutrally, "but you don't need to be religious to be impacted by religion. This programming has permeated the planet for centuries. And it has promoted a submissive, fear-based existence that's destroying our planet."

"You mean like living in a hierarchal society?" I venture.

"Exactly."

"But it's been proven that communism doesn't work either," Walker objects.

"I'm not saying communism is the answer!" James bursts out laughing. He composes himself and says, "The mere idea that our options are either communism, or free trade with taxation, or in some circumstances dictatorship shows how narrow the thinking is on the planet. But right now is a huge time of change, and people are starting to open their eyes to the possibility of a new way."

"And information is spreading like wildfire," I chime in.

"This is true; the internet is changing things dramatically and will continue to do so. It's the first time people who aren't at the top of the hierarchy have a voice."

"I suppose that makes sense," Walker says. "But what exactly does it mean for me and my issues with my dad?"

"Well, it's actually different for males and females. Emily, in this lifetime, you have replaced God with Daddy. Daddy is senior to you; he's the powerful one; he owns the money and is supposed to take care of you. In your case," he winks at me, "Daddy owns all the creativity too."

Walker and I stare at him silently.

"You aren't laughing," he says with another chuckle. "The last thing you want to do is lose your amusement. If nothing is greater than you, then you won't lose your amusement over nuthin."

I flash a courtesy smile and ask, "So, how do I get it back? My seniority, I mean."

"Females are naturally receptive beings, but it wasn't always bad to be a female. Early on women had much more power and there were many matriarchal societies. When religion was constructed for political and social control, female power eroded. Everyone is terrified to talk about it, but one of the cornerstones of religion was to make women the problem in an attempt to structure the world for male benefit."

"How did they make women the problem?" I ask.

"Females were too sexualized, so they needed to wear chastity belts; it was *their* fault that they were been raped. In some countries females still have their clitorises cut out, and do you know how many women I know that don't have a monthly cycle because there is so little permission to be female?" he asks incredulously.

"Yeah, I guess they don't really highlight that in church," I say, thinking about my own desire to be a boy.

"It may sound dramatic, but the reality is, everything has been structured for females to conform to a male ownership and worship. Just look in *Webster's Dictionary* at all of the words used to degrade women—slut, whore, trollop, hussy, floozie, an old maid... you get the picture. Meanwhile a man is a womanizer, a Cassanova, a ladies man, a lady-killer, an eligible bachelor. Not to mention, not so long ago, a female was the *property* of her father until she was the property of her husband." He pauses, "This was not the case before religion."

"But things are different now, aren't they?" I protest.

"In some ways, yes, but in many ways, still no," he says very seriously. "Who benefits if women are stripped of their power?"

"Men?"

"Yes, because then women need them and defer to them. And who has power positions in religion?"

"Men?"

"That's correct. The paradigm on the planet has shifted and now the predominate thing controlling folks is money. But from A.D. up until midway through the 20th century, it was religion. It's a much easier step for women to take to seek approval and acceptance from their fathers and husbands if the number one most important thing in the universe—the being that gave you life, and can absolve you of all of your sins—is a man."

"I always thought that was a little weird," I confess. "I remember being pretty young, maybe nine years old, sitting in Sunday school and listening to them talk about the Heavenly Father and thinking to myself, if there's something powerful and magical enough to create all of this, would it even have a gender?"

James shakes his head and exhales deeply.

"The world would be a *very* different place if women had the money and power. In controlling the money and power, men control women."

I try to imagine what the world would be like if women had the majority of money and power.

"But there are some women with money and power,"

Walker interjects. "Are they free of this need for approval and acceptance?"

"Good question, Walker! Even the most independent, financially secure women on the planet are seeking approval and acceptance from males on some level—unless they've done the spiritual work to transcend the imprint of rejection that comes from not being born a boy."

"OK, I see what you're saying way back when religion reigned supreme and women were obviously second-class citizens, but what about today? And, what if there are already four boys in the family, and then a girl comes along?" I ask.

"There is still very little permission on the planet to be female," he reiterates. "In some parts of the world, like China and India, female infanticide is still enacted because girls are considered so inferior. And in some parts of the Middle East, a husband, father, or brother can legally kill a woman if they believe she has dishonored the family in any way. But even here in the US, there's programming that impacts females and decreases the female vibration immensely." He closes his eyes for a few moments, which he only does when he's looking very closely at something. "Say Daddy has the tiniest, slightest fear about his baby girl being older and being sexual—even though being sexual is a natural part of having a physical form, and the only reason that there's any shame or embarrassment associated with sex is because religion says we should feel bad about it— as you've learned, all of our thought forms have vibrations associated with them, and baby girl registers the density of this fear-based thought as rejection of her innate self." He pauses. "Think back to the first time you remember being rejected. What did you want more than anything else?"

"To be accepted," I say immediately.

"Exactly. And from day one, whether you're conscious of it or not, you begin seeking approval and acceptance from males as a result of that initial vibration of rejection. And how ya gonna do it?"

I stare back blankly.

"Perfection. You can't possibly be rejected if you're puuuuuuuuurfect right?"

Wow.

"The cosmic joke is men created religion to control women, but women keep religions going. This daddy-worship programming leaves women feeling resentful as heck because they've spent a lifetime putting males before themselves."

"I mean, on a very baseline level, don't churches do good things for people in need," I say. "Offering people a sense of community, food drives… connection?"

"Well, on a surface level, yes, those things are true. Just as taking a pill for a headache will mask the feeling of pain but will not address the root cause." He takes a sip of water before continuing, "I challenge you to look beyond your programming. Religion tells us that we're not all connected but are separate. 'My God is better than your God' is singlehandedly responsible for countless wars and the deaths of hundreds of millions worldwide. And the fear of not being good enough or not being right enough perpetuates competition on the planet, so we have civilizations of people who view themselves and their lives as limited or lacking."

"But competition is good because in some respects it motivates people, and creates innovation, and drives prices down, quality goes up, and innovation moves forward," I counter, echoing the words I've heard my father say hundreds of times.

Daddy worship, 101. Repeat what your daddy has told you as absolute, ultimate truth. Over and over and over again.

Even though he's explained it before, James shows no sign of frustration, "When I use my sixth and look at the energy of competition on the planet, it has the same vibration as a virus. Competitive creations are like a race to nowhere, because whatever you achieve will never, *ever* be enough. People are motivated out of fear, and this creates emotional and physical pain. I'm not saying don't create, don't make money, don't innovate; I'm saying create from a place of *passion!* When we create from a place of passion, what happens?"

"It's more fulfilling?" I offer unsurely.

"Yesssss," he leads me, "and?"

"And you're not an asshole?" Walker suggests with a smile.

"Thank you," he says with a small smirk. "Your vibration skyrockets; making money is effortless; your health is good; and you're full of vitality, experiencing joy and meaning in your life."

Oh, is that all?

"Now with fathers and sons the competitive stakes are higher. Walker, you've made your father senior to you because he has all of the money and the toys."

I glance over at Walker, who seems just as fascinated by this discussion as I do.

"And when there's serious conflict between Mommy and Daddy—as you both have experienced—children, regardless of the gender, take it on. This conflict causes children to feel like there's something intrinsically wrong with them, which makes it difficult for them to really love themselves or others."

"What do we do about it?" I mock wail dramatically.

"Well, you are doing it. Both of you are taking big steps by making recognition of your spiritual path and doing this work to see beyond face value. Pulling back the curtain on the illusions you've agreed to that keep you in pain. Looking at your pictures! And as you let go of your parents' conflict in your hearts, you'll both be way more loving to yourselves, and inner kindness translates to outer kindness."

Just then we're interrupted by Walker's phone vibrating on the table.

"Intake call," he explains, picking it and taking it onto the patio.

"I'm going to heat a few more slices of pizza," I announce, walking into the kitchen.

"That sounds like a good idea," James agrees, following me. "By the way, how is everything going with your first energy center?" he inquires, referring to our last conversation about my infection.

"A little better, I think."

"We are going to heal this. Actually everything we've just discussed helps us understand how these things work. Since you are a female, with built-in receptivity programming, you've taken in a lot of pain that isn't even yours. This is why we call it *illusion healing*—it's an illusion that it's possible to alleviate others from their pain; they have to do it for themselves. But in a desire to make things better for your family, especially your dad—which is really just an attempt to make yourself feel secure and safe—you inadvertently have accepted very dense energies into your universe.

This accounts for cancer wards around the world, especially breast cancer. These are your illusion channels." I wince as he presses down just below my clavicle. "You know if this is tender, you're illusion healing.

And the cosmic joke is your energy goes out of you and wraps around him, so he has all of your energy covering his pain, which numbs him to his own pain, meanwhile, depleting you of your vitality."

"Well if someone is numb, he's not really in pain then, is he?" I object.

"No, that's the illusion. It's still within him, directing his life and creations. In order to heal pain, you must be able to feel it. If you are numb to the pain, it leaves the density energy unattended. Over time, it will manifest into some form of *dis-ease*.

I think of my dad. I don't remember exactly when I let go of my crusade to heal my him, but sometime after Australia, I felt myself detach. Arah and my dad seemed suspended, neither willing to concede, and neither able to let go. Conflicted by lifetimes of loyalty to my dad and the understanding that my "help" wasn't really helping at all, I quietly slipped away, allowing him to face his own creations. But clearly, I still have more work to do.

Tuning into my thoughts, James says, "Illusion healing the men in your life has decreased your frequency as a female and diminished your own capacity for creating. This is quintessential Crazy Goddess behavior."

Yikes.

"I will assist you in releasing this energy, and soon you will find yourself in greater acceptance of yourself, and in turn, those around you will be in acceptance of you too. You will also come into your healer abilities as you become a more Vertical Woman."

"Well, I'm into that," I reply, more than slightly dubious that he can help rid me of a nearly lifelong condition that no traditional doctor, acupuncturist, or naturopath has been able to help me heal.

"Everyone needs assistance at some point," James says kindly.

"Even you?"

"Everyone," he repeats, "even me."

17.

"I will never, never, never grow
so old again..."
                        —Van Morrison

The next day I join James for lunch in Santa Monica. Climbing the steps to the Georgian Hotel, I spy him sitting peacefully on the deck, his eyes closed, the outline of his straight Greek nose tilted up towards the sun.

He opens his eyes and gets up to greet me with a big bear hug.

"Isn't this fabulous?" He motions to the flurry of activity on Ocean Ave. A teenage boy with long blonde hair whizzes by on a skateboard, an older couple feeds birds from a park bench across the street, and a tall girl with a thick mane of black curls is walking six dogs of all shapes and sizes on three leashes.

James takes a long sip of his lemonade. "This might be the best lemonade I've ever had. Can I get you a glass?"

We fall into easy conversation, and I'm relieved that he seems to have put his concerns about Walker to rest. A woman walks by in a kimono, which prompts James to share about the two years he lived in Tokyo while he was creating his "white" paintings. He describes the omnipresent smell of broiled eel fused with the grassy scent of the woven tatami mats. I begin to yawn uncontrollably as he recalls rushing out into the street in his wooden geta shoes on a snowy winter evenings to meet the yakimo man who'd be singing in the street, "yak-eeee-mo, yak-eeee-mo," announcing that sweet potatoes were warming over hot coals in his wagon. His eyes are alight. This is more than he normally reveals to me about himself.

"Has everything always been perfectly clear to you?" I ask. "Or have there ever been times when you've doubted what you see or experience?"

"Ah, ha! These are good questions to be asking!" he says, sipping his lemonade. "Well, early on, it was challenging because when I shared what I was experiencing, people told me I was crazy because *they* weren't able to see what I was seeing or what I was doing. I had to literally ask myself if I was crazy. I mean, what's more crazy than knowing the things you're experiencing are real, but no one around you can substantiate them?"

"Wow," I murmur.

"Say you do something on the physical plane—skiing, for instance—and someone tells you not only that you aren't skiing but also that skiing doesn't exist at all, right after you just had an amazing run down the slopes! They've never been skiing—or even to the mountains for that matter—so it *must* not exist."

"That *is* crazymaking."

"Although now it may sound easier than it was, I concluded that I am *not* crazy, and I've stood by my spiritual experiences and capabilities, which has allowed me to evolve as a healer and given me immense inner strength."

"In a way, it's like if you were to look through a window and see a bunch of people dancing—moving and contorting their bodies in different ways, but being that you are on the other side of the window, you can't hear the music, so, of course, the dancers are going to look like they're crazy."

The words rush out of my mouth. "Oh, but you're obviously the dancer in this scenario."

"You crack me up!" he starts laughing mid-sip, sending a spray out onto the table, which makes him laugh even harder, and then I, too, catch the giggles.

Finally, he composes himself and says, "This is the reason I say I don't have time to debate with people and can only really work with those who wish to heal and grow. The planet is no longer sustainable on a variety of levels but most importantly, the old beliefs no longer work."

You can say that again.

Our food arrives, and we stop talking. Then he says, "Isn't having a human body amazing? We get to taste delicious food; make love; create with these things!" He wiggles his hands and pinches his forearm, explaining, "These are creative channels! With these we can write poems, paint paintings, mold sculptures! Without these human forms it would be impossible."

His giddy appreciation is infectious. After lunch, we make our way down to the beach near Santa Monica pier. Most of James and my interactions up until this point have been in the privacy of my home or over the phone, and primarily centered on what I'm working through. Being with him now is like being with an explorer discovering a new world. Stopping every ten feet or so, he snaps a photo or points out an obscure detail that I wouldn't have noticed.

"Isn't this marvelous?" he remarks, running his finger over the stripped wood railing to reveal a rainbow of colors created from years of oxidation. *Snap, snap* goes the camera.

Something catches the corner of his eye, and he swivels around to witness a flock of seagulls diving in succession into Santa Monica Bay. James slips off his leather loafers and wriggles his toes into the sand. Picking up a broken branch, he untangles a piece of seaweed and starts tracing in the sand.

"You know what this is?"

"A piece of driftwood?"

"It's a magic writing wand!"

"Come with me down to the wet sand. And we need to find you a magic wand."

We head towards the water, and I find a long, thin stick with a curved head, while James starts drawing figures in the sand.

"You want to know what *true passion* to create looks like? It's when you are painting and you run out of paint, so you grab the charcoal and continue; and when you run out of charcoal, you get a pencil; if your pencil breaks, you find a stick or a rock. It's this passion to create that has sustained us as a species because when we are truly engaged in a creative passion, there is no fear of the future; there's no regret about the past. There is only the present moment. Cro-Magnon man and all the other tribes died out. What kept Neanderthal man going was the *art*. The caves of Lascaux in France were discovered in the 1940's filled with drawings of forty-foot-long bison, human figures, and stags from 50,000 years ago."

I carve out shapes in the wet sand as he talks.

James pauses, gazing out over the water, just as a red-tailed hawk swoops down low. We watch it glide over the water then angle up over the mountains. *Snap. Snap.*

"When I first learned how to go out of body consciously, I would transport myself into hawk bodies, floating above the valley near our home in Woodside; I experienced the flight and motion of the hawk as it drifted through the sky. I also gained great consciousness during that transition into that hawk's form."

"You flew in a hawk's body?" I can tell he's not making this up, but I still find it hard to believe.

"Yes, and I still do that meditation today," he says pensively. "One day you will do it too, if you choose."

"I choose!" But then I feel doubtful. "Is it really as simple as just *choosing?*"

James looks at me intently. "Neutrality is the key to consciousness. The greatest understanding is the tiniest judgment will freeze you out of consciousness. So when I say that you can *choose*, I mean you can choose to heal into acceptance, which will allow you to vibrate beyond your competition and judgments. Then you, too, can have greater consciousness and fly around in hawk bodies amongst many other very amazing things!"

We walk in silence for a few steps until he asks, "Do you remember the hawk that lit your path on the astral the night after you saw me at your sister's apartment?"

"That was you?!"

"I saw you needed some assistance," he says with a wink.

I remember how I almost turned and ran from dark, terrifying path I was facing, and how it changed instantly when the hawk illuminated my way.

"Do you have *total* consciousness?" I turn to face him.

This causes him to laugh out loud. "If I had total consciousness, I could instantly transport both of us to the Champs-Elysées in Paris right now in our physical forms, where we'd be sharing a croissant and drinking café au lait!"

"Oh." I smile back, slightly embarrassed.

"I have very little information in the whole scheme of things."

I purse my lips and raise an eyebrow skeptically.

"Well, sure, I have more information than a lot of folks, but when we understand how much there is to know, that's when we come into understanding of how little information we really have." His voice softens. "Does this make sense to you?"

"Yes."

"Remember, acceptance and neutrality—*not IQ score*—are the keys to wisdom and consciousness, and ultimately a more passionate and meaning-filled life."

"Did you ever have to work on your own judgments? I mean, when you were younger?" We begin to walk down the beach, the sun on our backs.

"Neutrality is something that I brought in with me from my epic. But, yes, I did have to learn how to heal myself from judgments that I'd accepted before I knew what they were. And I still work on things every day! Consciousness isn't a line you cross. It's more like a practice. If I have a judgement come up, I know it's giving me info about me."

"In some of the spiritual books I've read, they explain the judgments and the thoughts of fear and jealousy that we have as the work of the ego. And we have to release the ego to let our true spirit shine through. It's described as something that we think is the real us, but it isn't. Is that what you mean?"

"Hmmm... the Freudian Ego?" I watch as he accesses information I can't see. "Well, I suppose that would be a very accurate description if you weren't using your sixth. Essentially, how it works from an energy perspective is from the minute we're born, we accept programming from the thoughts of people around us. On a very simplistic level, it's things like, girls should wear pink, and boys should wear blue. As you grow older, you must have a certain job, live in "the right" neighborhood, go to such-and-such a school, and if you don't, *you are not good enough!* These opinions and judgments are essentially fears that carry a very dense energy vibration, and ultimately program you to believe these things as truths, which they are not. These fears cause this part of your head" he explains, tracing a finger around the crown of my head, "to swell, crushing down on the sixth energy center, so you believe this programming to be a truth about who you are rather than *seeing* who you are with your sixth."

I rub the grooves on the side of my head—they aren't so bad today.

Nothing I've read so far has described what's going in this level of detail. My mind churns as I try to pinpoint what programming I've received and what my true thoughts are.

"And don't forget, judgments can carry over from other lifetimes as well. This is an epic imprint, which can range from amazing artist talent or musical ability to great pain and agony."

"How do you avoid bringing in pain and agony?"

"Running the energy of creative passion is one of the most healing things you can do."

Oh, here we go again...

"Also, transmuting energy in your meditations is critical for removing abandonment from your heart, so you aren't attracted to those who will abandon you. And one day, you'll get a heart healing, which will allow you to feel love on a whole new level."

We walk in silence for a while, the cool water lapping up over our toes. I consider how ingrained judgments can be and how

I've never witnessed James to have a judgmental tone. It's why I feel so open with him.

Six or seven butterflies flutter past us, and James exclaims, "How fun!" *Snap, snap.*

"They look like they're playing! Wait what is a group of butterflies called? I mean like a gaggle of geese... is there a term for a cluster of butterflies?"

"How about," he pauses to rip off his sunglasses dramatically, "a flurry of butterflies? I just love how in the movies they rip their glasses off their face. How about a tangent of flamingos?"

"Or a bevy of bees?"

"Or a harem of horses?" he says with a big belly laugh.

"A circus of crawdads!"

"A tide of terrapins!"

"A paw of pandas!"

We soon enter nonsense territory: a flagship of indolent eyeglasses; a terse temptation of wax-less candles, choking on our own laughter.

After our laughter subsides, James turns to me. "You know something?"

"Hmmm?"

"You're a lot less serious than you used to be."

"I am?"

He nods his head. "You've been pretty serious for most of your life, but since you've started coming more into body, you're starting to find your true playful spirit again—the essence of who you really are."

I briefly contemplate this bizarre concept that I somehow know is true, but the thought is eclipsed by the sudden realization that James is the most lighthearted person I know. In nearly three years I've never heard him complain once, he's never been ill to my knowledge, physically looks younger than his sixty years, and has more childlike playfulness than I've seen in many children. Whatever "rational" holes I can poke into his teachings doesn't change the fact that James is undoubtedly the happiest, most creative, appreciative, and generous person I've ever met. And it would seem wise to take advice from the person who has all the qualities you want.

18.

"Anyway, the thing is,
what I really mean
Yours are the sweetest eyes
I've ever seen..."
—Elton John

Within a month of my session with Ava, my old friend Mike finds me on Facebook *and* another Mike—an old love that I haven't thought of in years—leaves me a voicemail. And just as she predicted, one week after that, Walker asks me to move in with him, *and* I do run into some issues with my car: a parking ticket, a fender bender, and a tow in the span of about a month. Normally I'd be extremely hassled by it, but now I just wonder: *If she was right about those things, is she right about the whole soulmate/happily ever after/being a writer and helping people change their lives for the better thing?*

Despite almost three years of healing work and the love of this kind man, a heaviness still lurks around my heart, and I can tell it's holding me back from loving as deeply as I'd like.

In response to Walker's invitation to get a place together, I tell him that I want to stay in my bungalow until my lease is up in four months' time. I don't mention that it's always dandy for the first year and then everything goes to hell and I'm not completely convinced that this loving, patient, and thoughtful man won't disappear as easily as stars competing with city lights. But as the days turn into weeks and months, my confidence grows that this is not just his putting his best self forward at the beginning of the relationship.

With long weekends to Sayulita for surf, New Orleans for the Jazz Festival, Dallas to meet his family, Aspen for camping and more music, my job, and the spiritual work I'm doing with James, the summer zooms by. And, just as Ava predicted, come July, I'm number one in my division with the biggest commission check I've ever earned. Which comes in handy since my lease is up and it's time to move again.

On our second scouting trip, in an area called Los Feliz, Walker and I find an incredible craftsman house with elevated ceilings, new hardwood floors, fresh paint throughout, and lush, tropical landscaping. The owners had been hoping to flip it, but then the housing market crashed. It's a few blocks south of stunning Griffith Park, with views clear to the ocean and dozens of hiking trails.

After one month in our new home, just as the domineering heat of September gives way to a balmy October, I pull into the driveway and see that Walker is home early.

"Lovey?" I call out as I set my keys on the table, still not totally used to the fact we live together.

"Schweeeeeets!" I trace his voice to the backyard.

As I lean over to give him a kiss hello, a high-pitched yelping—quite possibly the sweetest noise in the world—fills the air, and little paws press against my calf.

"Oh my! And who is this?"

"He turned up at Sagebright without a home, so I thought since I'm traveling so much, you might want to have a companion. Plus, he has nowhere to go."

I bend down to pick him up, his entire furry body fitting inside my two hands. Horrifying images of the dog pound flash through my mind.

"Do you want to keep him?" His blue eyes crinkle as he smiles.

I'm not exactly what one would call a dog person, but there is something about his innocent amber eyes that I let him nuzzle into my hair.

"I think I do," I answer, surprising even myself.

I've never had my own dog before, and as his tacky little tongue explores my neck, it's strange and delightful.

"So we need to find the right name for him," I announce as my declaration of custody.

"What about, Harvelle? You know, after that little blues joint in Santa Monica."

"Harvelle seems like a dog with a mangy, oatmeal-colored coat and a goofy look on his face. Although, it *would* be fun to talk to him in a thick Southern accent: *Harvelle, git ur skinnae lil' hinny in here or Mama ain't gonna be pleased.*"

Walker laughs, pulling me and little Harvelle onto his lap. "It'll be like I never left the South."

For the next three days, I try calling him Harvelle. Around lunchtime on day two, my faux Southern accent has lost its luster. With his caramel-colored coat and black tiger-stripe markings, he looks like he should be running free on the open plains of the Serengeti.

Apparently, he feels the same way because that night on the astral he comes to me with his little ears pinned back politely and says, "Mama, my name isn't Harvelle. I want to be called, Disco. Okay, Mama? Got that? *Disco*."

Even for me, who lives out dozens of realities each night on the astral, this was a special experience. When we wake up I tell Walker, "Our dog's name is *Disco*."

We can't tell what Disco's genetics are. He has the dark snout of a German Shepherd, the freckled tongue of a chow, the curled tail of a Sharpe, the lean body and short hair of a boxer, the defined tiger stripes from—who knows... and short floppy ears that make it impossible for him to hide his emotions, and I soon find out that he has predator instincts like a bloodhound. He seems to sense that I have no experience raising dogs and does his best to help me; after only one accident inside, he's housetrained.

Disco and I are soon inseparable. We go on regular walks in Griffith Park where he frolics with other dogs, "hunts" squirrels, and never strays far from me. My heart hums with love for this furry little creature who has come to depend on me. At home, I hear the soft click, click, click of his nails against the hardwood floor trailing behind me wherever I go. I discover reserves of patience and delight I never knew I had. He eats when I eat. He drinks when I drink and he looks at me with eyes so sweet, I'm convinced they could end wars.

I become acutely aware that I've never experienced this mixture of pride, adoration, and amusement before. I knew that having a dog was going to be a big responsibility with a lot of extra work and our weekend trips would be cut down dramatically, but what I was in no way prepared for was how tightly connected and deeply in love I would fall with this little creature. I think I even feel the lingering darkness in my heart beginning to wane.

I realize the magnitude of this love a few weeks after Thanksgiving. Out of nowhere my normally vital little pup isn't eating his food and his loving eyes are staring back at me with a look that says, "I'm in pain. Help me, Mama."

Concerned, I call Walker at work. He tries to reassure me, but when we get off the phone, I do what any concerned mother would do: start combing the internet. Not eating and depression yield over 10,000 results, and I work myself into a mini frenzy by the time Walker gets home.

"I think he has parvo," I say before he can close the front door.

"What's parvo?"

"I know, right? Well, apparently it's a very common and highly contagious virus that is spread through dog feces and has a 91 percent mortality rate!" My words rush out all in one nervous breath.

"Wait, hold on, slow down. Why do you think he has parvo?"

"Because his symptoms match the description for parvo most closely. He's barely moved and has been having horrible diarrhea and threw up twice after I talked to you."

Walker kneels down next to Disco and rubs his head softly. "You OK, little bug?" he asks affectionately. Disco just stares back at him with those sad, droopy eyes.

"If not treated, he might die in 48 to 72 hours."

"I'm almost positive that we got him vaccinated for parvo," Walker says, walking into the kitchen and rifling through the drawers for Disco's papers. He finds a printout with nearly a dozen things we had him inoculated for, and sure enough, parvo is last on the list.

"All I know is something's very wrong, and we're going to the vet," I declare, gathering a few of Disco's things.

"Mama knows best," Walker concedes, grabbing the car keys.

After several hours of sitting in the waiting room, the vet comes out and tells us that Disco does, in fact, have parvo. The vaccine is more effective in some breeds than others; some part of his gene pool must be a weak link. He's in bad shape by now, shaking on the cold tile floor.

"I don't care how much it costs; we want to do everything possible to save him!" I proclaim.

"Whoa," Walker reins me in. "What if it's, like, ten grand?"

I bite down on my lip, willing myself not to cry.

How do I explain that we can't put a price on Disco's life? And that when he looks up at me through his gold-flecked eyelashes, I SWEAR he is reading my mind?

Before I can tell him that I will find a way, the vet smiles kindly and says, "Don't worry; it's not ten thousand dollars. It's probably closer to three thousand, depending on what type of care you want and how long he needs to stay. He will be receiving medicine intravenously around the clock, and although it isn't clinically proven, we have had a lot of success with Tamiflu, if you want to add that."

"We do," I assure her hastily.

If this is how I feel about my dog, which I have had for three months, I can't begin to imagine how parents who are watching their children fight for their lives are managing.

The vet brings us paperwork to sign and says, "There is nothing more you can do. Why don't you go home and get some sleep and call and check on him in the morning?" She gingerly hoists Disco up over her shoulder like a baby. "Since you brought him in early, the probability of a positive outcome is increased." Walker gives my hand a little comforting squeeze.

When we get home, the house is eerily quiet, and I wonder how I've lived so many years without a dog. Lying in bed, trying to sleep, all I can think is, *What if Lil' Discie doesn't make it?*

The following morning, I finally get ahold of James to see if he can predict if Disco is going to recover.

"There you are!"

"Sorry, Sweet Pea. I have been doing a healing up in Sebastopol with no cell service and I just got your messages."

I fill him in on the events of the past twenty-four hours.

"He is filled with a dark inky energy right now, but there *is* a little gold-green coming into his heart, which is good."

"Do you think that he is going to make it?"

"I will work on him."

"You didn't say if you think he's going to make it."

He stays quiet for a few moments and then says, "I think he will, but I *do* need to work on him."

"I don't know what I will do if he doesn't make it. He has been such a..." I pause, considering what it is exactly he is to me. "He has been such an unexpected gift in my life." My chest feels tight.

"He has been helping you heal," James says in that slow, knowing way that means he is reading me.

"You know, I can feel it. He *is* helping me heal."

"Do you know why?"

"Because I'm feeling unconditional love for the first time?" I ask hesitantly.

"Well, that's part of it, but it's because having an animal forces you to be in the present. It's very difficult to engage with an animal and drop into a past-time vibration or get ahead of your-self in a future-time vibration because they live in the present."

"Hmmmm... I never thought about it like that before."

"Which essentially is helping you to shift your vibration out of the past, where you have been vibrating for a long time. Don't worry, Sweet Pea. He's going to be OK. Just imagine bright green healing energy from your heart to his."

"Oh, I will! And thank you for working on him. It means so much to me."

That evening, sitting in my office, unable to concentrate on my expense report, my eye wanders over to the books piled up every which way in our bookshelf and settles on one of Walker's contributions: *The Power of Now*. I make a mental note to ask James why *exactly* having a present-time vibration is so desirable. I slide it out and start reading.

The premise is that time is purely a construction of the human mind, not the essence of what we actually are, and this creation is the root of all suffering. It's not only the biggest obstacle to us being free of our personal problems but also the primary thing keeping us from living in harmony as a civilization.

The author, Eckart Tolle, explains, *"All negativity is caused by an accumulation of psychological time and denial of the present. Unease, anxiety, tension, stress, worry—all forms of fear—are caused by too much future, and not enough presence. Guilt, regret, resentment, grievances, sadness, bitterness and all forms of non-forgiveness are caused by too much past, and not enough presence."*

He gives a few examples of spiritual teachers who have all pointed to the NOW as the key happiness, abundance, and enlightenment. As I read how the great Zen master Rinzai would often times raise a finger and ask, *"What at this moment, is lacking?"*, this prompts me to consider what is lacking in my life.

Well, aside from a healthy Lil' Discie, nothing at the moment. Or, wait! Is that really just my fear that I will be lonely in the future without him?

I abandon my expense report, fill up a hot bath with honey and sage aromatherapy salts, and hungrily devour Eckhart Tolle's wisdom on how the NOW is our only chance at freedom—*freedom from our thoughts.*

The next morning, when I call the animal hospital to check on Disco, they inform me that they've never seen a dog recover from parvo so quickly. They want to keep him one more day to be on the safe side, but his tail is wagging, and he is definitely going to make it.

19.

"I don't blame you anymore
That's too much pain to store
It left me half dead
Inside my head
And boy, looking back I see
I'm not the girl I used to be
When I lost my mind
It saved my life"

—Mozella

When I finish the *The Power of Now*, a startling truth dawns on me and I realize that I have uncovered a big piece of the puzzle as to what went so wrong with Aidan and my relationship. Our entire existence became about what the future had in store for us. We both invested so much in the future—namely when his company sold—that when it actually arrived, the future wasn't what either one of us has been fantasizing about at all.

It's easy to see now, that the future meant very different things to each of us. To me, it meant I would have my sweet, funny boyfriend back and we would have the resources to travel around the world like we planned, and hopefully a ring, which, for some reason, I believed would save me from my feelings of "fear, need, lack and incompleteness," which as Eckhart Tolle says, "are part of the human condition in its unredeemed and unenlightened state." And for all that, I would just perform the daily duties of your everyday, dime-a-dozen, *Crazy Goddess* mercenary.

I think Aidan had an even taller order for the future: He was counting on all those extra zeros in his bank account to ease the burden of inadequacy he'd been hauling around since he was old enough to form the illusion that millionaires were better and happier than everyone else.

The magnitude of our differing visions didn't come to light until the company actually did sell for hundreds of millions, and even though things weren't exactly daisy chains and laughs between us, I was still surprised when he told me the trip was off. What shocked me even more was the reason why. It wasn't his new pseudo-celebrity status, or the yes men surrounding him; it wasn't even the endless stream of women that were suddenly very inappropriately chummy with him. The trip was off because if he left now, he would get *behind*.

"Behind *who?!*" I sputtered.

"You know, just behind." He shrugged.

"Um, actually, no, I don't know. You have been promising me for almost four years, as soon as we could, we'd go on our trip."

He looked at me unapologetically. He'd clearly already made his decision.

I finally understand: When the moment we'd been waiting for arrived, when our dreams were to be realized and fears washed away, nothing was different. We were the exact same unfulfilled, unaware people we'd always been. I was still holding out that my future-time fantasy of us traveling around the world would serve as an asylum from my regret over turning my back on my inner voice all these years, while he needed to create something new, somewhere out "there" in the future; once he accomplished that, *then*, he would be happy. With the notion that salvation existed at some future point outside of ourselves, we didn't stand a chance.

It wasn't his fault! It wasn't my fault!

Like a stubborn condensation that's been lingering on the bathroom mirror suddenly dissolving, the blame I've been directing towards Aidan—which pales in comparison to blame I've been inflicting on myself—evaporates.

We were both just so unconscious. Not to mention, I was so terrified of creating for myself, I depended on his dreams and successes to fill me up. Suddenly, it hits me; all this time, I've felt like I was betrayed, but the reality is, I betrayed myself. I knew in my heart that there was something else for me—something that my spirit was calling for me to do, but I silenced that voice in favor of the security that came with approval and acceptance from Aidan and my old group of friends. I'm overcome with compassion for both of us as I think about how the two of us genuinely tried in the only ways we knew how but always ended up back in the same place of hurt and frustration. It's taken me three *freaking* years, but I think I can finally start to let it all go.

～

A week later, after not crossing paths for nearly a year, I come face to face with Aidan. Widespread Panic is playing at the Orpheum Theater. Walker and I arrive a little late, and the place is going nuts. I walk in completely sober, in jeans and a boyish tee shirt, and I can't help but marvel at how times have changed. A year and a half ago, I met Walker in this same theater, dancing on front row in a white crochet dress and heels, waving around a lavender feather boa, looking for trouble, with one too many whiskeys under my belt.

Thank freaking Gaaawd, or Buddha or the Universe, or whoever's running this joint for growth. That's all I know.

At set break, standing in line for the bar, we bump into Aidan and my old crew. Much to my surprise we share a few jokes and they invite us to come hang with them in the front. Dancing with my new boyfriend on my left and my old boyfriend on my right, I can't help but to think, *amusing!*

After a couple of drinks, I decide to share my realization with Aidan. As everyone is filing out at the end of the show, I tug on his shirt and ask, "Can I talk to you for a minute?"

"Sure," he agrees, unable to hide a look of confusion. We take a seat on two of the theater chairs.

"Hi," I say awkwardly.

"Hi," he echoes, with equal awkwardness.

"I just want you to know that I don't blame you for what happened," I start out and am mortified to feel my eyes pricking with tears.

Not now! It's been well established that I cry more frequently than some people change their undies, but now is really not the time.

By the look on his face, I can tell this was the last thing he was expecting.

"I don't blame you, either. I only remember the good times," he says kindly. Just then a theater employee comes over and shoos us out of the seats.

As we start heading up the graded walkway, I explain, "The thing is, I wasn't following my dreams. I was depending on your dreams to be enough for the both of us."

"I never thought about it like that," he says. His eyes cloud over like they do when he is processing something for the first time.

"And we were just so young..." I trail off. What I really mean to say is, "*We were so unconscious!*" But for some reason, it doesn't come out.

"OK, folks, let's go!" We're ushered into the bright, chaotic lobby.

I don't have time to get into the whole present-time, future-time salvation bit, but that doesn't matter. What matters is that *I* recognize it and can finally start releasing myself from the oppressive blame and resentment that have been fixtures in my life for years.

We give each other a hug and head outside where our friends are all waiting.

"Ready?' I ask Walker.

"Sure," he says, lifting me off the ground into a big hug. I melt into his big, strong arms and nuzzle my face into his neck, which still smells fresh from his shower.

As we walk to his car, I'm overcome with relief, like a sailor lost at sea for years who finally sees the curvature of the shore.

20.

"It will soon shake your windows
And rattle your walls
For the times they are a-changin..."
—Bob Dylan

"OK, lay on your back and spread your legs as wide as you can," Leia commands.

"I know, I know," I grumble as I hug my knees into my chest and grab my ankles as I'd been told.

"I just can't believe that it isn't working on you," she says as she inspects my bikini line. "I mean, how any times have you been back now?"

My mind skips through the various LA neighborhoods; visualizing all of the different spots Leia has moved her business to over the years. Initially, I'd go up to her house where she lived with her doctor baby-daddy in Bel Air, then the office building in Brentwood, then there was the stint in Mar Vista when she was a blushing, newlywed to the ex-cop who ended up transitioning to a woman, and then freshly divorced back in Westwood in her new apartment with her teenage son, and now in her bungalow in Santa Monica.

"I started coming to you when you were over in Bel Air. So that was at least five years ago, I guess."

She flashes me a dubious look. "Well, you might want to consider giving—"

"Don't even say it. I'm not giving up. It has dramatically improved the situation, and this time it's going to be permanent," I finish determinedly.

"I just don't want to you waste your money," she says apologetically. "Most people who have hair this dark don't have to come back after five or six times. Seven, max."

"Maybe most people that come to see you aren't hairy Portuguese women."

"Oh, you don't even have the first clue what hairy is! You can't even imagine what I see. This is hardly what I'd call hairy! I think it's just that you are too damn healthy. Your repair cells must work too well."

"You're just being kind."

Leia gives me an exasperated look. It's hard to believe that she is in her 50s. With her lean, tan body and wrinkle-free skin, she could easily pass for late thirties. All of a sudden, we are interrupted by three bangs on the door.

"Oh, no," Leia groans. "It's my ex dropping off my son."

I look around in panic for something to shield myself with. I'm not really what one would call a modest person, but even I draw the line at meeting people with only saran wrap covering my lady bits.

"Do you mind if they come in?" Leia asks desperately, already unhinging the accordion style door from the side of the wall. "I can pull this over, and they won't be able to see a thing."

"It's cool," I say and close my eyes tightly. Almost every time

I see Leia, there's some interruption that leaves me lying, slightly uncomfortable, wrapped in saran wrap. I know she juggles a lot: her regular day job as an RN, the laser/dermatology business she runs on the side, two kids, three exes, volunteering on skid row, her sobriety, and attempting to have a social life. Visiting her is a bit like going to the Mad Hatter's tea party.

But her customers, many of whom are celebrities, put up with the bedlam because she is extremely skilled at her craft and has a generous heart and a wonderfully goofy sense of humor. Which does not translate into business savvy; she rarely charges full price, and when she does, it is still dirt cheap.

I listen through the makeshift door as she greets her son with a kiss and his father with a friendly hello, then sends her son in his room to do his homework, gives her ex a tabouli salad from the fridge, and then is back by my side in less than three minutes.

I hear James' voice inside my head, "Don't be fooled by face value!"

Maybe it isn't sheer chaos after all but rather a set of systems she has in place, making things appear chaotic to an outsider.

"OK," she says, snapping on a new pair of latex gloves, "spread 'em. Has the numbing cream been on long enough?"

"Well, I put it on at least an hour ago."

"OK, you're good. And if I remember correctly, you don't even really need the numbing cream."

"I just have a really high pain tolerance." I shrug.

Leia stares at the chart. "Do you realize that your last three appointments, I have had the machine turned up to *fifty*?"

"What does that mean?"

"It means that the only logical explanation is that you must have been a prisoner of war in your past life who endured extreme torture because you don't even flinch." She looks at me incredulously and then starts laughing.

"Maybe..." I muse, envisioning myself chained up in a dank cave in some remote war camp being whipped and beaten but refusing to divulge any secrets. I'm slipping deeper into my daydream when what could only be a porcupine bathed in hot coals slams into my labia. My entire body recoils into a tight little ball, managing to kick Leia's elbow in the process, knocking the laser out of her hand.

"Agggggggggghhhhhh, ooooooooooohhhhhhh, eeeeeeeeeee!" I shriek and moan, clutching the injured area. Leia gathers herself and rushes hastily to my side. "Are you OK? What happened?"

"*What the hell was that?!*" I cry, sure if I pull my hand away it will be covered in blood.

"What do you mean?" Her eyes are concerned, but her pink lips are beginning to twist into a little smile. "Is this a joke, Emily?"

"Are you... What was that?" I start to laugh, confused and a little embarrassed that I kicked her.

"That was the same laser we've always used for you..." she references my chart for a second then says, "for the past fourteen visits."

"I've never felt so much pain in my entire life," I whine.

"Are you on your period?" she asks, studying the laser.

"No... I finished my cycle almost a week ago."

"Are you taking any sort of medication that may cause sensitivity?"

"Nope."

I'm completely baffled, and so is she.

Much to my surprise and relief, when I finally pull my hand away, everything is completely intact, just a little red.

I decide to try again, this time applying an ice cube to the area immediately after she zaps it. We continue on like this for what seems like eternity. Although the ice cube helps a little, it's basically as if the porcupine is still doing his thing, minus the hot coals.

When it's time to leave, Leia thoughtfully packs a "to go" ice pack for my drive home, but that doesn't stop my yoni and neighboring vicinities from burning like hell the whole way home.

Disco greets me happily at the door, ready for his afternoon walk through Griffith Park.

"You're gonna have to give me a minute, little bug; Mama can barely walk."

Perched on the corner of the carpet, showing me how well behaved he can be, his tail swings wildly behind him, completely giving him away. I look closer and see that he isn't even sitting but crouched down on his hind legs, ready to pounce up when I say the word. I can't help but to smile at this effort at such exemplary behavior.

So stinkin' cute!

"OK, we'll go," I promise, suddenly less aware of the scorpion sting between my legs.

Disco follows me into my office, his freckled tongue wielding around my legs, trying to get in as many licks as he can. I sit down and flip up my laptop to find James sent out his monthly newsletter.

Are you ready to shift your vibration into the much higher frequency of the HEART MIND?

Yes! Wait, remind me what that is again?

J: This means consistently vibrating in the spiritual

wisdom of inner kindness—no negativity, no blame, no complaint, no competition, no looping thoughts.

I'm certainly trying!

J: Heart mind is an integration of ACCEPTANCE of YOURSELF in everyday life!

I accept myself, others accept me, and I accept others. Even those shifty assholes in my entourage—oh, wait, no blame. I take that back.

The newsletter goes on to explain:

12 CONSTRUCTS OF NEGATIVITY THAT ENSURE NON-SUCCESS

I scroll quickly through constructs one through five, as they are already things we've discussed: fear of the unknown, fear of judgment, agendas, competition, non-belief in self, but when I get to number six, a surge of energy runs through me, and my entire body is covered in goose bumps.

#6. Pain has a meaning for YOU!

Many times I have mentioned body clenching, which leads to physical pain in your lower back, hips, and legs, and in extreme cases, numbing. This is a sign that you are operating off of a great deal of perfection and fear as well as holding onto old pain. There is no meaning in pain and punishment. Holding onto emotional pain as some kind of badge of courage means you are punishing yourself immensely. Whenever you hear someone say, "They have a high tolerance for pain," they are really saying they have a high tolerance for being a *victim*.

Wait, just a minute here! All this time I thought that having a high pain tolerance was lucky, like a fast metabolism. But it's really nothing more than a big fat stamp on my forehead that says "victim"?

I suppose it makes sense. It's become increasingly obvious that I allowed myself to be treated like punching bag to pull through an agenda so grand Napoleon would have balked. Of course, I had no idea that I was doing this because I was operating under a set of illusions that just seemed so *damn* real at the time.

Does this mean that I should actually be relishing in the excruciating, stinging, burning—whatever that was—I just endured? Just for the mere fact that I'm not longer numbed out and can feel again? Have finally shed my victim-nature skin, and am I no longer waging a vicious war on myself?

Of course, little by little, I'd seen signs of change and growth, but there is nothing more powerful than a physical manifestation of change. I pick up the phone and jam my index finger down on the letter J to speed dial James.

"Ummm, yes, this is Interpool; we have a search warrant out on someone called Sweet Pea," he jokes.

"I'm here, turning myself in," I say quickly, way too excited to indulge "James Theater" for a second longer than I have to. On another day we might conduct an entire discussion in French or Australian accents, but today, I don't have time for that. I launch into the whole laser hair removal incident.

If he thinks it's weird that I pay money to have the hair follicles on my body stunned to death, he doesn't let on and quietly says, "Well, congratulations, Sweet Pea. You really are changing. You are finally letting go of the notion that being rejected by Aidan has meaning in your life." He remains quiet for a few moments before saying, "I see that you are no longer defining yourself by him or that relationship."

I pause for a second to think about Aidan. Of course, I think about him from time to time—after all, I spent more than half my twenties with him—but I couldn't remember the last time I'd met someone new and had shared the story of what happened between Aidan and me. For a while there, whatever unsuspecting person I'd meet would know they had a wounded bird on their hands by the end of the conversation.

"Actually," I say slowly, "thinking about him now, I no longer feel like he wronged me in some way."

"Wow, big step, grasshopper."

"It *really* wasn't his fault, and truthfully I'm actually glad he pushed me away because I wouldn't have left otherwise, and let's face it—I had and *still have* a lot of growing to do!"

"This is an important recognition," he says softly. "Do you know what people say when I ask them what it is they want most in their lives? Without fail, everyone says they want *passion*. What most folks don't realize is: how can you keep passion in a partnership if you can't generate passion for your own creations?"

"Well, when you put it like that, it seems like the most obvious thing in the world."

"I know I've said this before, but so much of what you've done and who you've thought yourself to be in this lifetime hasn't really even been you. And *you* are on the brink of becoming a *passionate creator*!" he says with the gusto of an Italian delicatessen owner describing the nuances of his family's aged salami. "And, Sweet Pea, there is no greater vibration of vitality than that of a passionate creator!"

I want more than anything to believe him.

21.

*"I was looking in the mirror
and my eyes were getting clearer
You can't change the past,
you can only change the future"*
—Samantha Stollenwerck

With the New Year approaching, one pestering question I can't seem to shake shows up. She's there, all bright eyed and bushy-tailed, when I wake up in the morning, and then begs around all day, making it nearly impossible to cast her aside for other distractions as I've done for so many years before. She even has the audacity to lurk into my astrals, causing me to wake up and stare at the ceiling for hours in restless contemplation: "WHEN ARE YOU GOING TO DO SOMETHING THAT REALLY MATTERS TO YOU?"

Sure, Walker and I have created a happy home, where we cook dinner together, play board games, talk about everything, snuggle, and coexist quite peacefully together—certainly not the vibe in the house with Aidan when we were alone. And I'm really trying to remain in gratitude about my job, *really*

I am—especially since the unemployment rate is creeping above 9 percent. But mustering enthusiasm to promote pharmaceuticals after witnessing firsthand that my body can heal without them, coupled with this nagging feeling that *just maybe* my existence has significance beyond just contributing to the financial economy, is getting increasingly difficult.

Listening to Walker talk excitedly about Sagebright and the progress he's making in these kids' lives, I feel a little envious that he's created something he's so enthused about. In fact, I'm a little in awe that he realized what he wanted to do, wrote a business plan, raised millions of dollars and made it happen when he was just twenty-seven years old.

When I come clean to James about this nagging feeling of lack, despite all of the amazing things abundant in my life, he chirps, "It doesn't matter if you are a billionaire and own all the tea in China! If you are not a passionate creator, you will never experience the true joy and foreplay of life!"

If I'd never started working with James, I might've misdiagnosed this feeling as the need for a new Spring wardrobe, or the desire to knock back half a bottle of pinot grigio each night, but it's too late for disguises; I can no longer hide, especially not from myself.

"I know that we've gotten to the core of *why* I haven't let myself create, but that doesn't change the fact that I still don't feel very creative."

"Oh, please. When I look at your creative levels, they are off the charts!"

"Hmph." I look down at the flowers I've been doodling, thinking a first grader could do better.

"Well, I know I'm doing something right when I get one of those little grunts," he says, laughing. When I don't say anything, he lowers his voice a few notches and says, "You are a *writer*," with so much conviction, tears balance warily in my eyes before sliding down by cheeks. They aren't tears of sadness but of recognition. And it suddenly hits me, hard, like a ballerina tumbling to the ground on a crooked landing.

Simultaneously, my heart taps a little time-step in my chest cavity. The signs are small but very clear. Perhaps they've been there all along, but I've been too numbed out to notice them. Whatever the case, there will be no more excuses; I will write my story.

Never mind the fact I haven't ever really written anything aside from emails or... I dunno, maybe the occasional thank you letter in the past eleven years, and tack on the actual subject matter is about as exposed as I could possibly be, but before I can start talking myself out of the whole thing, I realize I don't ever have to show it to anyone.

James says firmly, "Just remember, write it for yourself and be the beginner. As long as you are the beginner, you won't judge yourself, and the words will flow."

"I don't even know how to begin; that's how much of a beginner I am!" I object nervously, feeling my entourage hover in around me.

"Just light a candle and set your intention that you're accessing the information woven in your spiritual DNA for your creative passions and see what happens," he says, his tone an odd *combination* of mystery and knowing. "And before you go out on the astral, set a directive that you are recovering your creativity."

By this point I'm used to James saying things like this; however, the likelihood that lighting a candle and making a statement before bed is going to get the words flowing is a little harder to swallow. Nevertheless, I can use all the help I can get, so a few days later, I carefully place a candle in my windowsill, strike a match, and set an intention for the coming year.

"This year," I say carefully, "I'm accessing my past-life information from spiritual DNA for my creative passions." I take a deep breath and hear some asshole in my entourage say, "What creative passions? HAHAHAHAHA!"

I sigh, my gaze locking with the golden flame dancing about atop the wick, and say out loud, "I'm not in agreement to any fear or apathy."

Then I pull my hands over my head front to back and clean my hands off, whisking away the energies that aren't mine, then I hold 'em an inch apart, allowing the vibration to rev up inside my hands. To my surprise it's much stronger than usual. Softly, I say aloud, "I am Emily; a beginner of life, increasing my spirit-to-body connection and vibrating in my highest affinity for self and spiritual consciousness. I give myself permission to become a fearless, passionate creator."

As I say this, I'm surprised to feel the vibration increases twofold and I perceive a golden color inside my hands. Adding the word permission, I carefully draw it up to my heart and deposit the golden energy infused with permission into my fourth energy center, watching as it spreads throughout my body.

I turn my attention back to the droplet of fire flickering in the dark night. I'm ready to blow it out and get in bed, when suddenly something so crazy crosses my mind that for a second I think it must not be possible. Scrolling through my memory reel, all of the candles I've blown out over the course of my nearly thirty-two years flash before my eyes, and all I can recall is boys, boys, and more boys.

Could this be the first time that I have ever come face to face with a candle and not made a wish relating to the male species?

Wish after insistent wish that he would call me, or write me, or still love me. A wish that he would pick me, remember me, or think that I was beautiful.

Ding-dong! Could the Crazy Goddess be dead? OK, maybe not dead, but definitely terminally ill; in hospice, probably.

My mind drifts to Walker. If like attracts like, I must've changed to create something so radically different. Buzzing with love, but not hanging off the edge of a cliff ready to jump if he says jump; secure, but not boring; connected, but not code-pendent. Of course, we have disagreements, but not sharp words designed to hurt, knock down drag-out fights, or manipulations loaded with blame and guilt.

Could it be that for the first time in my life, I'm not whirling in a perpetual tailspin, trying to make something other than it is? Not trying to fix or change or save someone.

I find myself wondering if I'm so comfortable and secure in my life that I finally have the space to create.

Is this why the omnipresent question about what I'm going to do has become my stalwart shadow and my bold reflection?

Suddenly, I remember that embarrassing list I wrote over a year ago and rush into the office, scanning the shelves, until I see the navy-blue spine with the word Yosemite printed in white block letters. I pluck it from the row, and sure enough, my neatly folded piece of stationary falls out on the floor. Scrolling through, I'm dumbfounded that Walker has almost all the items on the list, except he's not a surfer or skier. Well, he wasn't. In the time we've been together, he's actually started to do both. OK, and he isn't exactly laugh-out-loud funny, but he has a quick wit.

Nineteen out of twenty-one? I'm not really a math girl, but this ratio sounds pretty good. Is this list responsible for manifesting my relationship with Walker?

Whatever the reason, I've never felt more peaceful in a relationship and clear in my head to pursue what interests me. Later, just before I drift off to sleep, I remember to say, "My directive is to recover my creativity on the astral."

～

The next day, I sit down in my living room and open my laptop. As soon as I open a new word document, I'm tempted to close it. Instead I remember James' words: "Just *be* the beginner; as the beginner you can never fail."

I close my eyes, pulling my hands from back to front up over my head to clear away all the energies from my entourage who are laughing and pointing because *I* am going to do something creative. I take a second to ground myself deep into the planet with green chords and hold my hands an inch apart. Unfortunately, the vibration isn't very strong this morning. I say aloud, "I am a beginner of life. I give myself permission to create passionately, effortlessly, and fearlessly."

My plan is simple. Start at the beginning and tell the truth. After all, I'm just writing it for me. As I begin to type, I'm surprised at how easy the first few paragraphs flow, and before I know it, I have a few pages. Writing about a time in my life that was so painful and confusing, I run the entire gamut of my emotions. Tears stream down my face as I relive how rejected I felt by Aidan, Courtney, and my friends; my cheeks burn with embarrassment when I think about what a, literally, *crazy* (*goddess*) woman I became for a while there; and finally, I feel a sense of compassion for myself when I think of this radical journey I've taken towards accepting myself. When Walker comes home, I realize I haven't stopped in nearly three hours. I hold my hands an inch apart—they're scorching hot, and the vibration is so strong they feel like two neodymium magnets that I can't pull apart.

"I started writing my story," I tell Walker shyly.

"Aw Schweets!" he says, his eyes brimming with pride as he comes over and gives me a big hug. "How does it feel?"

"Amazing and terrifying."

"I think that's how it's supposed to feel."

~

We celebrate New Year's Eve at a friend's low-key party, and just before bed, I repeat the same directive I've been saying every night since the night with the candle. "I'm setting the directive to recover my creativity on the astral, and I'm a fearless, passionate creator!"

I wake up feeling energized, alive, and not hungover for maybe the first New Years in thirteen years. This itself is a first, but an even more unusual thing happens the following week. I wake up to hear Disco scratching at the door to go out to pee, and as I scoot across the mattress to get out of bed, I feel the sharpest, most excruciating pain in my ankle since I sprained it at a lacrosse tournament in college.

I rip back the covers and flip on the light. Sure enough, my ankle is swollen to the size of a grapefruit with a purplish bruise reaching across the top.

What the hell is going on here?!

For a moment, I feel like I'm on drugs or in one of those really lucid dream states where you think you wake up but you are still dreaming. I lay back carefully, trying to remember if there is any way I could've bumped it or sleepwalked or something. Since Walker is traveling for work on the East Coast, there really isn't anything I could've bumped it on under the covers. And if I got up and sleepwalked, Disco would've gone nuts and I wouldn't have stayed sleeping for very long.

What the hell?

I hopple out of bed to let Disco out to pee. I soon realize that putting any weight on it is out of the question and hop back to bed, leaving the backdoor wide open.

Who sprains her ankle… sleeping?

I glance at the clock, which is blinking 2:32 AM, and hesitate for just a minute before picking up my phone and holding the "J" key down to speed dial James.

You can call a good friend at 2:32 a.m., right? OK, I just decided we're now really good friends.

After four rings, I'm sure it's going to voicemail, but just before it clicks over, I hear a scratchy but curious, "Hello?"

"I'm so sorry to bother you at this hour," I apologize, "but the strangest thing just happened."

"Yes?" he asks, his voice sharpening into concern.

"I just woke up with a sprained ankle and I did absolutely *nothing* to provoke it."

"Hang on a sec; let me look," he says. I hear some rustling around for a few moments before he says, "It's your right ankle?"

"Yes," I confirm.

"Ummmm..." he says, looking for a minute before saying with certainty, "Aidan."

"What does that mean?"

"True of false, you have begun to write your story?"

"Barely. I just have one chapter completed."

"Well, remember that the energies that you don't see are far more powerful than the ones you do see, and whenever we get injuries of the knees or ankles it is energy to prevent us from moving forward with a directive. And this is true that part of your story is about Aidan?"

"Well, it's more about what I *learn* from going through that experience, rather than it being *about* him, but it's kind of hard to tell my story without him being in it since he was such a big part of my life when I was so..." I pause, searching for the word, "I guess, unconscious."

"Exactly. Well, he doesn't want to be exposed, and he doesn't really want to see you move forward with your life, so he threw a little energy at you."

"I'd love to tell you that you're crazy, but after that little incident with the knot the size of golf ball in my forehead, and the sore throat, I know better." I pause. "Is he aware that he threw energy at me?"

"On some level he has awareness that you're doing something different, but he has so much unconsciousness that he doesn't know what his negative thoughts are doing."

"Well, what do I do?"

"Put your phone on speaker; you are going to need both of your hands."

I do as I am told.

"You probably don't have a neutral stick handy, and you can't walk, so we are just going to have to do our best with your hands," he says. "Clean them off and pull them very slowly over the top of your head so we can clear your space of all of the energies that aren't yours, and then hold them an inch apart."

"OK, now what?"

"Now, repeat after me: I am in alignment with James to do this healing. I am safe and protected and not in agreement to any pain or harm. I give myself permission to heal my ankle and change and grow so that I can vibrate into my highest affinity, consciousness, and grace."

I repeat what he says word for word, and I can feel the energy vibration begin to tingle between my palms.

"Now see a healing color inside your hands—I'm using an emerald green—and pull it directly into your ankle."

Even after all the times he has healed me, I'm a little skeptical that he can really help heal this.

Apparently a lifetime of medical programming is a difficult thing to shake.

"Now, press down on the top of your right hip," he commands.

"Ow!"

"I had a feeling that might be tender," he says with a chuckle. "Now press down twice, all the way down your right thigh, and then all the way down the front of your calf. And remember to see that emerald-green color at each point that you press." He is silent for a long time as I press down my whole right leg. I can tell that he is in deep concentration. Finally, he says, "If you can handle it, I want you to lightly pinch the webbing in between your toes." I wince a little but gently press down on the skin connecting my toes.

"OK, let's monitor. The swelling has increased, decreased, or stayed the same?"

"Ummmm... I think it's stayed the same. Or maybe gone down a little."

As I say this, I spy a very confused Disco flashing me a side-eye out of my peripheral vision.

"So on a scale of one to ten, ten being the most swollen and painful, where are you?"

"I think it has decreased by .001."

James laughs out loud. "You are hilarious!"

Oh to be as easily amused as James...

"OK, let's do the other side," he instructs. And so we go on like that for nearly an hour until the telltale yawning begins. One, two, three, I yawn deeply into the phone.

"Thank you," he says in response to my yawns. Finally, after thirteen yawns, I confirm that the swelling has decreased to at least a six.

"You need to get out on the astral, and I will continue to work on you," he tells me. Barely able to keep my eyes open, I don't object.

Although by now I know I shouldn't be, I'm shocked when I wake up and my ankle is almost back to normal. It takes me a minute to fully believe that it wasn't a dream. The swelling has completely disappeared, and the only indication that there was ever a problem at all is a faint bluish tint on the top.

When I walk, I feel no pain, aside from a little tightness on the side.

"*It's real, Disco!*" I whisper into his face with such intensity that he sits perfectly still, staring back at me as if he knows that I'm telling him something very valuable. "*It's really,*

really, real!" I kiss him on the nose and do a little twirl down the hallway.

I consider for a minute what I would've gone through if I didn't know James. I would have tried to get an appointment at a joint doctor, or worse yet, gone to the emergency room. I would have waited, gotten x-rays, waited some more, taken drugs, missed a few days of work at least, paid money, and most likely would still have an ankle the size of a grapefruit.

Before I can finish asking myself why people don't know about energy healing, I'm back at money, and lots of it. Medicine is big, big business, and I, being a pharmaceutical rep, am right at the heart of it. My stomach churns at the complexity of it all.

The entire day, I can't stop thinking about what just went down. Aidan throwing energy at me, which caused my ankle to swell like a grapefruit, James' midnight phone healing and now, I'm... well, just fine.

Almost unbelievable... if I hadn't experienced it first-hand.

The next few weeks sail along without any hint of discomfort in my ankle. Even though my enthusiasm for it is under a table drunk somewhere in Tijuana, I force myself to work as usual, but all I can think about is getting home as fast as possible so I can write. Then, suddenly, I start to notice a dull aching in my left ankle, this time, accompanied by a slight swelling. I try and call James at least a dozen times, but his phone goes immediately to voicemail. I think he mentioned something about going to Mt. Shasta where there's no cell service. Kind of desperate, I decide that maybe it isn't the craziest thing in the world for me to try and do what we did on the phone the first time.

Or let's be honest, it's the most bat-shit crazy idea ever, but let's face it; I'm not exactly winning any normalcy awards these days.

I pull my hands over my head and say my little monologue: "I'm safe and protected. I give myself permission to heal, to change and grow and vibrate in my highest consciousness and affinity." But this time I say, "I'm in alignment with higher self to do this healing." I hold my hands an inch apart and see that bright emerald-green color and pull it into my ankle.

As I press and release, down my leg, I *transmute*, breaking big plates of glass with Aidan's face on them, and encase myself in a golden bubble. I attach a grounding cord to my left foot and visualize dark energy draining from my ankle down into the center of the planet. Almost to my complete disbelief, after about thirty minutes of doing this, the aching subsides and the swelling appears to be decreasing.

Healing myself? This is even more nuts than having James heal me!

I continue on with the same technique for about twenty minutes until, much to my astonishment, it has completely gone down. I'm high as a kite for days and can't wait until James gets back on the grid so I can tell him what happened. Finally, almost a week later, I get a call.

"Sweet Pea? Are you OK? I just saw all of your calls come through," his voice cracks through the line, and I can tell he is somewhere really windy.

"You are *NEVER* going to believe this!" I shout into the phone.

"Try me!" he shouts back. I can hear him grinning on the other end.

"So after you healed my ankle the first time, the other ankle started hurting and swelling. And since I couldn't get ahold of you, I tried to heal it myself doing the same things that we did—and you are never going to believe this—*I healed my own ankle!*"

"Whoo hoo, little healer girl!" I hear him cheer from the other end of the line, and my cheeks literally ache from smiling so wide.

"This is one of the biggest cosmic secrets, Sweet Pea; we can heal our own bodies," he cries out through the crackling wind. "It isn't something that you are supposed to believe you can do." Then, as if on cue, the wind dies and he says, "Congratulations, Sweet Pea. You are starting to learn a little more about who you really are."

PART III:

WHO WE

REALLY ARE

22.

"Who's to say
What's impossible?
Well they forgot
This world keeps spinning
And with each new day
I feel a change in everything
As the surface breaks reflections fade
But in some ways they remain the same
And as my mind begins to spread its wings
There's no stopping curiosity..."
                        —Jack Johnson

Still jazzed from healing my own ankle and the reality that everything James has been saying about me being a healer might actually be true, I'm way more inspired to do my meditations every day, and motivated to make some external changes. Sure, alcohol isn't the mainstay in my life that it once was, but just a few glasses of wine a week are still enough to leave a sort of filmy residue hanging between me and that next level of clarity.

Of course, Walker hasn't had a sip of alcohol in four years, but left to his own devices, his eating habits boarder somewhere between animal flesh and pixie sticks, so I decide that for our birthdays, which are only a week away, we could both benefit from doing a five-day raw-food cleanse.

At first Walker looks at me like I've asked him to hike the Himalayas in high heels but eventually comes around when I tell him I heard that by age fifty, meat eaters will have five pounds of undigested red meat in their colons.

So each day we ingest shots of algae, wheat grass, chlorophyll, cayenne pepper, lemon and ginger; a cup of raw oatmeal; veggie nori rolls; a mango, kale, and coconut water smoothie; and juice made from green leaf, celery, coriander, apple, and lime. When day four rolls around and I still haven't done any real *detoxing*—if you know what I mean—a friend suggests that I get a colonic. In fact, she says that if I don't get a colonic, I'm doing myself an incredible disservice because all the stuff I am trying to release is just getting reabsorbed back into my body.

The thought of someone sticking a tube in my butt and pumping water through my body, then sucking out all of my poop while we both watch it go by in a plastic tube, all the while analyzing it's quality is somewhere on my list of things to do near getting my clitoris pierced and dropping acid with the Hells Angels. But if I don't do any actual *cleansing*, the whole thing is a waste. So I ask around and am referred to a woman named Natasha.

"Allo," she answers the phone in a thick eastern European accent.

"Um, hi..." I start off nervously. "My name is Emily, and I got your number from Lisa. I was wondering if I could come in for a colonic?"

"When you want to come?"

"As soon as possible."

"I can take you at three, one hundred dollars, 612 San Vicente in Santa Monica. Number 311. I take only cash. See you then," she says and hangs up.

It's not that I need the person who's sucking poop out of my ass to be my best friend or anything, but jeez...

I'm surprised to find that her office is in an apartment building. I'm buzzed into a grandiose entryway, with twenty-foot-high ceilings and a marble staircase.

I knock lightly on her door, and a guy, probably in his late twenties with a dark thick beard and ringlets curling down the sides of his face from under a woven Rastafari-esque cap, opens the door.

"Ummm... I... Hi? Is Natasha here?"

"She stepped out for a minute. Come in and have a seat," he says, welcoming me inside with kind blue eyes.

I follow him to a big square room with high ceilings and white walls covered with art I can only describe as mystical fantasy with Jewish undertones.

"You can wait here. I'm Ishmael. Let me know if you need anything," he practically whispers. With his bare feet, loose white pants, and a pale blue poncho, he looks like the front man for a Hasidic Grateful Dead cover band.

After a few minutes, a woman, probably in her early seventies, with silver hair chopped like a boy, standing no more than five feet, hobbles in, leaning heavily on a cane.

"You are Emily? Allo, I am Natasha. Come with me."

In the room stands what looks like a massage table encased in plastic like a giant condom. Next to it is a big white machine with small gauges, big tubes, and a frightening-looking lever. My asshole constricts just looking at the setup.

"I'm sorry you must see me like this. I fell today and hurt my hip."

"I'm so sorry to hear that."

She readies the bed. My eyes widen as she sets out an apparatus that looks like a vibrator.

"You've had colonic before?" she asks, not looking up from what she is doing.

"No, and actually I'm a little nervous. Is there anything I need to know?"

"Just like sex, everyone nervous first time. Then piece o' cake." Then, without looking up from her work, "You eat lots of sugar."

"Actually, I don't really have a sweet tooth at all."

"Pastas and bread is not your favorite food?" she demands, now looking right at me.

"Oh, well, yes, pasta and bread, but not sugar."

"Pasta and bread is sugar." I'm so sure she hates me that I barely wonder how she knows my favorite foods.

She leaves the room while I change into a hospital gown. Then we start the, uh, *procedure*. I do anything I can to keep my focus away from the cramping caused by the water filling my colon.

"Did you paint those?" I say, motioning to some oil paintings on the wall.

"Yessss. But you know that already, don't you?"

"I don't know. I thought maybe..."

"You already know because you are psychic," she says matter-of-factly, looking at me intently with her watery blue eyes. "You know you are psychic, no?"

"Um…" I think about James always saying *you are so darn capable*. "I'm not sure."

"You are. I know this because I'm an intuitive. Now breathe."

"I can tell that you suffered great pain, and you are still holding it right here, she says, jamming her fingers into my abdomen. Some pain you have been holding for twenty years or more."

I let out a little yelp, and tears slide down the sides of my face, into my ears, and I know with complete certainty that she is right.

Twenty years?! Crap. Literally. Crap.

"You are getting married soon." It's more of a statement than a question.

"Uh, maybe… I mean, I'm with someone and we're very much in love, but we aren't engaged or anything."

"You will be soon."

I smile to myself, close my eyes, and turn my attention back to my breath. When we are finished, I hand over a fist full of twenties and say thank you.

"I like to see beautiful woman take care of herself," she says, the harsh edge in her voice softening as she affectionately touches my face.

Of all the colonic, um… dooers in the Los Angeles, I somehow manage to find the psychic one.

In the weeks that follow our cleanse, we continue to eat vegan. It isn't easy, and we have nobody to go out to dinner with, but our energy skyrockets, and we find ourselves to be more optimistic and generally happier than we ever remember being.

We become inspired to make permanent changes in our diet, exchanging regular multigrain bread for sprouted, rice for quinoa and millet, and eating as many things in their alive, raw states as possible.

This means letting go of some foods I have been eating my entire life, which is challenging, but the rewards encourage me to keep it up. I say a tearful goodbye to the store-bought pesto sauce I have been eating since I was a kid, sharp cheddar cheese, and produce that isn't organic and fresh. The Sunday morning farmer's market becomes our religion.

One rainy winter night as we relax by the fire after a hearty meal of sesame seed burgers and kale chips, we get a surprise knock on the door and Disco goes wild, making his delightful little noises of complete torment because he already knows who is on the doorstep. I open the door to hear the unmistakable, soulfully sweet voice of my friend Samantha. *"Happy Birthday to you! Happy Birthday to you! Happy birthday oh, oh, oh, happy biiiirth-a-day, my beautiful friend, I sure do love yoooooooooou!"*

Tears well up in my eyes as I see Samantha holding an acoustic guitar with a big red bow around it in her hand.

"Sorry it's a few weeks late," she apologizes unnecessarily, as I know she's been on the road, "I thought it was about time you start making your own music," she says with a smile. I'm literally speechless. I squeeze her as tight as I can.

Finally, I whisper, "Thank you! Thank you! Thank you! This is quite possibly the grandest gift a friend has ever given me."

"Well, come to think of it, I don't think I've ever really given anyone a present like this before," she says, tears now brimming in her bright green eyes as well.

Mind you, I don't have the first idea how to play the guitar and have always placed learning an instrument somewhere near the category as learning a new language: if you don't learn it before you're like fifteen, then sorry bud, it's probably *not* happening. I've always idolized people who can play instruments and better yet, sing along. It just looks so damn complicated.

Music has always been a big part of my life, and as a child I loved singing. Sophie and I would make up songs and perform them for our dad. Then, in the sixth grade, when perfectly adorable little girls turn into perfectly adorable little monsters— myself included—one of the girls in our clique told me that some of our friends were telling everyone, "Emily thinks she's a good singer, but she isn't." From that point forward, I believed that I couldn't really sing. In high school, I didn't try out for the choral group for fear that I would be laughed at. I came to believe my place with music is in the audience.

The "I'm so perfect I hate myself club" really is something.

It wasn't until a few months ago, when Walker overheard me singing quietly to myself and told me I had a beautiful voice, that I've even been able to let go of this belief a little. And Samantha's gift is tremendously encouraging.

She leans down to give Disco's belly a rub, just as he jumps up to lick her face, getting his paw stuck in the straps of her purse. Then, all I see is a mass of blonde curls and paws tumbling to the ground and the contents of her purse spraying across the floor. She erupts in laughter as she and Disco roll around on the carpet. He climbs all over her, licking her face ecstatically.

The guitar feels foreign in my hands, but I remember the conversation James and I had about being the beginner.

I do not need to be Eric Clapton; I just need to be the beginner.

"I made sure to get you one with a thin neck because of your tiny hands."

"Teach me something!" I say giddily.

"Alright, let's begin with the basics. This chord is called is C." She effortlessly spreads three of her long, thin fingers across the strings and strums a few notes. Then she hands me the guitar and says, "Now you try."

I give her a nervous little smile and prop it up on my thigh, just as she did. I have to use my right hand to physically spread apart the fingers on my left hand and position them on the strings.

After a dozen unsuccessful attempts, the hum of the chord finally comes to life. We spend the rest of the evening learning "open" chords.

"Your fingers are like muscles and soon they will be flowing naturally into the chords without even having to look," she assures me.

I raise an eyebrow. "Riiiiiight..."

She gives me an encouraging smile and turns to Walker, who is rubbing Disco's belly in front of the fire.

"So how are things coming along at Sagebright?"

"Good. We're still in the start-up phase and figuring things out, but I'm really excited about our program; there's really no other program like it anywhere." His passion bubbles up in his words.

"Raaaaaad," Samantha pipes up, sounding more like Keanu Reeves in *Point Break* than like the 5'8" blonde beauty she is. "So what makes it unique?"

"Well, the fact that we have separate houses for the boys and the girls allows them to really open up and talk about past traumas so they can heal. And our family program is the secret sauce because addiction is a family dis-ease."

"What types of things do you do in the family program?" Samantha asks curiously as I fumble between the G and C chords.

"Well, our philosophy is that in order for people to get sober they have to heal their underlying issues. For instance, our speaker last weekend focused on forgiveness being a powerful tool for people to heal. One thing she said is that when someone does something mean or spiteful to you, it's really just that they are filled with pain themselves, which—when you think about—it is pretty obvious, but clearly a lot of people don't think about it that way."

"She explained that forgiveness isn't about the other person; it's for you. A big part of getting sober is forgiving yourself and forgiving others so you can let go and move forward with your life. So if you don't involve the family, the kid shifts and has to go right back into the dynamic that created the *dis-ease* in the first place."

"Um, yeah, lots of dynamics at play," Samantha says ruefully.

Samantha and I've been friends since we met in our freshman year dorm at the University of Colorado, bonding instantly over being native Californians adapting to life in the mountains. But it wasn't until I introduced Samantha to James two years ago, and she also started to become more self-aware, that our friendship deepened. We both have our own "pictures" to work through, but being able to bounce things off each other and support each other as we tear down lifelong illusions has been a connective neither one of us could have imagined.

After Samantha leaves, I hop in the bathtub with lavender essential oil, ready to dig into the latest issue of *Vanity Fair*, but my mind keeps wandering back to our conversation about forgiveness. Suddenly it's *painfully obvious* that any time I did something hurtful to someone else, it was just an outside reflection of the pain I'd felt.

I wonder what would happen if I consciously forgive?

I decide to give it a try. I start at the beginning and go through each year of my life, forgiving people I believed have wronged me in some way, apologizing to the people I've wronged, and then, possibly most importantly, forgiving myself. With each act of forgiveness, I visualize the memory of the incident leave my body and swoosh down the drain.

I apologize to you, Shannon, for passing a mean note about you in the fifth grade and trying to exclude you. Now it is clear to me I was jealous of you and that was my pain acting out. I'm so very sorry. And I forgive myself for doing something so hurtful. *Swoosh.*

I forgive you, Sophie, for excluding me and not being able to share with me as we were growing up. I get it's just the nature of being the first born. I apologize for not always being the best sister. I forgive myself. *Swoosh.*

I forgive all of my girlfriends who decided they didn't want to be my friend anymore once I went off to boarding school. I apologize for the gossip and pain I helped perpetuate in middle school. I forgive myself for contributing to something so destructive and petty. *What a waste of time! Swoosh.*

I apologize to all of the people I've abandoned and wasn't more accepting towards. I see now it was a reflection of not accepting myself. I forgive myself for not always being a good friend. *Swoosh.*

I forgive that girl who said I couldn't sing. I forgive myself for believing her. *Swoosh.*

I apologize, Courtney, for all the drama and pain I brought to our friendship over the years. I am truly sorry. I forgive you for not being there for me when I needed you. I forgive myself. *Swoosh.*

I apologize, Amber, for not being compassionate to you when you needed it most. I forgive you for abandoning our friendship. I forgive myself. *Swoosh.*

About halfway through, I notice I'm already feeling different—lighter but stronger somehow, in a peaceful way.

I continue on, touching on some of my resentments that still linger deep inside of me:

I forgive you, Aidan, for making promises that you didn't keep. Actually, thank you for not keeping those promises; I know now it was best for both of us. I forgive myself for trying to make it something it wasn't. *Swoosh.*

I forgive you, Mom, for leaving. I understand now how unhappy you must've been and that you were just following your heart. I understand now how difficult it is to be a woman and how much courage that must've required. I apologize for not being more patient and accepting of you. I forgive myself. *Swoosh.*

Dad, I forgive you for abandoning the magical little world you created for us. I apologize if I've let you down with my life choices. I'm learning what it means to walk my own path. I forgive myself giving up my seniority to you. *Swoosh.*

I forgive myself for being a Crazy Goddess and giving up all of my seniority to a man and expecting him to take care of me emotionally and financially, thinking that would keep me safe. *Swoosh.*

I forgive myself for destroying my spirit and body with alcohol and drugs. *Swoosh.*

I forgive myself for not following my dreams. *Swoosh.*

After all, there's no time like the present to begin.

23.

"If you want to sing out,
If you want to be free be free"
—Cat Stevens

"You're looking *really* bright," James says on the phone.

It's been almost a month since the great forgiveness act, and I tell him that I feel significantly nicer to myself in my thoughts. I'm amazed by how many people from my past have reached out to me and wanted to connect.

James says, "Remember, every single thing you do in life is for you. People are under the illusion that forgiveness is something you do for someone else, but when you forgive, you release resentment, which has a very low frequency; this allows you to free yourself from chains to the past and gift yourself with love that's available in the present moment. Only, when you're truly loving to yourself, can you be genuinely loving and compassionate to others."

"It's really so simple." I shake my head in disbelief.

"Truth is simple. It's illusions that make things complicated," he chirps matter-of-factly. He goes quiet for a minute, reading me. "You're much clearer than I've seen you in a while. You're about to enter a time of terrific growth."

"I am?" I ask excitedly.

"Yes, but that's all I'm saying because I don't want you mucking up the white beaches of the future with your muddy footprints."

"When are you coming back to LA?"

"It doesn't look like I'll be there for another month or so."

"Another month or so! Do you know how long that sounds?"

"What can I say? I need to stay in New York a while longer because people are cheese melting all over the place," he explains dramatically, but I can hear him smiling on the other end of the phone.

Even though James has been a spiritual teacher and healer for twenty-five years, recently word of his abilities has spread, keeping him on the road for months at a time.

"Is this the most people you've ever worked with?"

"Hmmm... I'd say it's ebbed and flowed over the years. And there have been stretches where I've been so focused on art that I haven't had the time to dedicate to it. Other than when I had my clairvoyant group, I'd have to say this is probably the busiest time."

"Why do you think that is?"

"Well, it's a few things. This is really the first time in centuries that healers have had permission to do this sort of work on the planet. And our planet is traveling through an expanding universe, which is very challenging for people, but also an opportunity to wake up."

"I don't think I've had any meltdowns lately," I say, realizing it's been a while since I've even cried. There was a while there when tears were just daily life.

"It's because you are doing spiritual work, which has helped you heal your heart, and as a result you've raised your vibration."

"So, I'm not attracting as much lower level funk as I was before?"

"Exactly. You're vibrating above the densities the planet is traveling through, not to mention the densities that already exist here. These densities are really impacting folks," he continues, "and more and more people are turning to drugs, alcohol, prescription drugs, and other escapist behaviors just to deal with their everyday lives. We're in a cycle of greed that perpetuates people to want more, more, more of everything because they are operating under the illusion that *more* will fill that feeling of lack inside of them. When in reality this feeling of lack is the feeling of being so disconnected from our true spiritual nature."

"I wouldn't know anything about that," I comment dryly.

"When we get in-body, we are vibrating with the passion to create—a vibration I'm starting to see around a certain someone. You wouldn't know anything about *that*, would you?"

"I have three chapters completed."

"Whoohoo!"

"*And* Samantha gave me a guitar for my birthday!"

"Wow..." he trails off, and I can tell he's "reading" something. "Just be the beginner, and amazing things will transpire."

After we hang up, I make a kale, banana, and coconut water smoothie and nestle into the couch to write. Taking a few moments to ground myself into the planet with golden chords, I pull my hands over the top of my head, clearing away the energies from my entourage, before holding my hands an inch apart, ready to set my intention: "I'm Emily. I'm a beginner of life connecting my spirit to body."

Saying this, the vibration inside my palms skyrockets, and I cradle the energy gingerly.

"I give myself permission to vibrate in my highest affinity, grace, and compassion and to write effortlessly, with great fun!"

Another surge of energy swells in my hands. I bob my hands back and forth a few times, feeling the energy grow and develop into a magnetic sensation before visualizing it as bright green with flecks of gold and drawing it into my heart. I close my eyes and imagine it flowing into my heart, through my shoulders, and down into my creative channels before opening my laptop.

I can hardly believe that I've been writing for nearly four hours straight when Walker busts through the door with a mischievous grin on his face. "Guess where we're going?"

"Where?"

"My brother's getting married in July, and we're going to the wedding in Ecuador, where Gabriella's family lives!"

"Whaaaaaaat? When?"

"In July!" he confirms excitedly.

I hear wedding and Ecuador, but all I can think of is the Amazon Jungle and Peru.

"Peru! Peru! We're going to Peru!" I jump up excitedly.

"The wedding is in Ecuador."

"Which is right by, *Pe-ru!*" I look Walker square in the eyes and say intently, "Do you want to go to the Amazon?"

"Sure," he says easily.

"I mean do you *really* want to go to the Amazon? Like *deep* into the Amazon?" I lower my voice a few notches. "As in off the beaten path style..."

"What does that mean?"

"It means go stay with actual indigenous, tribal people, explore the jungle, and take part in their ceremonies, like Ayahuasca."

"Ayahuasca?"

"Ayahuasca's a vine native to the Amazon. All I know is that it's very powerful, and that Amazonians use it for healing the mind, body, and spirit."

Walker props his laptop up on the coffee table and is already researching Peru, the Amazon, and Ayahuasca before I can finish my sentence.

"Interesting. Here's an article about therapists using Ayahuasca to treat addiction."

"I've heard that the actual ceremonies can be pretty intense— as in possibly scary at times," I relay, "but regardless of what your experience is like, there are supposed to be benefits that carry over into your life later. I'm not sure exactly how it works." I think back to what my friend Dominique told me. "Dominique and her parents went and stayed with a shaman in Ecuador for a week and did it a few times back when we were in college."

Suddenly, I realize that Ayahuasca might not jive with his sobriety.

"If you are not feeling it, we can totally go somewhere else," I add quickly.

I don't say anything for a while as I watch as his eyes comb through what Google has to offer on Ayahuasca.

"This is so interesting. Everything I'm finding on the internet is about Ayahuasca's healing power in addiction. I wonder why I've never heard of this."

"The people I know who've done it say it is a tool for deep spiritual healing, and is in no way anything you would—or could— ever use for recreational purposes..." I trail off, recalling what

I'd heard about people seeing snakes inside them—not really my idea of "recreation."

"I'm going see if I can connect live with someone in recovery who's participated in a ceremony first."

"Of course," I agree. "I want you to make sure it's the right decision for you. And no pressure at all; if you aren't feeling it, there are plenty of other things we can do."

"Let me check into it, Sweets," he says, lifting me into a big bear hug.

"And we can check out Machu Picchu too."

Within three weeks, Walker has our entire trip to Peru and Ecuador organized, which I'm thrilled about because I'm not really what one would call a planner. Not only does he find dozens of accounts of people kicking severe addictions with Ayahuasca, but he talks to a few people in recovery who've participated in actual Ayahuasca ceremonies—one in Peru and two in the US. What's interesting, they all—more of less—have the same description: the ceremony itself was amazing and at times intense, but they all felt it strengthened their understanding of their spiritual path, and they're all even more peaceful in their sobriety now.

The itinerary Walker mapped out starts with us landing in Iquitos, where we will meet up with the group and take a boat down the Amazon. Walker found an American journalist, Peter, who's been staying on and off with the same family in the Amazon for twenty-five years. We'll have the opportunity to participate in an Ayahuasca ceremony and see the Amazon "in a very different way than most tourists" he promises.

I flip flop between being wildly excited and scared stiff. I've heard that it's not uncommon for people see horrific images.

And there's also the purging part. I've thrown up less than five times in my post-infant lifetime, and that is *not* by accident. I've been known to do any number of things, including curling in fetal position for days, rather than succumbing to hurling my insides, outside. And now here I am, about to intentionally ingest something that will undoubtedly make me vomit.

I amp up my meditations, some days doing more than one, which I find helps keep me from jumping into the future imagining every little detail of the Amazon Jungle like, where will we sleep, go to the bathroom, and shower? I suspect it's the same place where the snakes sleep, the jaguars go to the bathroom, and the crocodiles bathe.

I focus more to my writing, getting lost for hours in the world of my story. Letting the whole truth of how I'd been creating my life—dramas and all—spill onto the page restores a sense of integrity in me that I'd lost somewhere along the line.

And nothing prepares me for the happiness I find in learning how to play guitar. It's the first thing I want to do in the morning, immediately what I pick up when I get home, and the last thing I put down before I go to bed.

Each time I lift its hollow body into my arms, I carefully remind myself to be *the beginner* and that I'm doing this for me. At first the noise I force out of it sounds like it's in as much pain as the tips of my fingers. I close the windows tightly and send silent apologizes to my neighbors—one of whom is a pianist with the Los Angeles Philharmonic, the other a successful music producer.

But like slow stirring on a lazy Sunday morning, I feel something awaken inside of me, and little by little, calluses form on my fingertips and the fragmented notes morph into a melody.

I even write a song—well, the lyrics anyway. I rip off the tune and most of the chord structure to "This Land is Your Land." My muse is my inspirational, loving, adorable, hilarious best friend, Disco. I play it over and over for weeks. If I'm driving Walker and Disco crazy, they don't let on. Actually, I've caught Walker singing the chorus under his breath:

Because your name is Dis-co
But you're not from Fris-co
Although you've been there
That's where you shed some hair

Just like a seesaw, as my desire to create soars, I watch my competition teeter in the opposite direction. Less am I consumed with what I'm lacking, what anyone else is doing, or what I need to do more of. Instead my mind is alight with sentences puzzling themselves together. Melodies, chords, and lyrics swarm about, wanting to structure themselves into songs. An unexpected feeling of camaraderie amongst other women, especially those who are also daring to live their dreams, springs forth, while I'm also filled with a deep compassion and understanding for the women who are still stuck in their prisons of perfection.

The more I write and make music, the more I trust that I *am* actually a creative person. I start taking guitar lessons from a guy named Matthew, a classically trained musician who fronts a hipster band. After a few months' time, I've written three totally original songs: "Sheikky-Skeikky Boom Boom Room"—a rock and roll tune about a wild night at a speakeasy in San Francisco; "Lovey and Sweets"—a little love ballad for Walker, and "The Sailor"—a finger-picking song about my spiritual journey.

Singing my heart out while strumming my six string is every bit as glorious as I imagined it would be, but I'm surprised to discover that nothing rivals the act of creation itself. It's in those moments of inspiration, when I'm in the uncertain process of crafting the song where I feel an odd sensation that my energetic body is expanding beyond my physical form taking with it any old, dense debris. It's as if new pathways are forming in my mind, as I tread down the forgotten footpath to my heart.

I wonder if it was the fear of the process that kept me from knowing this wellspring of joy all those years. After all, the process is messy; it shows the cracks and reveals the imperfections. Yet turns out, the process is also a portal to that present moment aliveness that feels so damn good.

Is the sweet promise of completion a trojan horse holding within it what spirit actually craves? The Quest. A journey into the nooks and crannies of self, to an otherwise inaccessible level of expansion. Is it through this quest that we begin to understand the truth of who we are? And as we expand, the light comes bursting in.

I finally get why James promotes the creative so much. Like a well-matched doubles team, the creative and the spiritual propel each other forward. Instances of inspiration connect me to who I am and why I'm here, and there is *literally* no place I'd rather be. Much to my surprise, this magically transforms whatever stubborn resentments that were still lingering into gratitude. It's as if an invisible crane has come and lifted a fifty-ton weight off my shoulders in a single motion.

One afternoon, as Disco and I are returning from a walk in the park, I stumble upon an old easel and a set of paints being sold at a yard sale for ten bucks that I lug three blocks back to our house. I discover childlike delight just from mixing different color combinations, and the simple act of making a vibrant red to contrast with sunny yellow feels like success. Next thing you know, my office has morphed into a makeshift art studio, and I can be found splashing bright colors on big canvases. Walker surprises me and immediately takes to painting, and soon we're spending a few nights a week lost in our creations.

One evening, as I'm drying my face in the mirror, I'm surprised to find a very different looking woman staring back at me. There's a distinct softness about her as her eyes, full of wisdom, meeting my gaze. Feeling a deep connection, I stare back at her as if we share a secret. And then—as ridiculous as this sounds—I realize that this woman is me. Despite looking into a mirror thousands of times over the course of my life, it's as if I'm seeing myself for the very first time.

∿

When James returns to LA, I excitedly share all three of my songs.

"I just love being validated," he says breezily.

I can feel my face flush with happiness.

"I told you that you're a creative spirit!" he reminds me smugly. "How does it feel to be a passionate creator?"

I think for a moment, trying to find the words.

"This might sound weird..." I start off, working it out in my mind for the first time. "But, it's like, I'm excited to go to bed so I can wake up and start the day. Even though I'm not leaving the house to go anywhere or do anything, it's as if some wild adventure awaits me."

"There is no more daring adventure than the journey inward, Sweet Pea. The creative is a big part of that. You're vibrating very, very differently. I see a much more authentic, feminine vibration."

"The crazy thing is, before, when there was so much, it never felt like it was enough. And now, strangely, I have less by so many people's standards, and it feels like more.

"It feels like it's enough more of the time because you are starting to feel like you are enough more of the time."

To think all these years I've been hopping from one party to the next and creating drama-rama-roo all around me, distracting myself from the very thing that brings me sincere joy!

"Up until now, you've followed a very narrow script about how to be, think, and act. It's prevented you from knowing your authentic self. It looks like you are going to have some terrific visions in the Amazon that will give you even more certainty about who you are."

I bite my lip, thinking about doing Ayahuasca. It must be what he's seeing. There's no way I'm telling James about Ayahuasca until *after* the trip. He gets uncomfortable if I do acupuncture, insisting that everything is energy and we need nothing but our organic selves to see and heal.

∾

The next afternoon, I go to Barnes and Noble. I get in line at Customer Service to ask where the travel section is. My eyes settle on the promotional table before me, from which a sea of familiar faces, bare midriffs, and pearly whites stare out: Nicole Ritchie in a sparkling tiara, Sarah Palin dolled up in red, Paris Hilton sprawled across pink satin sheets. My body temperature begins to rise.

Is every single book on the table written by a "celebrity"?

David Hasslehoff? Fabio? Tila Tequila, Jesse James, Britney Spears, Vince Neil? Bristol-*freaking*-Palin? They all have books.

Beads of moisture pick my hairline. Carrie Prejean and Regis Philbin? Now in a full-blown sweat, I shed my top layer of clothing.

This is what people want?

I haven't actually read any of these people's books, so I'm in no position to judge the quality, but there isn't a single book on this table written by a non-celebrity.

I haven't really allowed myself to think about what happens after I write the book because when I think about people reading about things I've never shared with anyone, I get so uneasy, I can barely continue. But as I'm confronted with all of these celebrity authors, I can't help but to wonder if anyone even reads about regular people's stories anymore.

Or, err, maybe not so regular per se, but a reformed Crazy Goddess discovering the magic of truth and beauty of who she really is in a world hellbent on telling her otherwise...

I begin looping on: unless you're a celeb, nobody cares about your story. I know it's my entourage, but I can't quiet them. They are a raucous bunch, lighting up my core pictures of non-belief.

Just as I'm rounding the corner to the exit, my jacket grazes the corner of a table, sending a pile of books on the floor.

Bending down to retrieve them, I see that of all the books in this mega store, I've just knocked down three copies of *My Horizontal Life* by Chelsea Handler, which is one of the funniest books I've ever read—written *before* she was famous.

Some might say the universe is intervening on my behalf. James would say I and I alone created this to encourage me to continue writing. Whoever's responsible, I'm grateful and mostly just embarrassed that I let myself get so flustered and invalidated my path just because others have been successful on theirs.

Sigh. And just when I thought I was doing so well!

Back in my car, I call James. He picks up, saying, "I've just got a couple minutes before my next session, but I wanted to say hello."

"Hiiiiiii..."

"How we doing?" he asks, knowing full well something is up.

I tell him every embarrassing, competitive little detail from the bookstore.

"Oh, Sweet Pea, it doesn't matter how many times you fall in the toilet; making recognition is what matters."

"Hmph."

"If you could see what I see, you'd see what a destructive virus all of this competition really is. We're all on our own and very unique paths each lifetime, based on what we've created before, the agreements we made, debts we have to pay, and debts other people owe us. Everybody is on a spiritual path, whether they know it or not, and making recognitions is what helps us change and grow out of our painful judgments and into affinity."

"It's just that..."

"Yessssss?"

"It's just that I really was noticing a decrease in my competitive levels, and then on an innocent trip to Barnes and Noble to find some travel books, I hit the skids."

"Spiritual growth is *not* linear," he repeats for the 42,367th time.

James is a patient man.

"You can be going along, doing great for one, five, or even ten years, and then hit a picture. It's like pulling back the layers of an onion. This may have been a time of great significance in another lifetime. As long as you make recognition of what is really going on, and don't get caught up in illusions, you will work through it and become more neutralized to it."

I let out a long sigh and I realize I haven't really been breathing since I left the store.

"I haven't wanted to talk much with you about outcomes, because it impedes the creative process, but it takes real courage to share your story with the world; in fact, it matters *even more* that you aren't a celebrity because you have the opportunity to show other women they, too, can change their lives when they embark on an inward journey.

The thought of helping other women find their way out the darkness makes my whole body buzz with purpose. I can't think of anything I'd rather do with my life. Suddenly, it seems like everything I've done up until now was designed for that very reason.

"And there are *no* accidents. You knocked this other woman's book over to remind you that you don't need to be a celebrity to have a story to share. Celebrities are no better or worse than anyone else; they're just people on a spiritual journey too. If you can get past your competition to recognize anyone—celebrity or not—who is passionately creating as an inspiration, your creations will flow even more easily."

Well, if Bristol Palin publishing a book on her journey so far isn't inspirational, I don't know what is.

Damn you, competition.

24.

"I could hold you in my arms
I could hold you in my arms forever"
—Ray La Montange

As the dusty twilight descends upon the city and a few brave stars show their twinkling faces, Walker and I make the short walk to our favorite Italian restaurant, Little Dom's, for an impromptu date. The air—still warm from a day spent in the blazing sunshine—is rich with gardenia's sweet, pungent smell. Our hands, joined together, swing slightly as we stroll past tightly clipped hedges, manicured grounds decorated with velvety roses, and unkempt gardens wild with overgrowth. Something about my outfit—flats, a soft cotton tee shirt, and faded black jeans, with nothing but a Chapstick in my pocket, makes me feel younger than my thirty-two years.

"The bees are working late tonight." I point out a handful of dutiful honeybees buzzing around a spattering of bright yellow Gumplants.

"Or are they?" Walker asks, a twinkle in his eye. "Maybe buzzing from one blossom is the best thing ever, like stopping into eat at all your favorite restaurants for free and never getting full?"

"More is always better," I tease, and we exchange a knowing glance that nothing could be further from the truth.

Because it's still very early, we score a table on the patio, under the black and white striped awning—an almost unheard-of feat for a Friday night. With its laid-back vibe and big wooden wrap-around bar, mixed with a New York City aesthetic, Little Dom's is the hippest restaurant in Los Feliz—some say in all of Los Angeles.

We order drinks and apps as our neighboring tables fill quickly, lighting up the patio with cheerful chatter.

"Ah, my happy place." I sigh, taking a sip of cabernet as our waiter strikes a match, letting it hover over the wick of our candle until it ignites. I notice the corners of his mouth curl into a small smile when he hears this.

"Whatcha thinkin', Sweets?" Walker asks, his eyes on the menu.

I scan the menu, even though I already know what I really want.

"Oh, this is so hard! I haven't had it in so long!"

"Really? You're going to do it?"

"It's just the most delicious thing ever."

"When was the last time you had meat?"

"Four months ago."

"Cheese?"

"Four months ago."

"Vegan no more," he declares.

"Can I be an inconsistent vegan?"

"You can do whatever you want, Schweets," he says. "Let's not get trapped in dogma. Maybe I'll get a steak?"

"Ah ha! The Texan surfaces!"

Walker flashes me a wry smile.

"There's something about tonight. I feel like doing something crazy." As if ordering sausage and cheese pasta is the wildest thing I've ever done.

Absence has totally made my heart grow fonder. My pappardelle pasta with homemade rosemary sausage and goat cheese is even better than I remembered.

I suppose inconsistent vegan is better than no vegan.

Our first fall off the vegan wagon is hard, and before I know it, Walker's ordered three desserts and a decaf Cappuccino for me.

"More is always better." He winks at me.

After dinner, we take the long route home, and seeing as the button to my jeans has been unfastened since mid-meal, I'm grateful there is a long way.

As we round the corner of Cromwell and Observatory, I spy the just barely there sliver of the moon, just as Walker points up to the sky and says, "Look, it's a new moon. You know what they say about new moons, right?"

I purse my lips together, trying to remember what I know about new moons.

"Our galaxy is clipping its fingernail?"

"Nooooo..." he says, pulling me close to him. It means that whatever new things are started during the time of a new moon are more likely to last." He kisses me on the nose.

"I see. So, what you're saying is, if I'm the one to initiate a game of Scrabble tonight, it's more likely that I will win?"

"Maybe so," he says as we start to turn down the street to our house.

"Does that mean you're in?"

"Sure, why not?"

Disco greets us excitedly at the door, yelping and jumping as if we've been gone for months.

"Set it up. I'm just going to change!" I call from the hall, already wriggling out of my jeans.

When I return to the living room, I find the board set up, Van Morrison's *Astral Weeks* playing softly on the speakers, and a few candles burning. As I take a seat, Disco races to position himself in the crook of the couch, getting stuck under my legs in the process.

Walker walks in with two cups of steaming lemon water with cayenne.

Immediate detoxification. That's how remorseful, inconsistent vegans roll.

The game gets off to a slow start, with us laying down words like "bug," "face," "tire," "rust." Finally, I manage to lay down "lizard" for a triple letter on the z, pulling into the lead and opening up the board.

My lead doesn't last long after a lengthy spell of drawing all vowels. Which means Walker is getting all the good stuff. As the bag lightens, and my score hovers around seventy as Walker's pushes one hundred and forty, my interest begins to wane. I start plucking my guitar in between turns.

"Sweets, you have one draw left!"

"I do?" I ask, surprised, looking down at the board covered with tiles.

Walker hands me the blue felt bag, which feels empty.

"There's one left," he assures me.

As my fingers reach into the bag, they feel something very unfamiliar—certainly not a flat, smooth Scrabble tile.

Then it hits me. My mouth gapes.

"Wha-?"

Walker has a huge grin plastered across his face.

I pull out the most sparkly, brilliant-cut, stunning diamond set in pave diamonds that wrap around the sterling silver band.

In shock, I begin to slide it on my finger to see if it fits.

"Wait, wait, wait!" Walker rushes over to me and takes the ring, bending down on one knee.

"Emily," he pauses getting his words together, "you are the love of my life, my best friend, my greatest teacher... We have the relationship..." he starts off, getting a little choked up, "that I always envisioned. Will you marry me?"

"Yes," I say, nodding as he slides the ring on my finger.

It fits perfectly.

He lifts me into his arms and kisses me deeply before pulling me into the tightest hug that lifts me off the ground.

Tears are streaming down both of our faces, and Disco is on his hind legs, trying to get into the hug action with us. We fall back onto the couch, without letting go of the embrace, letting Disco, for the very first time, join us on the beige couch.

After some time, we call our families and tell them the news that they already knew was coming. After rehashing the story a few times, since both of our parents are divorced, and we have three siblings between the two of us, we snuggle up with fresh mugs of hot water with fresh lemon and cayenne.

"Did you know?" Walker asks.

"Know that you were going to propose tonight?"

"Yeah."

"Um, not in the slightest."

"Promise?"

"I like to think that if I had even the faintest, itty-bitty idea that I was getting engaged, I would've washed my hair, shaved my legs, and had something a little more sexy on than my dog pajamas from eleventh grade."

This seems to satisfy him. I nuzzle my head into his chest.

This is it! This is my partner, my family, and the future father of my children!

"Was this planned?" I ask, thinking back to any signs I must've missed.

"I've had the ring for months, taped to the back of the wall behind the washer and dryer. I was trying to hold out until the top of Machu Picchu, but..." he pauses, "you said you felt like getting crazy."

"That's the truth, Lovey."

"The truth is, I didn't want to wait any longer." He gives me a sheepish grin. "The most important thing to me is that you were surprised, because I know you love surprises."

"Lovey," I say, rubbing my still very uncomfortably full belly. "Trust me, if I thought there was a one in fifty million chance you might propose tonight, there is no way in hell I would've ordered that sausage pasta."

25.

"Traveling light, is the only way to fly
Traveling light, just you and I..."
                                        —J.J. Cale

Through the scratched plastic window, I see an expanse of dense, green jungle with muddy tributaries of the Amazon intersecting and converging, creating estuaries and lakes of varying sizes.

We descend upon the city of Iquitos, the tiny plane shaking as we dip disturbingly close to the marshy jungle, where I'm sure *tribes* of crocodiles wait with little bibs around their necks and saliva dripping from their snaggle-toothed smiles. I close my eyes and dig my fingernails into the fleshy part of Walker's hand; he's nice about it. Finally, I feel the rickety landing gear touching down.

"We made it, Schweets!" Walker gives my hand a little squeeze.

That means the Ayahuasca ceremony is just days away, and I'm in a bit of a panic that having to pee every ten minutes for the past three weeks might not just be "fear" and "survival," as James says, but possibly a real bladder infection. Which left untreated can become a kidney infection.

James has helped me heal so many ailments that when he told me it's a result of clenching the first energy center in fear, I believed him. After all, I *am* mildly terrified about everything the Amazon has in store for me, and there has been none of the pain associated with bladder infections.

But what if James is wrong this time?

I may have to take antibiotics, which I've sworn off unless it's absolutely necessary.

Soon after we get off the plane, a lean man with neat hair, probably in his mid-twenties, approaches us and asks in heavily accented English, "Peter Gorman group?"

"Yes," Walker says, outstretching his hand.

"I'm Jorge. I work for Peter." He has a sweet smile full of silver and gold teeth.

"Me llamo Emily. Mucho gusto."

"Ah! Español!"

"Un poco."

I actually *do* speak Spanish proficiently, but the comprehension escapes me. I'll string together a few sentences that give the impression I know what I'm doing, which evokes a rapid-fire response and expectations of a decent conversation. But then I generally have to ask, "Como? Otra vez. Una vez mas? Que?" every other sentence.

We sputter out onto a busy road with dozens of other rickshaws jockeying for position. After about fifteen minutes, we pull off the highway and onto a congested city street lined with Spanish Colonial buildings in pale pastels, then curve down a narrow road and slow to a stop at a cluster of rickshaws and climb out. We're swarmed by vendors selling trinkets. Jorge leads us to a tired but roomy hotel that's crowded with a group of Americans gathered in the lobby. While Walker hands over our passports to the guy behind the reception desk, I study the group with curiosity. They are awfully quiet for Americans. With their blonde hair and pale blue eyes, I wonder for a moment if they might be on a family trip, but then rethink that when I realize they all appear to be somewhere around twenty-five years old.

Why are they all wearing white short-sleeve button-downs with navy slacks?

Then I see them. Carefully tucked in breast pockets, back pockets, and hands are navy-blue leather-bound Bibles.

Mormon missionaries?

An uneasy feeling bubbles up inside of me. Before I have a chance to put my finger on it, Walker grabs my hand and pulls me toward a big winding staircase.

"Come on Sweets, let's go."

Big and airy, with high ceilings, velvet drapes, and a window overlooking a promenade, our room was clearly once very posh— like a century ago. We take turns rinsing the travel off under the slow, cool trickle of water from a single pipe in our shower, then head down to the lobby to meet the others.

We recognize Peter from his photo on his website. He's a big guy, maybe in his early fifties, with a wild shock of almost black hair streaked haphazardly with grey. He's holding court at a plastic table crowded with gringos of all shapes and ages, donning nylon and cameras like us. He wears knee-length jean shorts and a faded yellow golf shirt with a popped collar. As we walk toward them, Peter says something that causes everyone, including himself, to erupt into laughter; as he laughs his corpulent belly heaves up and down, revealing a stone-washed fanny pack slung loosely around his hips.

"You must be Walker and Emily." Peter transfers his hand-rolled cigarette into his left hand so he can shake our hands.

I feel my first energy center clench at the realization that I'm about to follow this man—who looks like he may keel over at any moment—deep into the jungle.

"Nice to meet you," I say, meeting his gaze with a nervous smile, then introducing myself to the others.

We all head to dinner. Including Peter, we're a group of thirteen, ranging from ages twenty-five to sixty-six. I fall into step with Andrew, a lean forty-something father of two from Atlanta who prefers to eat organic, and Carter, a friendly Brit and an alien enthusiast with a tattoo to prove it, who is the youngest of the group, as Walker strikes up a conversation with Sam, a musician, educator, and sound therapist living in Sedona, Arizona with a Southern accent.

As we follow Peter through the humid streets stricken with toothless beggars and drug addicted drifters, my attention returns to the missionaries. I have no doubt they believe they're part of the solution. After all, this idea of white saviorism is programmed into us from elementary school, with stories of gallant explorers and altruistic pilgrims bringing education, medicines and religion to "Indians" and savages" to improve their way of life. Now landing in the richest eco-system in the world, this version of history suddenly seems preposterous.

"Oh, you guys gotta try these." Peter's enthusiasm rips me back to the here and now. He stops at a stand selling big worms covered in a sugary glaze. He buys a bunch and passes them around.

Even though I'm starving, I slink away as the group devours the shiny morsels. Walker—who, aside from our engagement night, has been sticking to a vegan diet with the same resounding discipline as a monk who's sworn off sex—lobs a worm into his mouth.

"Hmmmm... Amazing! You have to try one, Sweets!"

I shake my head skittishly. "You go on with your worms. I'm all good." He eats five more.

"I'm tellin' ya, Sweets, you're missin' out."

"I believe you, but you know I have texture issues," I say under my breath, wishing more than anything that I didn't have texture issues.

I'm distracted throughout dinner. Even though I *really* don't want to take antibiotics, my discomfort forces us to leave early and get some Cipro at a Farmacia.

We hail a rickshaw-taxi and speed toward our hotel. As we ramble across the potholes and ditches with the proud South American sun setting behind us, a hint of *that* feeling washes over me—the thrill of bravery contrasting with the gravity of fear; a liberation from routine coupled with the promise of self-discovery that comes from thrusting yourself into the electrifying unknown.

∿

The next morning in the lobby, Peter tells us, "The Belen Market isn't a place for tourists and definitely isn't a place where you want to *look* like a tourist. If you look like you don't know what you are doing, you'll be pick-pocketed. Just be smart, don't go off on your own, and you'll be fine. OK, let's go."

"Maybe you should go leave the camera in the room," I whisper to Walker, who's taken no less than fifty photos since we left the room.

"It's cool, Sweets."

Amid the chaos on the street out front of the market, Peter's team rallies us together and gives us one last warning that if we act like stupid tourists, we will be sorry. Even though I'm dressed like a boy in baggy, loose clothing, my hair twisted into a low bun under my Fidel Castro cap, which is pulled low over my eyes, and my money is on my person, their words carry a vibration of fear that infuses my core. I quickly wrap myself in an orb of golden light.

I'm safe and protected; I'm not in agreement to any pain or harm.

As we follow the group into an open-air structure with a dirt floor and tin roof, the noise of people yelling excitedly to each other rolls over me, along with the overwhelming stench of rotting flesh. I struggle not to gag. I pull my bandana up to my nose and breathe into it and cast my eyes into the dirt, sure I had a recent past life working in a slaughterhouse.

I draw my gaze up, but there is nowhere to rest my eyes except on hoofs, and ears, and snouts, headless chickens, and indiscernible hunks of meat proudly displayed on long crowded tables as opportunist flies swarm hungrily. At a table directly in front of me, a small man raises a sharp cleaver high above his head, and before I can avert my gaze, he hacks down into a barracuda, sending juices and blood and guts ricocheting in every direction, including my hair. A woman laughs at something the woman in the next station says as a stray dog attempts a nip at a carcass laying limp on her table.

"Aye, ya, ye! Perro vaya! Vaya perrito!" she scolds, shooing him away, but not before he gets a few licks in.

The air is hot and still, with no sign of ice or refrigeration. As we walk up a slight incline to where whole, hairy boars and hog-tied crocodiles hang from the ceiling by large metal hooks, my head begins to spin, and I feel like I might pass out. I grab onto Walker as we keep walking in an effort to keep up with the group.

"Are you OK, Sweets?"

I nod my head yes, even though I'm not sure I'm OK at all. I stare down at the ground for a while until I feel steady again.

As I lift my head, I lock eyes with a beautiful little girl in a stained white dress. No older than two, sitting in the middle of a table piled high with turtle meat and whole snails the size of rats, she has a look of total peace on her face as she sucks on a banana leaf. Her big dark eyes search mine for a few seconds before she flashes me the sweetest smile I've ever seen. I want to scoop her up and take her with me; shield her from this bacteria-infested existence.

I try to stop myself from attaching to her or wanting anything different for her, remembering this is *illusion healing* and creates a chord between us, allowing all of her energy into my space and all of mine into hers. I try to neutralize this aspiration, reminding myself that her spirit made conscious choice to choose this physical form, to be with those she had agreements, debts, and oaths with. I realize very quickly that I'm about as neutral as Chairman Mao mid-revolution.

I tell Walker I'll be outside and stumble out into the crowded market. The stalls are overflowing with everything imaginable: hand-woven baskets of fine-milled grains and spices of rich hues share space with shoelaces, dolls, candle wax, shrunken skulls, tonics and elixirs, eggs, and bananas. People are exchanging goods for money, money for goods, and goods for goods.

A few minutes later, the group emerges, and Peter leads us through one narrow corridor after the next as vendors urge us into their stalls. Walker stops in front of a huge tray of glazed worms and forks over a bill. His first bite makes an audible crunching noise as I back away, mildly horrified. A sour looks spreads over his face, and he spits the mashed-up worm out five feet in front of him, gagging and coughing as people start to stare.

Note to self: glazed worms are not all created equal.

Walker fumbles around in the backpack until he finds some water as I drag him along so we don't get separated from the group. They've stopped at a table of people busily rolling cigars and cigarettes using this little invention, which is basically a piece of cardboard attached to a stick.

"This tool they use to roll is called a banderilla," Peter's deep voice booms over the noise of the market, "which means flag, and if you want to buy mapachos, this is the place," he instructs.

A few people make their purchases.

"Are mapachos just rolled cigerettes?" I ask Susan, an addiction specialist from upstate New York.

"They're all natural, made with tobacco indigenous to Peru. The smoke is supposed to help get rid of evil spirits, I think," she adds with a smile.

We continue to the far edge of the market, where it's quieter. Peter arranges for us to go up on a rooftop so we can get a view from above. A sober mood falls over us as we take in the vast Floating City of Belen where the housing ranges from sun-bleached mint-green and flamingo-pink concrete homes on stilts to three-walled wooden shacks on balsawood platforms, tied together so they don't drift away with the currents. Power lines dip dangerously close to the mucky, debris-filled water. Peter explains that Belen has its own schools, hospitals, and mini markets. They transit via canoe, and it's not uncommon for fifteen people to live in a two-bedroom house with no indoor plumbing. Children's laughter wafts up from the floating city.

Gratitude. Gratitude. Gratitude. I will never complain again. Ever.

We head back to the hotel, and the next couple hours are a flurry of eating, showering, packing, and getting ready for our journey. Getting fitted for our jungle boots, I notice a tangle of snakes painted in bright colors hanging in a frame on the wall. Jan notices me starting at it and says, "It's a painting of an Ayahuasca vision."

My first energy center clenches a little tighter as I resist the urge to pee. The *Cipro* hasn't started working yet.

Maybe James wasn't wrong after all.

We congregate in front of a bar Peter once owned. He warns that we're about to experience mayhem like never before, but nothing could've prepared me for the chaos on the sixty-foot-long, twelve-foot-wide stairway down to the port, where the three-story, flat-bottom riverboat waits.

Three hundred people disembark as an equal amount of people fight to get on, with a couple tons of cargo in hand. Blocks of ice, canoes, toilets, radios, chickens, children, tables and chairs, motorcycles, crates of food, amongst countless other items are rushed up and down the steep grade. Meanwhile family members say tearful goodbyes and heartfelt hellos, while vendors swarm with candies and cokes, magazines, and jewelry. Urgent-eyed, barefoot children push little trays of brightly colored *chiclet* up in the air. My heart leaps into my chest.

We need to get these children out of here! Surely, they will be crushed in the charge!

But they persist, untrampled—their sweet pitches of *chiclet, chiclet* deafened by the commotion.

I put my backpack on my front, clamping down on it with one hand, and grab tightly ahold of Walker with the other as we fight through the masses of people, trying to keep sight of Peter.

We ascend to the top tier of the boat, where Peter's sectioned off an area on the bow.

"Do you have any idea how long we're on this boat?" I ask Walker, taking a swig of my water.

"I think around sixteen hours."

"What?" I choke, a little bit of water dribbling down my shirt.

"Well, I know we're sleeping on it."

Seeeeeeee. Had I read that itinerary and saw that we were going to be on a boat for sixteen hours, there is a very good chance I wouldn't be here right now.

I usually get seasick on boats, but the water looks pretty smooth. Peter says to get ready for the best night of our lives as he passes around a few squares of balled-up tinfoil filled with something that looks like cornmeal we're supposed to eat with our hands for dinner. The sleeping quarters are small cabins with narrow cots arranged like bunk beds.

A loud whistle signals our journey is about to begin. I wish I felt more relaxed.

I sit on the deck while Walker takes photos of everything; nothing seems to him too small or insignificant. I've cooled on taking pictures since I realized it takes me out of the moment; plus, I don't want to look like a tourist, but I can tell it's bringing him great satisfaction, so keep my mouth shut.

After about an hour, I relax a little and Walker and I decide to explore. In the back of the boat is a web of brightly colored hammocks, a few-stray chickens waddling around, and dozens of content locals. A man leans off the stern, jabbing a long piece of bamboo into a sandbar. We realize we're not moving.

Are we stuck?

My breath shortens into shallow divots. But these people were raised on this river; they *must* know how to get a boat off a sandbar.

Walker asks a portly man with a bushy black mustache, "Que pasa? No movamos."

"Es normal," Bushy says with small smile.

My breath evens out. I follow Walker's lead and practice my Spanish.

"So that bamboo jab off the stern is effective?" I ask brokenly.

"Si. Pero, un barco como este se hundidio."

No small smile this time.

"En el mes pasado."

"Did he just say a boat just like this one sank?" I ask Walker.

"Uno como este?" Walker verifies.

"Si, y dos cientos personas se ahogaron."

My mouth falls open, which prompts Bushy to give me another small smile.

"Se ahogaron?" I repeat, looking to Walker.

"I think he said a boat just like this one sank, and two hundred people drowned," he says slowly, the color draining from his face. A month ago."

Bushy is now talking excitedly and waving his hands in the air. Desperate to diminish any parallels from *that* barge and ours, I focus the attention of every single cell in my body on his words and gestures. I manage to gather that if we do go down, I should understand that beneath the surface of the Amazon is like a range of rolling hills—some are very tall, hence, the one we are stuck on, and conversely, there are also very deep crevasses.

"Si nos vamos más, no trate de nadar y solo trata dejar de que la corriente le llevará a la orilla del río." He moves his arms like a swimmer doing the crawl, while simultaneously shaking his head no, then a small smile.

"They didn't know how to swim?" I demand, pulling on Walker's sleeve. "That's why they drowned?"

"No, he said if we go down, don't try and swim. Just let the current take you to the edge. When people try and swim against the current, is when people drown."

I scan the river's edge, about half a mile away. With the sun beginning to set, all I can see is the dark, dense jungle.

OK, so even if I make it to the edge in one piece, what'll I do once I'm there?

I bristle into silent fear, nodding my head in thanks for the information and force a small smile of my own.

Surely, James would've said something if we were going to sink. He wouldn't have said it looks bright, would he?

"Let's go deep into the Amazon Jungle," I said. "Let's go off the beaten path," I said. "Let's drink Ayahuasca..."

Who do I think I am? Freaking Indiana Jones?

26.

"If you smile at me, I will understand,
Because that is something
everybody everywhere
Does in the same language..."
      —Crosby, Stills & Nash

My eyes open suddenly, yanking me back from the astral and onto the two-foot-by-seven-foot cot I'm sharing with Walker. I swing my legs to the floor and stand up, raising my arms high above my head, stretching out my stiff body. As I unlatch our door, I'm hit with a cool breeze and am surprised to see a dense fog has settled on the river. Quite a contrast from last night as we powered quietly through the moonless night under an astonishing spectacle of stars.

Hanging my head over the railing, watching the mist evaporate, I feel far more at ease. Whatever chaotic energy I'd been carrying around slipped away into the night. Suddenly, the momentum from the back of the boat as everyone begins rushing to the front indicates we must be arriving. Peter rallies us all together.

"This is it, the final stop. We're going to let everyone else off first, then you guys will head up those stairs and meet me at the restaurant on the corner. You'll know the one because there's only one restaurant and there's only one corner. You'll get a bite to eat as we get your stuff organized for the next leg."

Did he just say, the next leg?

Everyone disembarks. Families reconnect with a flurry of hugs and kisses before climbing the plank staircase, splayed across the muddy hillside, with plastic buckets filled with fruit and bread supported by their heads.

It's before eight o'clock, so the tiny town, Guerra Herrera, is still quiet, but Peter is friends with the owner, Fernando, who makes us breakfast. Under the shade from a thatched roof of palm leaves, we hungrily gather around small wooden tables and devour bowls of sopa con vegetales y maiz.

This is the last stop on the Amazon permissible for tourists. And to get clearance for where we are headed, Peter will "talk" to the cops when they wake up. So while we wait, we explore the tiny market. We buy a soccer ball for kids and start a juggling circle until we realize we're all horribly sweaty and out of shape. We take part in a flag raising ceremony, and I get skunked in chess by the fourteen-year-old girl operating the soda stand out of a plastic cooler.

Mostly, we wait. And wait. Shade is scarce, the air is heavy, and the sun is scorching at 9:00 a.m. Finally, Peter gives us the signal, and we all file back down to the dock. As I stare down at the peque-peque, painted bright blue like a toy, I wonder how this oversized canoe, outfitted with a small motor on the back, is going to carry all of us. Like a puzzle, Peter ushers each of us into specific positions based on our size and weight. Carter, seated right behind us, is holding a plastic bucket.

"What's that for?" I ask curiously.

"There's a hole in the boat," he responds with his cheerful British sarcasm.

Riiiiiight.

As each person steps in, the boat teeters back and forth and sinks a little deeper. We have less than an inch to spare before water will start spilling into our little craft. Everyone goes silent as Peter hops in at the bow; a single oar tucked under his arm and a lit mapacho dangling from his lips.

Juan revs the motor a couple times before pushing us out into the wide expanse of water. Peter huffs and puffs, wielding his oar like a sword, slicing through the current that wants to drive us into the chalky cliffs lining the river. Finally, our little vessel sputters past the resistance and out into the middle of the murky channel. The journey will take about two hours.

The farther we push along, the jungle grows even more lush and dense. Ragged lean-tos, tarps, and hammocks dot the shore, with people slowly milling about and chickens pecking in the dirt.

Everyone on the boat is quiet, lost in his or her own thoughts as Sam weaves a gentle melody from the flute he picked up at the Belen Market. An unexpected peacefulness descends upon me. I close my eyes and notice my lungs expanding as my breath slows and deepens and my shoulders lower for the first time in days.

Peter steers us into a tributary, which ushers us out onto a lake, which is home to pink and grey river dolphins, before finally turning onto a much smaller river.

"It won't be long now," Cameron, who's been on the trip before, calls out from the back of the boat.

"And this, my friends," Peter announces proudly, lighting up another mapacho, "is the Ayucacu."

Leafy vegetation creates canopies over the calm water. After another thirty minutes, Peter announces, "And here we are!" I follow his gaze and see a clearing up a grassy slope, shaded by thick palm trees with three open-air wooden structures supported by stilts. Peter's team, who'd rode on a separate barge, has already arrived with our food, supplies, and gear; Ruber and Jorge, donning knee-high, rubber boots, help us out of the boat.

Juan leads us up the staircase formed out of chopped logs sunken into the sodden mud and stops in front of the first structure overlooking the river. A long row of brightly colored hammocks strung around tree trunks makes up the foundation of the platform.

"Ustes van a dormir aqui." Juan leads Walker and I into one of the two private rooms at the back of the sleeping porch.

Peter introduces us to the Julio's family, who will be hosting us for the week. Julio was Peter's shaman and teacher for twenty-five years. He recently died at ninety-two, but Peter is very close with the rest of his family as well, who we learn are direct descendants of the Matses Tribe, and many still have the tattoo markings on their faces. Lean and muscular, with cheekbones that look like they were carved with a blade, they welcome us with bright eyes and gentle smiles. Eighteen hours away from Iquitos, far away from any outside influences, the native people appear to be flourishing.

We change into our suits and head to the river to bathe. Two children run gaily down the steps ahead of us, hop off a log, and dive headfirst into the murky water. They float lazily in the water, doing somersaults and pretending to be fountains. They don't seem at all worried about crocodiles, piranhas, or that bacteria that's attracted to heat and will supposedly swim up inside you if you pee in the water.

Walker goes into the water and pops back up in one piece. After a few minutes, he seems to be doing OK, so I follow his lead. Balancing on a fallen log, I'm careful not to let my feet sink into the doughy riverbed. I keep one hand resting on the peque-peque. Arching my back, I'm able to soak my hair in the cool water without having to dunk my head. I wash my hair and give the important parts of my body a quick scrub before hightailing it back to land. The whole operation goes down in less than two minutes.

We spend the rest of the afternoon lying opposite of each other in one hammock, swaying gently beside our new friends. Some of the others who've done Ayahuasca start sharing stories. Cameron's done several extended trips with Peter and has lots of experience, and so does Susan, who's participated in a dozen ceremonies with different shamans.

My ears perk up as she recounts a ceremony when she saw a vision of her son sitting on the foot of his bed crying. It was a Tuesday night. When she finally got to a phone four days later, she asked him what he was doing on Tuesday. He replied that he and his longtime girlfriend had broken up, and he was indeed crying in his room.

"People who've never done it before say that you have hallucinations, but my experience has been that you gain access to your third eye," she muses thoughtfully.

"Have you ever seen a snake before?" I pipe up.

"Oh, yeah," she says casually.

"No big deal?" I ask.

"You'll see they're there, but you can manage 'em."

"I actually kind of like seeing them," Cameron chimes in.

"You *dooooooooo?*" I demand.

"It's all just part of it."

∼

Our hosts have been busily preparing us dinner since our arrival. We all gather at long picnic tables covered with a blue and white checked plastic tablecloth. The meal of brown rice and vegetables is delicious.

When everyone's seated, Peter stands and says, "I hope you all are getting settled in OK. When it gets dark, you are going to go on a little expedition that will help you get better acquainted with the jungle. I know we've had a lot of travel today, so it's not going to be a long expedition, but you're going to head out in the canoes with Jorge, Ruber, Mauro, and Juan to hunt for a couple hours."

Hunt?

"You may want to put your jungle boots on for this part."

An excited murmur skips across the table.

Less than an hour later, covered head to toe in Deet, we tread down the hillside where two canoes are waiting for us at the water's edge. Everyone looks excited and a little nervous.

Peter explains that in order to successfully hunt and fish food for the rest of the week, everyone needs to be as still and quiet as we are out on the water.

This is no joke, Indiana.

They arrange us in the canoes. This time I'm in the very front, just behind Jorge, who's holding a paddle in one hand and a long spear with a sharp head in the other. I watch as the other canoe gets smaller and smaller until it disappears, in the direction we haven't gone yet. I swivel around to see Mauro—with a shotgun strapped to his back—push us off before hopping in as we glide off in the opposite direction. As I turn back around to face the front of the canoe, I see a pair of yellow reptilian eyes staring at me from the exact same place we swam earlier today, with rows of neatly organized scales shimmering in the moonlight.

27.

"I am who I am who I am who am I
Requesting some enlightenment?"
— Dave Matthews

The morning of the Ayahuasca ceremony, I wake up early to the clattering rhythm of birds calling out to each other, trees rustling, distant cries of creatures I can't place, and Walker's even breathing. My bladder infection has not eased up at all, and I'm annoyed that I have to break out this peaceful morning snuggle to go pee, yet again. I exit at the foot of the bed, trying not to wake him and tucking the mosquito net in behind me.

In the pearl-gray light of dawn, I watch the native women laughing as they carry baskets of laundry on their heads down to the river as yellow-winged butterflies flit about behind them. Over on the kitchen platform, smoke curls up from the morning fire. The contrast between the destitute, frenetic vibe of Iquitos and the abundant harmony radiating from deep in the Amazon is unmistakable.

Once upon a time, before the Spanish conquistadors arrived, was Iquitos also a place of abundance and harmony?

As I crawl back under the mosquito net, Walker murmurs, "What time is it?"

"Sunrise, "I whisper back, careful not to wake the others, who are only separated from us by a thin lath of wood.

I slither into the crook of his armpit, enjoying the last hour of wanting to actually be close to someone before the coolness of morning evaporates into the suffocating heat of the day.

When I wake again, Walker is gone, and I have slid down into a gap between the wood planks that make up the sleeping platform, and my tailbone feels like I am eighty-two. My stomach feels very empty, and I remember that Peter said we would be eating breakfast a little later today, as it would be our last meal before we begin our fast. He couldn't have made it any more clear that when it comes time to vomit, it will be very obvious who followed these instructions and who didn't. I'm prepared to do exactly as he says, even if it means running through camp with nothing but my river boots on.

"Schweeeeeets! Time to git up," Walker calls as he clambers up the stairs to our room, laying his Texan drawl on for effect. He's dripping wet.

"Did you just go swimming?" I ask stupidly.

"I just *showered*. And now it's time to go on that hike to cut down the Ayahuasca, so, you, little lady," he says, pulling me up from the under the net and into a tight hug against his cool wet body, "need to git up." He leans down with little water droplets on his eyelashes and kisses me on the mouth. A year and a half later, and his kiss still tingles on my lips.

Our hike to cut down the Ayahuasca is relatively short. Jairo (pronounced hi-row), Julio's son, leads us on a path alongside small fields of yucca and plantain before we cut in front of a one-room, mint-green schoolhouse with a tin roof and then traverse a field where some locals are playing soccer. With temperatures in the mid-90s and humidity to match, I'm grateful for the shade of the towering trees. Soon, we arrive at a platform house perched on a bluff overlooking a bend in the river.

"This was Julio's house," Peter explains very respectfully. "And this is Ayahuasca," he says as if he's introducing us to a person.

It's a common understanding in the selva that all living things have a spirit—a flower bud, a mountain, an ant. And the spirit that is Ayahuasca lives in the vines of this beautiful tree standing before us. It's said that if you find yourself in a position to take Ayahuasca, she has summoned you to her.

I look around at the dozens of trees surrounding this one and wonder how the very first person came across this particular tree. It is the only one like it for at least a couple miles. She is so tall that I can't even see her crown. Her slender body shoots straight up into a canopy of leafy green bunches with long, ropelike vines hanging parallel to her trunk but several feet away, giving the illusion that they could be growing right out of the sky. And then I realize that person must've been *summoned* as well.

Watching Jorge effortlessly scale the trunk with his machete, looking for the best place to cut the vine Jairo has selected, eighteen hours down the Amazon river, deep in the jungle, I've no doubt that I've indeed been summoned.

He slices it with one clean swipe while Jairo chants and blows smoke from his mapacho, before passing the vine around to each of us so we can set our intention. The group is full of curiosity, awe, and respect. When it gets to me, I say silently and with great intention, "Please let me see what I need to see, so I can live life full and free."

"Oh, and please be gentle with me," I add nervously.

Jairo begins chanting again as he chops the vine into smaller pieces to be transported back to camp.

As we retreat back to camp, I repeat what I said to Ayahuasca quietly to myself, addressing her by name this time: *Ayahuasca, Ayahuasca, be gentle with me, be gentle with me, show me what I need to see, so I can live life full and free, be gentle with me, be gentle with me.*

Soon my little mantra slides into the tune of Frère Jacques. I sing quietly to myself for the rest of the walk back.

The women are waiting for us with a feast fit for kings: papaya salad, rice and beans, pescado, and ratone—also known as guinea pig—all prize catches from our midnight canoe hunt last night. Where I somehow, after six clumsy attempts, managed to spear a fish.

As Sidalee hands me a bowl overflowing with rice, beans, and veggies, Peter goes over what we can expect for the rest of the day and for the ceremony that night.

"After this meal, there is to be no eating for the rest of the day," he reminds us *again.* "It would really be a shame to come all this way and spend the entire night vomiting up that candy bar that you snuck in the afternoon, rather than vomiting up the things you want to vomit up, like that time that you stole the test in fifth grade, or the time you cheated on your girlfriend and never told her," he bellows to the group, and it's obvious how passionate he is about the healing that is going to take place tonight.

Apparently, after the initial purge, you just dry heave, and it releases the negativity stored inside you.

"I cannot underscore what a tremendous opportunity this is to let go of the things from your past that are no longer serving you," he says intensely. "That baggage that has been holding you back from getting to where you want to be."

"I don't know about you," he goes on, "but I would rather get rid of it here in the jungle on Ayahuasca in one night than sitting on a shrink's couch for fifty years." He pauses. "That is the power of this medicine." Another pause. "And for some of you, all you will do is spend the entire night vomiting because you have that many things that you need to let go of before you're ready to see. As Julio used to say, you need to clean the room before you can paint it! And hopefully for many of you, you will have amazing visions that can assist you, as I have so many times on Ayahuasca. But either way, Juan and Jorge, Ruber, Gastalia, and Sidalee, and I will be there to help you out. They will wipe your ass for you if they have to, and don't worry about it. This is part of their life, and they're used to it."

My stomach does a nervous somersault in anticipation. Let's be honest; I'm *fucking terrified*. I'm terrified of what I will see, terrified of what I won't see, how I will feel, what I will do if the snakes approach me, the vomiting...

You have been summoned! You have been summoned! Freaking RELAX! You have been FUCKING SUMMONED!

I hang on Peter's every word. In an attempt to experience the ceremony as organically as possible, I haven't read anything about Ayahuasca. I'm already carrying around the experiences of those friends of mine who have tried it, and for some it wasn't positive.

After breakfast, we take a four-hour hike. Sweating in pants and knee-high socks, long sleeves tucked into gloves, and a goofy hat, I'm ready for the deep jungle.

Mauro fluidly wields his machete effortlessly through the thick brush, carving a narrow path for us to follow. Juan, who's bringing up the rear, instructs us to tread as lightly as possible, and if we have any interest in encountering the animals of the jungle, "then quit yapping."

We ascend into the jungle that has always existed in my imagination. The trees are at least 100 feet high, leaving visible only the bottom layer of the canopy. The thick trunks are so wide a car would fit inside them. I've become increasingly nervous about the ceremony, my belly growing big and bloated, and it's a relief to get lost in the trees' peace and strength. I remember the Shel Silverstein book, *The Giving Tree* as the wide branches, dense with enormous leaves, shield all but a few splintered rays of sunlight.

Juan explains the significance or medicinal properties of various shrubs, vines, trees, and flowers we encounter—therapies for everything from arthritis to cancer. I pull Juan aside and ask if he knows of a plant that could help me. He assures me, "Yes," and will get it for me by the end of the week.

Clearly, Juan has never had a bladder infection before.

I thank him and we forge on.

After walking for about twenty more minutes, we stop at a clearing. Juan says this was Julio's favorite place in the entire jungle. He motions to a cluster of five or so trees, which have peculiar 360-degree circles shaved off the middle of their trunks.

He shares that when Julio was alive, he was so powerful that nobody dared come near this area of the jungle. But when he passed, vindictive people from neighboring tribes came and carved circles around these trees, which would normally be a rapid death sentence for them.

"However, it is quite curious," he says, "because it's been three years, and the trees, as you can see, are still alive and thriving. Julio's spirit is watching over them and keeping them safe," he concludes, full of emotion.

I let out a long sigh, realizing I'd been holding my breath.

Julio was, err, is a badass.

"You all carry water. When we're thirsty in the jungle, this is what we do," and with that he takes his machete, slices the vine in two, and water rushes out. He tilts it to his mouth, and then offers us a sip. I close my eyes and let the water glide down my throat. It's sweet and cool, and I have a strange awareness that it too is alive.

When we get back, I spy the large cauldron where the Ayahuasca has been brewing since morning. The ceremony is in a few hours. I start singing over and over my song to Ayahuasca hoping she'll hear me.

Sticky from sweat and Deet, the muddy water of the Aucayacu River feels like pristine mountain spring water, reviving all the cells in my body. Still, I'm back on land before I can be lunchmeat for that baby crocodile that *was* indeed in our swimming area last night, confirmed by the other canoe.

Seconds after I step onto land again, Oshmar comes running up behind me. "Piranha, Piranha!" he shouts, laughing as he pinches his nipple that is dripping with blood. Nobody seems concerned.

I head to our room and dig out the outfit I have been preserving for the ceremony. Susan shared with me that having her favorite things with her comforts her in the ceremony, and I'm willing to take any tips I can get.

Once dressed and completely coated with multiple layers of mosquito repellent, I lay down a towel and set my iPod to the meditations that James recorded for me, hoping to calm my nerves. The familiarity of his voice and the routine of the meditations I've done so many times before instantly relaxes me, and my breath begins to even out. Unfortunately, it's mosquito-feeding time, and apparently, they put a buzz out on a girl sitting on a striped towel.

Eventually, I give up and join the boys, who've formed a little circle a ways up the hill. As I listen to Blake, a seven-foot-tall twenty-something, talk about how difficult it is living in Scotland because people are generally just unkind, I'm aware of a deep affection I have for these people. Bonded by our desire to change and grow, to rip down the walls of perception that we know exist only in our own minds, the support amongst us is tangible and incredibly comforting.

The sun dips behind the trees on the opposite side of the river, and we all migrate up to the platform where the ceremony is taking place. The mats are laid out in a U-shape, and people have already staked claim to the edges, which was my plan as well. The only place where there are two spots together is in the middle, right across from the stool where I assume Jairo will be leading the ceremony. Walker and I put our things down and look at each other apprehensively.

He squeezes my hand firmly and says, "No matter what happens, I love you with all my heart and am right here."

"Me too," I say, squeezing his hand back. "Love you."

Peter lights kerosene lamps and sets up chairs outside the platform where he, Jorge, Ruber, Mauro, Sidalee, Gastalia, and

Malbec will be sitting and waiting to assist us. Gastalia and Sidalee keep giving me encouraging winks and nods.

Jairo takes his seat directly opposite me and spreads his things out before him: the tall dark bottle filled with Ayahuasca, a pile of mapachos, a bottle of camphor, and a very pungent holy water native to Northwest Amazonia called Agua de Florida that apparently Ayahuasca loves. Peter sets the *acrana*—the invisible barrier enclosing us and the outhouses—preventing unwanted spirits from joining the ceremony. A shiver crawls down my spine as he warns us that if anyone goes beyond the walls he has set, disastrous things will unfold with dangerous spirits that none of us want to deal with.

Peter says, "OK, I'm going to give you guys a few tips before we get started. First off, don't be a pig. You can always have more later, but you should wait an hour to see where it's going to take you before giving yourself permission for more. If you see something you don't like, blow through it. Whether it's with real air or psychic air, just blow it away, and it will disappear. If you run into a tough spirit or two, just make yourself one hundred and fifty feet tall and step over them. You have no physical limitations in that world. Just think it, and you can be it. If a spirit comes who doesn't disappear quickly, ask it if it's your teacher. If it's not, it will go away. If it says it is, ask it what it has to teach you, and then go with it." He lights a mapacho. "The spirits don't have a lot of time to spend on you, and if you hesitate, you will lose opportunities. Remember that no one was ever hurt by the medicine and remember that no spirit can physically touch you. Lastly, remember that you have a right to be in that world. You have permission to be there. If you remember these few things, you will have a great, great time and a tremendous learning experience."

Oshmar, sitting at one end, is the first to drink. Jairo says a quiet blessing into the cup before each person's turn.

I take this time to do the things that James has taught me. I clean my hands off like I'm whisking water off them and pull them very slowly over my head, clearing away whatever energies do not belong there. I ground myself to the ball of energy in the core of the planet, with lines of energy connecting to my feet, hips, and first energy center. I imagine a big sphere emanating from just below my diaphragm or my third energy center and wrapping around me, protecting me.

I am safe and protected. I'm not in agreement to any pain or harm.

I then put my hands in front of my heart and hold them an inch apart. The vibration is stronger than usual.

I'm a beginner of life, healing me. I give myself permission to see what's holding me back from living a life full of happiness, prosperity, health, and freedom. I give myself permission to let go of all that's no longer serving me.

I envision a golden energy inside my palms and pull it into my heart and picture it traveling through my body. Then, one by one, I close my first five energy centers, picturing each one as a flower closing up its little buds. With my sixth energy center, my third eye, I do just the opposite; I visualize a closed flower opening up wide, ready to receive.

Ayahuasca, Ayahuasca, be gentle with me, be gentle with me, show me what I need to see, so I can live life full and free, be gentle with me, be gentle with me.

I hear Peter tell Jairo, "Ella es muy flaca"—she is very skinny— and I assume that means don't give her too much, and I say a silent thank you. Jairo blesses my cup, Peter brings it to me, and Ruber follows with the Agua de Florida and camphor and a hard candy to mellow the aftertaste. I take a deep breath, exhale, and take down the thick, bitter drink in three gulps. Saliva gushes into my mouth from the tart yet smokey aftertaste.

Ruber extends the Agua de Florida, which I rub all over my hair—a move I immediately regret because the stench is intense.

Now all I have to do is keep it down for as long as possible. I lie back on the foam pad and close my eyes. I continue to pull energy up from the core of the Earth and carry it through my body. Jairo begins chanting a rhythmic, nasally melody.

Maybe twenty minutes has gone by when I begin to feel a gentle swaying, as if I am on a boat.

I begin to see countless formations of beautifully colored dots floating upward, and immediately I feel like I'm going to be OK. A force courses through me that I have never felt before, and suddenly I'm overcome.

I open my eyes for a moment to see if the dots are there as well but am surprised to see everything has pixilated into a matrix of very thin red lines. I have a certainty that those lines are always there, but it's just now that I'm able to see them.

When I close my eyes again, the dots are in full force, swarming upwards in many different patterns, all different shades of green. Though James has been telling me for years my spirit originated on a planet of healing where everything is green, it's been hard for me to fully believe—until now. Light green, sea green, mint green, forest green, pea green, sage green twisting and twirling and layering themselves on top of each other in an upward motion. They resemble bubbles under water or blood platelets moving inside the human body. Their movement has an intention, a purpose, an order.

I hear people rustling around and starting to puke off the platform. The vomiting is raw and forceful, echoing into the quiet night. I reinforce my protective bubble and repeat my mantra: *I'm safe and protected; I'm not in agreement to any pain or harm.*

Immediately, an influx of soothing green swoops in, assuring me I'm OK.

Then, suddenly, I know I'm going to vomit. I stand up quickly and fall to my knees on the platform and barf in my mouth a little. I crawl to the edge of the platform where Gastalia rushes to my aid, and I heave the bitter liquid out onto the dirt.

When I'm finished, Gastalia leads me back to my mat. The dots are still there when I close my eyes again, traveling up and counterclockwise into what appears to be a giant orb. I say: *I'm safe and protected; I'm not in agreement to any pain of harm.*

I mean... you can't be too safe and protected, can you?!

Nothing is constant; dots and lines and grids are layering upon one another and moving, the colors soft and in lighter and darker shades, like paint samples. The pictures are very sharp, like high-definition TV. I hear Jairo singing, *"Ayahuasca, medicina..."* and shaking his scapa, and I'm surprised at having such clear awareness to both realities.

Instantly, the backdrop changes—now the orb looks like eyeball wallpaper; one different colored eyeball per square, swirling in a counterclockwise circle. Peter says we're pulling back the veil between the spirit world and the physical world, and not to be scared if you see people staring at you. I take a deep breath, trying to assess if I need to be afraid. I decide I don't. I sense some sort of surface, like a clear partition separating me from those eyeballs.

Then, dozens of green butterflies swarm around me, communicating in a language that I don't know. I say, *I am safe and protected; I am not in agreement to any pain of harm.* As I say this, the butterflies sew me into a green gossamer cocoon, cozier than anything I've ever felt before; I instantly feel safe and protected. I'm overwhelmed with love for my new friends and get the feeling that they are connected to the green planet.

A yellow brick road—like the one that Dorothy takes—unfolds before me, and suddenly, I see a young cartoon girl, with yellow pigtails, a cheerleading outfit, and a backpack. She's me, yet I'm me as well, watching her from a distance.

The butterflies rise upwards and settle on the very top right side of the orb, looking down on her/me. In a young valley girl accent, she says, "Thanks, guys!" and gives the butterflies an air high five and hip bump. She's very cute and very happy.

I remember what Peter said and ask the butterflies if they're my teachers. They flutter wildly around the little girl.

"What do you have to teach me?" More happy fluttering.

I hear myself blurt out the question that has been burning inside me for so long, but I've been too afraid to really entertain: "What am I supposed to do with my life?" And then hear myself ask, "What will happen if I follow my dreams?"

Seeing as I don't even know exactly what my "dreams" are, I'm caught a little off guard.

The background of lines and geometric images transforms into a foreground of shooting stars, hearts, and rainbows shooting up from below, swirling all around me like a tornado.

"Whoa, OK, sold me," I hear myself say in a bit of a joking tone. And then it immediately all disappears.

I feel a twinge of sadness that it stopped so quickly. I guess they sense my disappointment because an elaborate fireworks display explodes right over me.

"Oh, thank you, thank you, thank you," is all I can say.

I'm overjoyed by this connection with the butterflies. When I ask if they're associated with the green planet, the rainbows shooting through my body increase fifty-fold. I finally know what it feels like to be one big energy center—the constant, and up until now, unattainable goal of my meditations.

I see a shark but I'm not scared; I think of my old friend Claudia, and little rats scurry out of the walls. I look down and see a big paw. It's mine. I'm in the body of a lion or tiger, looking out over a vast land. The trees, bushes, shrubs, and mountain have a green tint to them, like I'm wearing night vision goggles. I'm tremendously excited that I've inhabited an animal body; just as I'm figuring out how to operate it, a force pulls me out, down into the lower part of the orb; everything is darker—more dense—and suddenly, fear closes in around me. I call up to the butterflies in my little girl voice, "Hey guys? Are you there?" A few flutter down to my side.

"Oh, thank you. I was just wondering if, you know, you could just give me a sign every once in a while, you know, to just let me know that you're... that you're there?" I ask shyly.

More fluttering before they sew me back into the cocoon, and immediately, I feel safe once again and float up in the top part of the orb where reality is lighter.

I feel my stomach big and bloated, and I sneak a peek at what is happening down there. There appears to be a gray-green sludge all piled up, and I foresee the need to vomit again in the near future but think I can put it off for a while. Just as I focus back to the top of the orb, the vomit comes flying up, fast and furious.

Rushing to the edge of the platform, my legs feel like noodles, and I trip off the edge. Somebody very big and strong catches me, and I begin projectile vomiting with a force I've never experienced. I see the origin of this need to retch deep inside my second energy center. I feel myself barfing up the pain I've caused myself in being hurtful to others over the course of my life. I hurl up my mom and my sister, and the anger and sadness I've been harboring for them buried deep inside of me for not being able to connect with them as deeply as I've longed to.

The vomiting subsides for a few moments, and I realize that it's Peter holding me. I have no feeling in my legs. His presence is very comforting as I feel my insides stir again, ready to blow. This time, it's images of actual memories of individual events I'd pushed deep in the recesses of my memory come flying out of me like polaroid pictures: a summer day sitting in the hall outside my sister's room, crying because she wouldn't let me inside to play with her—a very deep, acidy rejection for her not treating me the same as she did her friends; the time my mom and sister wouldn't let me play Monopoly with them because they said I was too young; the time my mom took my sister to the Rolling Stones concert and left me at home; my mom going out at night, while I wrapped my body around her leg like a Koala bear, begging her not to go.

They're memories I'd stuffed deep into my unconscious mind. A sadness washes over me as I think about how I'd always wanted my mom to talk to me honestly about her life choices and experiences. I longed for her to be someone I could trust and tell the truth to and get honest advice from—to be my best friend.

A large funhouse-like mirror comes into view; it's my mother's face staring back at me. She's weeping, and so am I. Instantly, I know why she has kept her shell around her.

It's so obvious now; how could I not have seen it before?

We've behaved in the exact same ways—hiding our vulnerability—the way the patriarchy teaches us to be strong. But in doing so, we began to forsake our authenticity, and in the process became victims of perfection, locked in a prison of judgement that makes nothing ever feel like it's enough.

Especially after seeing the floating city of Belen, I know many have suffered far more than my mother. But even the most beautiful externals in the world do little to stave off the pain of abandonment and non-permission. My mother's lineage assured great wealth. Her paternal grandfather founded the first advertising agency in Chicago in the 1920s. As the story goes, he summered with his clients Henry Ford and Harvey Firestone, liked his steaks rare, his drinks stiff, and adored my mother. His spoiled sons shunned the idea of taking over the business in favor of chasing goldrush dreams out west. In 1949, my mother's parents packed up the three children and drove to California to make their mark. But the ghosts of World War II were close behind, and my grandfather swilled the family fortune away. My take-no-shit-from-anyone Grandmother kicked him out and raised her children on a public teacher's salary. Her father sobered up, remarried, and moved to Florida, but my mother never had a relationship with him.

Mom doesn't wallow; her motto is: *onward*. She rarely speaks of her childhood, but whenever she is asked about it, everything was just fabulous. Staring at her image in the mirror, we are both weeping. We unconsciously accepted the patriarchal programming to exchange our dreams and creativity for the promise of approval and acceptance, in a misguided attempt to feel safe.

I suddenly understand that in an effort to "illusion heal" my dad, I took on his anger toward my mother and made it my own. With this recognition, a big wash of vomit comes flying up and out of me in three long gags. I long for my hair clip. Gastalia instinctively comes over and pulls my hair off my face. Staring at my mother in the image in the mirror, I feel boundless love for her. Shame for not being more grateful towards her for doing everything in her power to protect me and give me opportunities she didn't have sails out of me in one long purge.

After maybe a half an hour, I motion that I want to head back to the porch. Peter and Gastalia carry me back to my spot, and make sure that I feel secure. I plump up my sweatshirt as a pillow and lay back, exhausted, grateful to be free of the urge to gag for the moment. I put my hands over my ears to block the noise, and, once again, form my protective layer as I look forward to going into whatever world or dimension is waiting for me.

The minute I close my eyes, I'm just where I let off. Floating bubbles of color rise and swirl in rhythmic formations. I see faceless mouths, big beautiful straight teeth, and pretty lips.

I ask, "Is anyone going to talk to me?" Then, before anything can answer, I retract, "Wait, I don't need talking; pictures are good. Well, I guess some talking would be OK," I resolve. Then I laugh at myself for rambling on and my desire to control what is happening in my vision.

A mouth spreads into a slow smile and then curves into an eye. A third eye, a female eye, and I remember that I saw her drift by briefly a while back. She bats her eyelashes seductively at me, and I say excitedly, "What do you have to teach me? Oh, wait, I forgot to ask if you are my teacher," I say sheepishly. She answers me with more eyelash batting. The eyelashes curl up on the ends, beckoning me to follow her.

Before I can, the noises of several people hurling up lifetimes of pain bring me back to the porch, which causes me great anxiety. I close my eyes tightly, pulling my purple windbreaker over my head, which instantly comforts me. My arms ache from holding them tightly over my ears, and I wish I had earplugs. Then I hear something say, *You have superpowers, silly. Use them.*

Oh, right. One by one, I secure little shields around my ears. Sure enough, the noises dim.

As I get situated, saying my mantra, the butterflies busy themselves, sewing me back into the cocoon. The backdrop of colors floats rhythmically in the counterclockwise motion. I spy a snake with beautiful iridescent scales woven into the folds of the orb.

Ah ha! The snake that everyone talks about!

I watch her peacefully observing all that's present inside my orb; she's still and wise and just seems to be keeping an eye on things and me. I respect her but do not fear her.

Bobbing gently in back of the orb is the top half of my face, with my eyes the most clear and light hazel-green they can get. I'm looking at something off in the distance and do not see myself watching me. Although it is undeniably me, I'm amazed at how beautiful I am; this is not how I see myself on the physical plane. I turn my focus to the left side of the orb and see a dark-haired woman I understand to be Jody, even though we've never met in person. Bright rainbow colors spin around her. I feel an overwhelming desire to know her better, and then she vanishes.

I could stay in the top half of the orb and play for hours, but I must address the densities lurking in my first and second energy centers. My stomach has bloated out again and is sending me sharp pains.

I call out to my cheering section of butterflies, and my voice comes out so much more girlish than I'm used to. "Guys, I'm having such a good time," I say, like I'm leaving a party, "but I have to go down," I motion to my first energy center, "and do some work. Will you guys be here when I get back?"

They answer with fluttering wings accompanied by bolts of stars and rainbows.

As I slowly make my way down, hanging around my right ovaries is the image I've had since I was a little girl of the end of the world. Boiling brown soot, barren, trees curled like overgrown fingernails. Toxic air strangles the sky, and I recognize this dead land is Aidan and me. The very unhealthy lifestyle we were leading and the absence of true love between us.

I soon realize I can see into the minds and relationships of friends and family members. And just as if I am perfectly psychic, I read how much pain, sadness, and illusion so many people I know are struggling with and am hit with a wave of compassion for them. Aware that I'm holding it all inside my body on some level, I release it down my grounding cord and into the planet.

I see my friend Samantha, and a bright yellow line of energy connects our fourth energy centers. I see Courtney and feel like I'm seeing her for the first time since boarding school. I run to her and hug her tightly, telling her how much I've missed her; she says nothing and disappears.

I focus to the mounting gray-green sludge in my lower energy centers. Like a plow pushing snow into an embankment, I drive the chunky sludge into my grounding cord, letting it slide deep into the center of the Earth.

The more sludge I release, the more the bloating in my stomach decreases. As I pull energy up my grounding chords from the center of planet, a burst of rainbow colors floods my first energy center, healing the space where I've held Aidan and our toxic relationship for so long. It washes over the barren ground, bringing strong trees, green, fertile grasses, and clean rushing water to my right ovary.

Suddenly, prancing, as if up an invisible spiral staircase, a sexy Asian woman in a chariot pulled by white horses, adorned in a barely-there sequined dress, sashays into my uterus, trailed by vibrant rainbow colors, bringing joy and love and unmistakable femininity into my first energy center. Her jet-black pixie hair is tousled, and although she isn't singing, there is festive music surrounding her, and disembodied voices sing out, *"Chevere, chevere!"* I giggle with delight at witnessing this enchanting event. Which is taking place in *my freaking womb!*

And over on the left side of the orb, I see Walker. Oh, Walker, I've been so busy, I haven't thought about him at all. At one point I made awareness that he got up off his mat and hasn't returned.

As he approaches me in the orb, and we take each other's hands, hearts and stars and rainbows and butterflies encircle around us, in a tornado of love. We hug and kiss with the beauty of it all. It's the most loving feeling I've ever experienced.

Then the ever-changing orb pulls me back up near the top where one image dissolves into another, and I feel a strong presence rising up a few layers behind countless colored bubbles and geometric lines. I turn to see James' gigantic head floating up like the Wizard of Oz, a friendly smirk on his face, as if to say, "Look what little Sweet Pea is up to…"

"Pretty *amaaaaaazing*, isn't it, Sweet Pea?" he asks softly. "This is what I have been trying to tell you about."

I cry out, as if realizing it for the first time, "*You're my teacher!*"

James just smiles a knowing smile, his warm brown eyes crinkling in the corners as they do, and I feel like my heart is literally pumping love and gratitude through my arteries. It's the most incredible feeling. I suddenly realize how different this experience would've been had I not had the courage to call James when Aidan and I were breaking up.

Just then, I hear Walker return to the mat and Peter's voice call out, "How is everyone doing?"

"I'm fine," Andrew chirps, as if he has just returned from his morning jog.

"I'm good," a few others echo.

I, on the other hand, am still deep in the throes of Ayahuasca medicine, but I open my eyes and try and sit up. Immediately, I flop back down on the mat like a rag doll.

"Sweets?" Walker calls softly. I muster up all of my energy to roll on my left side to face him.

"Lovey! Mine was amazing!" I say far too loud, and he shushes me through his laughter.

His eyes are full of love.

"Are you OK? How was yours?" I whisper excitedly.

"Good. *Really good.* I had to leave the platform because all the noises from everyone were so intense. I went and laid out on a blanket under the stars."

"Wow, I couldn't even use my legs really. I don't think I can right now," I say, looking down to see I have one foot in a hiking boot and one in just a sock; the boot's pair somehow migrated to the middle of the platform.

"I'm staaaaarving," Walker says, rubbing his stomach. "They are putting out some crackers and fruit down in the kitchen platform. Do you want to come?"

Food? How can you think about food at a time like this?

Suddenly, Susan who's yet to acknowledge the ceremony has ended, gets up and hurls off the back of the platform, three long wretches, and then lays back down and pulls a blanket over her head.

Glad to know I'm not the only one who might be here for a while.

"I don't think you heard me." I repeat to Walker, "My legs aren't working right now.

"I'll bring you something," he promises, standing up and heading off in the direction of the food.

I close my eyes, and the colors are still swirling, but I open them again, not allowing myself to go back into it.

Walker returns with a cup full of freshly cut fruit and pops a piece of papaya into my mouth. The juicy fruit is sweeter than I remember, and I'm happy to finally get a better taste in mouth.

"Oh no," I groan. "I don't think I was ready for that. "I think I need to throw up," I inform him. "But I can't stand; you have to help me."

"What do you want me to do?" he asks, crunching into a saltine.

"Can you help me put on my shoes?"

"Sure," he says, putting his food in his pocket and kneeling down to try to get my hiking boot on. He carefully arranges the tongue and pulls the laces tight, like a shoe salesman at Nordstrom.

Once that's accomplished, he gets under my armpit and hoists me to my feet, which instantly buckle beneath me.

"Whoa, you aren't kidding," he exclaims, grabbing me at the waist and dragging me across the platform. We only go a few feet when I fall onto the ground and start vomiting into the base of a tree.

Walker crouches beside me, holding my hair and rubbing my back tenderly.

How are people who came on the trip alone managing?

The puking is intense and persists for a few minutes. Thankfully, when it's over, I feel a million times better.

Walker leads me back to our sleeping porch, where some of the others have gathered, chattering about their experiences. I give them a small smile and tuck into our mosquito net, grateful to lie back down.

As I close my eyes, I recognize the familiar clots of color swirling once again. Like soldiers marching in formation, they seem know their place.

Instantly, they all vanish, and a vast expanse of desert opens before me. Two grand sandships with billowing white sails glide gracefully before me. The one in front has the most gorgeous people I've ever seen—tall, lean, muscular, with glistening gold jewelry and gauzy white clothes that set off their creamy, almost black skin. Their dance is fluid and effortless, to the beat of a song I've never heard. But it's so captivating; I don't want it to ever end.

The exquisite second ship almost mirrors the one in front, with its magnificent sails and stunning men and women, but this one has an elephant standing on the bow with one foot raised in carefree delight.

Who are these people vibrating in pure joy and astounding beauty?

I can't drink in their presence fast enough. I want them to stay, so I can dance and play with them, but the breeze swiftly guides them to the left of my line of vision, and I watch as they get smaller and smaller and finally disappear into the horizon line. I fling my eyes open and realize I've been clutching my heart.

I curl up into fetal position, eyes open, listening to the sound of insects pumping their steady, metallic buzz out of the inky darkness. A tree frog that must be very close by makes his presence known with a loud, consecutive, steady *ribbbbbit, ribbbbbbit, ribbbbbit.* My body is totally exhausted, but my mind is surprisingly clear and humming with equal amounts excitement and bewilderment. I've done enough hallucinogens to know that this was something very different. Suddenly, I'm aware that the annoying sensation of having to pee hasn't pestered me since we finished the ceremony, a record for the trip so far.

I take a few deep breaths as my mind settles on the unnerving yet simultaneously hopeful realization that we don't have the slightest idea about who we are or what the heck we're doing here.

28.

"Two people were married
The act was outrageous;
the bride was contagious,
She burned like a bride"
—Paul Simon

After six nights in the jungle, we say goodbye to our new friends, river showers, and voluntarily purging and make our way up to Ecuador enlivened, empowered, and amazed by what we've experienced. Free of my bladder infection immediately following the Ayahuasca ceremony further validates my belief in the power of energy healing and my ability to heal my own body.

Amid the chaos of a delayed flight in Iquitos, missing our connection in Lima, and having to fly through Bolivia to reach Quito in time for the wedding, I felt none of the usual annoyance. Instead, I floated through those road bumps, vibrating in the wonder of life and relishing in this new, deeper connection that Walker and I forged.

Joining Walker's family, we gather for the wedding in a formal Catholic cathedral in the main square before heading to the countryside for an elaborate twelve-hour reception that has us toasting, eating, drinking, dancing, and singing—entirely en Español. At one point, Walker's sister and I attempt to join in on a choreographed dance routine with the bride and all of her friends, when I glance down to see a small circular burn mark still raw on my right bicep. A tiny reminder that, less than twenty-four hours before, I'd participated in another indigenous ceremony—*Sapo*. Which entailed burning frog poison (sworn to be an immense immune-system booster) into my arm.

~

We captured the frog, *Sapo*, on our midnight hunt and watched as Pepe tied its rubbery little arms and legs to four stakes stuck in the dirt. Believing his life was in danger, the frog excreted a poison off his back that was collected and dried into a paste. After the burn had been administered in the bicep, Pepe placed a small scoop of the Sapo paste onto the open wound. Our local friends had multiple scars up and down their biceps from years of ingesting Sapo into their bloodstreams.

I was a little hesitant, not about the poison aspect—I trusted that the healthiest looking people I'd ever laid eyes on knew what they were doing—it was just the whole vomiting thing again. When I asked Cameron what it's like, he very calmly explained, "It's like the worst stomach flu you've ever had, mixed with the worst hangover you've ever had, then multiply that by one-thousand. But it only lasts for fifteen minutes. Then you'll feel better than you've ever felt."

Well, when you put it like that.

I recalled something from a preceptorship I did at MD Anderson Cancer Center as part of my job training. The clinical trial staff was doing a study comparing traditional chemotherapy with frog poison, and apparently, now it's being studied at universities and various cancer centers around world.

After I watched everyone do it, I took my turn. And for fifteen minutes, exactly, I felt worse than I'd ever felt. Crouched over by the base of a very supportive tree stump, I heaved up my insides until there was nothing left to hurl.

Returning to the platform, I found Pepe blowing something called Nu-Nu into the nostrils of each person through a long bamboo cylinder. I watched as Oshmar took his turn, winced, and dropped his head into hands in pain.

I turned to Cameron expectantly.

"It's like a shotgun blowing your brains out. But afterward, you will be able to see fifty feet further, hear more clearly, and your sense of smell will be heightened. The Matsés do it before hunting trips so their senses are operating at the highest level."

"How long do the effects last?"

"A few days."

A superhuman sensory experience? I'm in.

Pepe positioned the long bamboo straw inside my right nostril and before I had time to reconsider, a steaming cannonball seemed to be ricocheting through the caverns of my brain, making even the most debilitating migraine feel like a slight pressure. Nausea swept my belly once more, saliva rushed under my tongue, and sweat dripped off my brow as I twisted in agony. This went on for what seemed like hours but was really just a few minutes, and sure enough, after the initial explosion of pain, I felt like I felt a clarity I've never known.

The brilliant beauty of the Amazon and all of its complexities shone even brighter.

Curled up on a hammock, immersed in the intricate web overflowing with more plant and animal species than anywhere else on the planet, confirmed that the natural world thrives in its unhampered state.

If we're part the natural world too, why aren't humans thriving?

Could it be that all of these fragmented ills of society, from racism, rape, war, poverty, dolphin massacres, child trafficking, GMOs, drugs, climate change, poverty, the banking crisis, even unfaithfulness, are really just branches of the same tree called not enough?

Suddenly, it is startlingly obvious that the same patriarchal machine that oppresses other races, annihilates species, destroys ecosystems, and exhausts resources all in the name of acquiring money and power is the same machine perpetuating the war on women. With clarity I've never experienced before, I see that for the planet to evolve into wholeness and harmony, the feminine spirit needs to rise. But first we need to find wholeness and harmony within ourselves.

∾

By the time we left the Ayucacu, I came to the conclusion that Peter—though a bit rough around the edges—is a deeply wise and sensitive man who knew exactly what he was doing all along. Every detail that I felt resistance towards: the Belen market, eating with our hands on the boat, hunting at night, and exploring the dense jungle had all been perfectly orchestrated so when the time came to drink Ayahuasca, we'd feel completely at ease in the jungle. And I did feel safe during the ceremony, and on the last day, I bathed in the river for nearly five whole minutes.

∼

After the wedding, four nights in Lima, and one in Cuzco, it's official: I love traveling with Walker. Unbeknownst to me, he spent hours researching, planning, and preparing every detail. As our journey unfolds, he handles everything—from flights, to cars, to dinners, to hotels, to sights I might want to see—in a very organized but low-stress way. I'm delighted by each new surprise.

From Cuzco we take the train—painted royal blue and bright gold and called the Hiram Bingham after a Western explorer—to Machu Picchu. I was instantly in awe of the vibrant green grounds of the citadel and the spiritual energy hovering around the scared site. Our guide tells us it was a retreat for the Incan royalty and their friends, and mesmerizes us with details of its construction, agriculture, and the royals' parties and games. It was cold and rainy most of the time we were there, and the misty fog, enveloping the jungle forests and the mountains, is incomparably beautiful.

Walker and I have decided that here in Peru we'll find the perfect spot to set an intention for how we want our lives to go together. At every cool spot we encounter, he asks, "Here? What do you think about here?"

"I have a feeling about The Sacred Valley," I stall every time. "Doesn't the name just say it all?"

As we board the Hiram Bingham once again, we make a list of eleven vows—a sort of visionary mission statement for our lives together. It's essentially the foundation for the happy life we've already been creating together, but it feels good to write something official—something we can fall back on in hard times.

On the final day of our trip, I wake up wrapped inside Walker's arms in the same position that we fell asleep. Gently untangling myself, I slip into the white plush hotel robe and venture into the sitting room where the remnants of last night's hot water with lemon peels and miniature jars of honey are splayed out across the table. I make myself a fresh mug before heading out to our patio.

Cool air tingles my skin as I curl up in one of the oversized armchairs. I hold the mug up under my chin, the steam warming my face, as I look out over the Urubamba River. Beyond it, the snow-peaked mountains glint in the sun like they are adorned with little diamond-encrusted yarmulkes.

"Mornin', Sweets." Walker emerges from our room bundled in a matching robe with the comforter from our bed slung over his shoulder. "How long have you been up?"

I look up at the sun that has now risen high in the sky.

"A half an hour or so," I guess.

He squeezes into the chair with me, tucking the comforter in around us, before wrapping his arms around me. I rest my head on his chest as we sit in silence, listening to the river gush and surge around the bend. I reflect on what we've co-created these past few weeks. I didn't know how we'd fare, never traveling together beyond an extended weekend trip before, and I'm surprised that after three weeks of spending twenty-four hours a day together, we haven't had a *single* heated word.

"You have twenty minutes before you're to be in the spa," he reminds me.

The spa! Oh, I've been dreaming about you since that bone-crushing ride in the peque-peque.

"Enjoy your day; I signed you up for the works."

"The works is just what I need," I say gratefully, thinking about my blister-covered feet and the dirt lodged deep underneath my toenails.

"You just need to be ready today at four o'clock," he says with a mysterious smile.

I slide into my slippers and I head for the spa, wondering what he's planned.

I love surprises!

～

Opening the heavy glass door to the spa, I'm hit with the scent of jasmine and lavender and citrus. A woman named Teh Teh escorts me into a dimly lit room with a massage table, and for the next several hours I give myself over to a series of delicious treatments: After the massage, I have lunch, then doze off during a facial as two more ladies begin to tend to my hands and feet.

"Hermosa!" the facialist announces proudly when she is finished, pulling me off the astral and back into the spa.

"What time is it?"

"I think we went a little extra," she says apologetically. "It's 3:30."

"I have to go!" I exclaim, jumping up. "Necesito estar en un lugar a las cuatro. In my frantic state, jumbled Spanish flies off my tongue, despite the fact we have been speaking in English the whole time.

I race up to the reception counter, quickly adding a tip before scrawling my name across the bill and calling out a dozen effusive thank yous, graciases, and adioses to the entire spa staff that has gathered to see me off as I backpedal through the glass doors before turning and literally sprinting down the log hallway.

Twenty minutes. I can do this.

As I push open the door to our room, my heart leaps into my throat. Red rose petals are scattered all over the floor, the chairs, the couch, and the bed. On the little round table beside the window is a flower crown and note with Walker's handwriting that says, "Wear me."

I spring into action, hanging my wrinkly dress in the bathroom to be steamed, hopping into the shower before the water heats up, scrubbing myself clean of massage oils. Then lotions, potions, and make-up. With just a few minutes, there's not much I can do with my hair. I run my fingers through it and cross my fingers that my curls will take shape. I slide into the long white sundress I wore on our first date in the desert and just as I'm putting the flower crown on, I hear a light tapping at the French doors. Walker steps in, donning his favorite pink and grey flannel shirt and a pair of worn blue jeans, with a big smile on his face.

"Schweets," he lowers his voice affectionately, and then opens his arms wide. We embrace tightly before he steps back to look at me.

"You look so beautiful," he whispers, and I can tell by the look on his face, my turbo beauty routine was worth every effort.

"Do you like your flower crown?"

"I love it! Thank you! Where did you get it?"

"I made it," he says proudly.

"What?" I demand, shocked. "It's perfect! How did you…"

"I picked the flowers down by the river and attached them with dental floss, because, well, it was all I could find."

I carefully lift it off my head to admire his handiwork. Sure enough, the periwinkle flowers are joined together by their dark leafy green stalks with waxy green dental floss. Walker takes it from my hands and places it gingerly on my head as traditional Andean music wafts in from the outside. Walker drapes my wrap around my shoulders before leading me outside by the hand. A man—maybe twenty-five years old—in a poncho and alpaca cap, pressing a fine wooden flute to his lips, falls into step behind us, filling the air with a rich melody.

The air is cool, but the sun, which still has at least forty-five minutes before mountains will mask its warmth, feels good on my face. We cross the grassy lawn and begin our descent down a handful of stone steps to a gravel walkway. In my long white virginal dress and thick flower crown, I feel like a young maiden from Robin Hood times, making her way through the forest to marry her love in clandestine ceremony. Suddenly, it hits me; this is not just a moment of intention. We're actually getting married!

Okaaay... I guess I'm down with that.

Walking along the riverbank, rays of light filter through the eucalyptus trees that infuse the air with their intoxicating scent. I spy a small woman with strawberry blonde hair crouched behind a shrub snapping photos of us. My mouth drops open, and I look up at Walker's face, which has a look on it that reads, *you ain't seen nothin' yet.*

My body buzzes with happiness as I try to soak up every detail: the soft glow on the jagged mountain's cape, wispy clouds against the bright blue sky, a rainbow of wildflowers dotting the riverbank, Walker's warm, dry hand encapsulating mine.

Farther down the path, a sea of red rose petals leads us up another set of stone stairs. When we reach the top, my breath catches in my chest. At first glance it's as if a magnificent flying carpet is floating through a bright green sky, a trail of rose petals in its wake.

Walker leads me to the oversized, cushy, white blanket, held in place by small stones and a handful of calla lilies—my favorite flower—in each corner. We sit facing each other, leaning against brightly woven pillows.

To my left sits the pink heart-shaped stone we found at an artisan market, anchoring down our list of intentions scribbled on the back of a Machu Picchu postcard, and a pair of matching rings carved with the Incan symbology for past, present, and afterlife lay touching, knotted together with a simple flower stem.

"You did all this?" I ask him in disbelief. "The music? The photographer? The calla lilies?"

He nods, a small closed mouth smile on his lips.

"Do you like it?" he asks, knowing full well I'm in complete awe.

"Love it, and love you," I answer quietly, holding his gaze.

I created this! I can't believe I really created this!

"What do you think about doing a short meditation and then go through our intentions?" He takes my hands in his, kissing the tops of each one.

"Love it, and love *you*."

"Love *you*, Sweets. *So* much." Then he begins. "OK. Take a deep breath and find a grounding chord into the center of the Earth."

I carefully attach a green chord to my hips, feet, and tailbone and watch in my mind's eye as the chords dive deep into the planet, connecting with a bright energy in the center of the Earth. We stay in silence for a few minutes, running brightness through us, as our breathing deepens.

"Now see a gigantic golden bubble surrounding us, and love is the only energy allowed inside this field."

I envision us encircled in gold and the hearts and stars and rainbows that enveloped us in the Ayahuasca ceremony as well.

"Here along the Urubamba River, nestled in the Sacred Valley, we recognize we've been on this planet before together and have come together again to co-create this lifetime to encourage, support, love, and nurture each other." His voice is low and husky amid the clear Andean music.

I mirror Walker, who holds his hands an inch apart, feeling the vibration, which happens to be really strong at the moment, and says, "I am Walker, a beginner of life," then looks expectantly at me.

"I am Emily, a beginner of life."

"I give myself permission to love and honor myself and Emily deeply and our partnership completely. To handle any challenges we may face with great kindness and compassion, and to always vibrate in great joy, gratitude, abundance, and laughter."

"I give *myself* permission to love and honor myself and Walker deeply and respect our partnership completely. To handle any challenges we may face with great kindness and compassion, and to always vibrate in great joy, gratitude, abundance, and laughter."

Walker slides our intentions out from under the stone.

"How do you think we should do this?"

"I could read one, and you could repeat it, and then you could read one, and I could repeat it?" I suggest.

"Love it, and love you," he says, picking up on my little phase.

I take a deep breath, letting the mountain air nourish my lungs, and begin with the first intention.

Holding the rose quartz in one hand and Walker's hand in the other, I say very clearly, "I vow to follow my dreams and live my passions and do whatever I can to assist you in following yours."

I pass the rose quartz to Walker, and he repeats after me, not taking his gaze from mine for even a moment. Then, glancing down at our intentions briefly, continues with the second one, "I vow to never get too serious or make anything greater than us."

"I vow to express my affection for you each and every day."

"I vow to consult you before any big life decisions."

"I vow to take care of my body and engage in at least twenty minutes of exercise every day—even if it's just stretching," I say with a smile.

"I vow to live a conscious life and be active in my spiritual growth and meditate every day for at least sixty seconds."

"I value my health and vitality and vow to eat vegan at least 80 percent of the time," I state as seriously as I can before we both crack up. "OK, 60 percent."

"I vow to always have at least one creative project in the motion."

"I vow to never stop exploring our planet."

"I vow to laugh every day."

"I vow to be intimate with only you."

Then Walker sets down the heart-shaped stone, gently untangles the rings from the stem, and takes my right hand in his.

"You are the woman beyond my wildest dreams, my best friend, and my greatest teacher, and the bravest woman I know. Let this ring be a reminder of the intentions we set today for the life we are creating together."

Tears of happiness slide down my cheeks as he slides the ring onto my right finger. It's a bit loose, but the width of my knuckle saves it from sliding off.

"When you look down at this ring, be reminded of the partnership we formalized today. You are the love of my life, my soulmate... I had no idea that a love like this was possible. Thank you," I add with a smile as I slide the ring on his left finger.

Then, amid the soft pinks of twilight, with the Peruvian flute singing in the background, we lean into kiss.

"We're married!" Walker says excitedly when we finally pull away.

Of course, we aren't *legally* married, but I can't remember the last time I looked to the California government to validate my commitment to anything. As far we're concerned, we just got married. It was like nothing I've ever imagined, and at the same time it was everything I've ever wanted.

29.

"It's a long long road
It's a big big world
We are wise wise women
We are giggling girls"
        —Ani Difranco

Back in our cozy home, the audacity of our trip begins to hit me, and I realize how different I felt just three weeks ago. Knowing that someone so courageous and loving as Walker has my back, offers a comfort I've never felt before, but even that pales in comparison to the comfort that this sense of certainty about myself, and this wild, spiritual journey I'm on, provides. If there was any doubt before that I'm a spirit having a human experience, rather than a human having a spiritual experience, it is one hundred percent gone.

Now, if only there was just a simple way to break the news to my parents, whom I suspect may not find our impromptu marriage as magical as we did. In Peru, anyone else's opinion about what we were doing was far from my mind. But immediately upon our return, I felt my parents' energy penetrating my protective bubble as guilt, and the sense that I've somehow taken something from them, began to set in around me.

Maybe Walker and I can just keep this between us?

I toil with the idea, reverting back to the little girl who tells them whatever they want to hear to stay in their favor. As much as I'd love to take the easy way out, I can no longer stomach lying.

I live and speak my truth. I do not need to make excuses for living my life how I want to live it.

∼

The next morning, I take a deep breath and call my mom. She's thrilled to hear about our trip. I highlight the parts of it I know she can relate to, dancing at Walker's brother's wedding in a ruched, boat neck dress paired with a patent leather, kitten heel and our stint at Spencer's lavish apartment in Lima, lingering on details like *staff* and *Balinese antiques.*

"Did you go to the place where Walker was originally planning to propose?"

"We did," I confirm, grateful for an entry. "It was actually so incredible we decided to just go ahead and have a ceremony."

"Oh, you mean a *spiritual* ceremony?" I could almost hear her rolling her eyes. A child of the 50's, she was raised to believe in things like the government, church, doctors, and well-established corporations.

"You got it, Mom," I say, straining for levity.

"Well, that's wonderful you could do that, darling," she says, brushing it away like a piece of fuzz on her Chanel blazer. "Time's ticking, now," her voice rises. "When are you going to come up here so we can start planning your *real* wedding? You know it takes months to have a wedding dress made."

"Let me look at my calendar, and I'll let you know."

"I'm *just* trying to help, Emily."

"I know, Mom, and I'm grateful. I'll let you know right away." I feel a mixture of gratitude and sadness for having a mother who sincerely loves me so much even though I'm probably not the daughter she wants me to be.

"Well, your trip sounds just fabulous, darling!" she exclaims, drawing our conversation to a close.

"Thanks, Mom, I love you."

I procrastinate calling my dad for a few hours until I remember that my dad and mom recently became friends again—after a twenty-five-year hiatus—while planning my sister's wedding, and now information travels through the family faster than a hot item of gossip hitting a sewing circle circa 1850.

He answers groggily on the last ring before his voicemail picks up, "Hello?"

"Hi, Dad!" I say cheerily.

"How was your trip?" I can tell he's trying to muster up some enthusiasm but can't disguise the fact that he's feeling less than chipper these days. He and Arah just finalized their divorce following an almost four-year separation, and as much as I know he's trying to snap out of out, I can tell he's still very sad.

I take him through the different legs of our trip, from the minute we touched down in Iquitos to arriving back in Los Angeles last night. Normally, I might conveniently leave out things like our Ayahuasca ceremony, burning frog poison into my arm, and bathing with piranhas, but I pack it all in, with hopes that spiritual wedding ceremony won't sound so glaring.

"So, you're married." There's quiet rage in his voice.

"Um. I mean, technically... it's not legal, but it was the real deal for us."

"Well, congratulations," he says uneasily, and I want to fall through the floorboards.

"It isn't personal, Dad." I want to alleviate his hurt even though I know it's just illusion healing. "We were just there in the moment, and it felt right."

Silence.

"I have pictures!" I add brightly, pretending his reaction was different and he'd actually want to see photos.

"Alright, send me the pictures. Happy you're home safe."

"Love you?"

Am I still his Ol' Em the Pem?

"Love you."

As I hang up the phone, I feel blanketed in his disappointment. The sense that I've done something horribly wrong hovers around me. I pace around the house a few times and drink a glass of water before I decide to try meditating. I return to the couch, planting my feet firmly on the ground, and pull my hands over the top of my head. I send both my parents love, letting them know it had nothing to do with not loving them, but I'm learning how to live my life for me on my own terms. I say twenty rounds of "I accept myself, I accept my dad, and my dad accepts me." Mid-way through doing the same thing for my mom, I feel significantly better, and my vibration must've shifted because Disco, who's been avoiding me like the stinky kid in class, comes and nestles himself between my legs.

I let my mind drift back to my colossal new understanding of what my inner body looks like as an energy system and this concept that healing myself really is possible. Suddenly, an urge to connect with Jody surfaces again.

~

The next time I talk to James, I find out if he thinks it'd be weird if I ask Jody if I can visit her for a couple of days.

"Oh, she'd love that!" he exclaims casually as if I just asked if she'd want to meet me for a lunch. "That would be so good for both of you. You know you two have quite an epic."

So I call her, and just as James predicted, she's happy to welcome a spiritual seeker for the weekend. She even invites Disco.

With Walker on the road for most of the month, I welcome the opportunity for a little adventure. That Friday morning, Disco and I head north under a blanket of patchy clouds. As we zoom along the coast, listening to old Bob Dylan tunes, I laugh a little at how brazen I've become.

Arriving in Carmel, where the houses don't have addresses, I zigzag through a maze of narrow streets looking for Jody's "moss-covered cottage between Spruce and Fifth." I finally see a gated English-style garden and behind it, a storybook cottage.

Nerves somersault in my stomach as I park, fasten Disco's leash, and walk up to the gate. A petite woman with a jet-black pageboy emerges from the darkness. "I thought that must be you!" Her welcoming, girlish voice warms the cool night, and immediately I'm glad I called her.

She unlatches the gate and hugs me enthusiastically.

"Thank you so much for having us," I say as Disco nips at her ankles.

"We'll, it's my pleasure, Emily," she exclaims sweetly, taking my canvas duffel out of my hand. "I hope the drive wasn't too long." We navigate the cobblestone path weaving through her garden, towards the light spilling out from the open door.

Stepping into her living room, she slips off her shoes in favor of a pair of silky slippers. I follow her lead, lining my boots up next to her other shoes.

"Excuse me a minute; I've just put on a pot of tea," she remembers, rushing into the kitchen. I look around her cozy cottage—rich antiques, Japanese lacquer tables, and lucky bamboo beneath dark wood beams. Disco darts around sniffing everything before scurrying up the stairs.

"Disco!" I scold.

"Oh, he's fine," Jody reassures me, returning with two steaming mugs, and for the first time I get a good look at her face. Her eyes—the color of Mexican turquoise—are framed with thick black lashes, while her high cheekbones are pink from the chilly air.

I dig a package out of my bag and say, "For you."

"Oh, my!" She unwraps the lemongrass candle and lifts it to her nose. "How thoughtful; we'll have to light it," she exclaims, crossing the room to get matches.

When Jody returns to the couch, Disco nuzzles underneath her legs. As we chat, it's obvious that Jody is very well-read and informed about politics and world events. She gets visibly enthused talking about her position as director of a well-established Carmel business. She laughs easily, shares openly, and lights up when she speaks about her son, who is about to graduate from college. She is clearly relishing her seventh decade, rather than being in opposition to it like so many people.

Over a delicious dinner at a quaint French restaurant called Bicyclette, Jody reads me for the first time. "When I look at you now compared to where you were when we spoke on the phone the first time, I see that you really *have* changed."

"It's been quite a journey," I admit shyly.

"It's has, hasn't it?" she says as if she knows every detail.

When we return to her house, Disco greets us with more fervor than usual, jumping and yelping and running up and down her stairs like he's just been stung by a bee.

"Disco!" I shout, pulling on his collar, but he keeps acting like a maniac.

"I promise he's not normally like this," I apologize to Jody, who's standing calmly beside me. I take him on a walk, and after ten minutes, his tail is wagging again and he's rubbing up against my leg affectionately.

Back in Jody's living room, Disco is calm and promptly finds his way onto the futon Jody laid out for me.

"He seems like he's back to his old self," I say with a shrug.

"Disco thought that you brought him here to abandon him," Jody says. Her voice is sure, and her eyes are kind.

"Oh no!" I exclaim, rushing over to his side. "Why?"

"You both have that as a matching picture."

"*He* has pictures?" I ask in amazement.

Her pink lips curve into a small smile. "Well, of course, he has pictures. His dog body is just his physical form. He's actually had many human lifetimes."

I look down as Disco, who's staring up at me with a very human look in his eyes. "I would *never* abandon you," I say, staring intently into his eyes. "*Ever.*"

"You were his mother in another lifetime, and it looks like there was a circumstance that separated the two of you, which left you both feeling like you were abandoned, but he knows how much you love him and came back to help you heal."

I lean down and wrap my arms tightly around him, nuzzling my face into his fur.

"I'm going to let the two of you get some rest," she says, covering us up with a fluffy comforter.

"Thank you so much for having us!" I call out, not letting go of Disco. "We haven't even done anything, and I've already learned so much!"

"It's my pleasure to have you both here," she exclaims sweetly.

With Disco's warm body tucked up next to me, I sleep soundly all night and wake to the sound of soft rain hitting the drainpipe outside. I curl an arm around Disco, raking my fingers through his chest fur. He arcs his back and whines happily. We stall under the covers, listening to rain, while thoughts of gratitude for shelter and warmth, Disco and Walker, and James and Jody flitter through my mind. Finally, I lean over to see what time it is. Just before seven—too early to wake Jody.

I text Walker that I love him and get up to brush my teeth and pee. I decide to take Disco for a walk down by the beach like I promised.

Just as I'm scrawling a quick note for Jody, she comes downstairs bundled up for the rainy weather.

"I thought a beach walk might be nice this morning," she suggests, eyes glimmering.

Nothing quite like hanging with a clairvoyant.

"My thoughts exactly!" I slide into my rubber rain boots and pull on Walker's yellow slicker.

Stepping out into the wet morning, Disco blinks quickly as he tries to make sense of the water droplets falling into his face. But after a few minutes of splashing through mini rivers, he's flashing a toothy grin as he tugs me down the street. We walk under a canopy of Monterey pines, Monterey cypress, and coast live oaks.

More fairytale-like cottages peek inconspicuously through the foliage with pieces of driftwood displaying monikers like "Will of the Wisp" and "Sticks and Stones" in lieu of actual addresses.

Reaching the wet-packed sand, I let Disco loose, and he yelps happily, trotting with delight up to the water's edge, until the stormy sea crashes onto his paws. He sprints back to me like he's just seen a monster. He stays close by my side until he sees some other pups rushing the surf and realizes that the monster he was frightened of wasn't really a monster at all.

Disco joins the other dogs. They seem to have a secret language of sniffs and barks and yelps that creates a specific order to their interactions.

"Do you know how dogs communicate with each other?" I ask Jody.

"They telepath," she answers matter-of-factly.

"You mean they read each other's minds?"

"They do!" she confirms, smiling.

"This is a language that all living beings use to communicate. It's just that most human beings do it unconsciously."

"So Disco can read my thoughts?" I ask, enchanted by this idea.

"He can. But sometimes being in an unfamiliar place causes him to go into fear, like he did last night."

I watch, absolutely amazed, as the dogs work their way around each other until the rain starts coming down in sheets and everyone clears the beach.

We race up to the top of the bluffs, and by the time we return to Jody's, we're sopping wet but giddy like children who've been stomping through puddles. While Jody showers, I towel off Disco and build a fire in Jody's fireplace. And by the time I emerge from the shower, I find two hearty bowls of steel-cut oatmeal with flax seeds and coconut shaving waiting for me. Eating beside the warmth of crackling wood, I feel so comfortable with her that every question I've ever wanted to know starts pouring out of me in a hurried rush: "Who are we? Why are we here? When did you know you had psychic abilities? Does a higher power exist?"

She bursts of out laughing. "I don't know *everything*, Emily. When I get into my sixth energy center and look, I always come back to the same thing: we are beings whose main purpose here is to recognize who we are as spirit through our connections with each other."

"When did you start using your sixth?"

I'm entranced as Jody explains that she first discovered this ability as a young girl. She had a dream that she and her little brother were in a car that rolled backwards down a hill, and sure enough, the following day, she and her little brother were waiting in the backseat of their parents' car when it rolled backwards down a very steep driveway. From there she regularly had dreams that would then manifest on the physical plane. When she got into high school, she began having psychic visions while she was awake but didn't really know what they meant until she took classes in her twenties from a psychic teacher who taught her about the energy centers, spiritual concepts, and psychic energy and essentially how to understand what she was seeing.

"So do you see anything about a higher power or a God?" I press.

"I don't actually see just *one entity* as a higher power. I do see an extremely powerful vibration that is essentially the vibration of love coursing through the universe."

"James says that we externalize our power by believing that there is something greater than us, which is at times confusing for me because there are instances when I've felt *something* there. I don't know what it is but it's... *something*."

"When I look at it, I see that this powerful vibration of love actually resides within us too, so it's not technically greater than us if it is us too, right?"

"Ahhhhh!" I exclaim, suddenly realizing that's what James has been saying all along.

"When we vibrate in pure love, which isn't the easiest thing to do, being on this dense planet, we are capable of anything that we understand to be Godlike. This is why our thoughts and feelings are so important. I see we have the power to create anything from entire planets in other parts of the universe to deadly illnesses. But I encourage you to use your sixth and see for yourself."

"I'm doing my meditations."

"I see you've had many healer lifetimes," she says, and goose bumps cover my body.

"Do you want to get into a reading space, and I can give you better communication?"

"Yes."

"OK, well, let's just situate ourselves." She gets up and drags two chairs so that they face each other, brings me a glass of water and a box of tissues.

Uh oh.

Just as James does, she asks me to say that I'm in alignment with her to do this reading and that I give myself permission to see truth so I can change and grow.

Right after I pull the energy into my heart, tears sprout from my eyes and roll down my cheeks like they did the first time I did a reading with James.

Why do I turn into an uncontrollable tear factory around them?

Reading my question, she simply says, "I'm recognizing you as spirit, who you really are. This is what we all want so desperately. Now create a grounding chord into the Earth."

I visualize gold chords attached to my feet and spiraling into the ground.

"Are you using green?"

"No, gold."

"Hmmm…" She closes her eyes again. "Green is all around you. This is a power color for you," she says before she begins navigating through the layers to my deepest fears of abandonment and rejection to my elation at discovering my creative self.

"Seeing how easy it was to heal myself during the Ayahuasca ceremony gave me hope that I can heal my transient yeast infection once and for all."

"We *can* absolutely heal our bodies. And I do see you are getting ready to let go of the energy that causes you discomfort and heal this."

My heart swells at the thought.

I ask her if there is any difference in what she and James can do and see.

"There are lots of people who can read," she says humbly, "but of all of the people I've known, I've never met anyone who can heal or who has more spiritual information than James."

Something about this gifted, accomplished, vital woman substantiating what I believe about James makes it easier to trust in his teachings, which—being so contrary to the programming on the planet—isn't always easy.

She goes on, "You know James' spirit originated in a different universe."

"He says my spirit originated from the same place that he's from. It's a place of healing where everything is green." I pause, anxiously shuffling my weight in her plush armchair, wondering what her read will be. "It was very difficult for me to believe it, until my Ayahuasca ceremony." I tell her about the green butterflies. "Do you also see that?" I ask timidly.

She closes her eyes again for a few seconds before saying, "Yes, I see that's true. That's why you and James have so much affinity for each other."

My entire body is buzzing as I relate every detail of my visions, from the vast array of orderly green dots and seeing my joyful younger self to healing my bladder infection, and the enormity of love and compassion I felt for my mother. The images are as vivid as they were that night: the bubbling soot in barren land that was Aidan and me and Courtney dissolving away as I tried to give her a hug.

"You created this for yourself to get information. All of which you can do through meditation, but regardless, this was an important creation for you to validate everything you've been learning."

"I understand why Aidan and I were a toxic wasteland, but why did Courtney disappear?"

"She didn't want to be revealed," Jody says without judgment. "What I'm seeing is that you want everyone to come along, but there are going to be some people who can't come along. As long as you continue to hold on to them, it's going to hold you back from some wonderful things, including many new friends that are in a more present-time alignment."

"I think I'm stuck on it because she represents an entire group of friends who rejected me."

"It is true they rejected you, and at the same time, why did *you* create it?"

I'd been so focused on their rejection of me, I never asked myself why I created it.

"Well, that wasn't exactly the healthiest lifestyle," I offer sheepishly.

"No it wasn't. And, when you're in a super tight clique of friends, you only get to grow as far as the group. You know more or less what life would be like if you were still there because there is an unspoken agreement of how to be, think, and act. There's nothing wrong with that; there's just not as much adventure—which is something your spirit deeply craves."

I'd never thought about it like that before.

"It would've been very difficult for your creative spirit to break through those controls."

A wave of nausea hits me as I remember the deadening apathy that once saturated my existence, locked in my own special prison of perfection. Jody's quaint cottage is spinning, and I feel like I might need to lay down, until I meet her pretty eyes, blazing with assurance.

They stabilize me instantly, and I know suddenly, in this moment, the rejections I've perceived are really keys that have helped set me free.

"It's time to let go," Jody says firmly, and for the first time, I think I actually can.

30.

"Call it magic,
Call it true"
    —Coldplay

Elated, I go home more inspired than ever to heal my body once and for all. When James comes to visit a week later, I tell him that I want to do seven days of healing work to heal my first energy center.

"Ah-ha, your first walkabout. I was wondering if you'd be ready for this after your Amazonian visions," he says with a little smirk, letting me know that he now knows what I was up to in the Amazon.

"I couldn't tell you before!" I cry. There's no way that you would've supported my decision, and I *needed* to do it!"

"Uh huh," he jokes, "*suuuure.*"

"It was something I had to do."

"You *did* let go of a lot of stuff down there; on an energy level you look dramatically different from when you left. And you're right, Sweet Pea. I wouldn't have encouraged Ayahuasca. Everything you did, you can *absolutely* do in your meditations *without* putting your body through all that stress," he scolds me like a loving father.

"James, not everyone can access the sixth as easily as you and Jody can! I had to trust the feeling inside me that told me that I needed to do it. Even you say there are no spiritual mistakes!" I remind him with a smile.

"Sweet Pea: Attorney-at-Law," he says, laughing.

I take him through my vision detail by detail, with extra attention to the vast array of orderly green dots, the butterflies associated with the green planet, healing my bladder infection, and the surprise of seeing his smiling face.

"Alright, I *will agree that it was an important step on your path to understanding who you are.* All of which you can do through meditation, but regardless, this was an important creation for you to validate everything you've been learning and your own abilities."

"True or false: you've gained a greater sense of belief in yourself that you can heal your body?"

"Seeing how easy it was to heal myself during the Ayahuasca ceremony gives me hope that I can heal this transient yeast infection once and for all."

"Yes, you can, healer girl. You can create anything." His eyes speed read the air before me, and I know he's looking deeper. He smirks and slides into his best Trucker James drawl, "What if I told ya, you ain't seen nuthin' yet?"

～

With Walker busy with the conference circuit on the East Coast, it's easy for James and me to completely immerse ourselves in my walkabout, which is more like spiritual boot camp. From the moment I wake to the instance when I literally crawl into bed completely exhausted, James guides me each morning through a series of meditations designed to heal my first energy center, afternoon charts to illuminate illusions, cleansings, and, thankfully, evening healings.

"We're essentially doing the equivalent of heart and brain surgery, so if all you know is your name and how to get to the bathroom, you're doin' *gooooood*," James says gaily when I peel myself out of bed after twelve hours of sleep.

James is right—there are still many layers of the onion to peel back. I'm surprised that the tiniest recognition can evoke a rush of tears or uncontrollable yawns, that my appetite is so voracious, and if I didn't know better I'd think I was eating for two, and that a short meditation can knock me unconscious. On day three, in the middle of a chart, when the gravity of how much I've held myself back in this lifetime, or as James says, "all the things I've *agreed to*," settles in around me, I boil into a heated rage.

My anger feels like a step backwards from the contented bliss I've been enjoying since Peru, but James assures me that anger is indeed a powerful tool because it means that I'm allowing my authentic emotions to surface, no longer burying, denying, medicating, or hiding my true feelings to make it OK for anyone else.

"Anger is an important step to reclaiming your power."

"Just by being angry, I reclaim my power?" I don't know if I'm more irritated that I gave it away in the first place, or because our planetary paradigm is rigged for women to give it away.

"Anger serves as your compass. We get caught in the trapping of being nice and perfect, so instead of letting the energy of anger run through us, leading us where we need to heal, we deny it, medicate it, block it, lie about it. We do all kinds of crazy things except listen to it."

James turns and walks down the hall, leaving me standing in the living room. I hear him rustling around in my hall closet before returning with a tennis racquet.

"Tennis? I'm supposed to reclaim my power playing tennis?"

"Now that would be *good*," James says, amused at my aggravation. "No, you're going to walk into the bedroom, pile up as many pillows as you got, and don't hold anything back," he says very seriously, extending the tennis racquet.

I accept it, reluctantly.

"The thing that prevented the cave people from being sabertooth kitty-cat sushi was when they discovered that using a club could level the playing field. This tennis racquet is your club, and using it will assist you in reclaiming your power from the people you've handed it away to in order to gain their approval and acceptance."

"I thought I'd resolved all that stuff with Aidan," I say, exasperated.

"Did you say you thought you still needed to get your seniority back from your father?" he asks with mocking sarcasm. "Well, you're right on."

"Hmph."

My father was noticeably absent from my Ayahuasca visions, and I was so absorbed with everything else I was experiencing that I forgot to focus to him.

"Now go and try it before you burst into flames."

I purse my lips, raise my eyebrows, and head to the guest room. I tear the pillows out of their neat order and raise the racket over my head. I pause for just a second at the top; my chest feels like it's being stretched in opposite directions before smashing the racket down into the pile, prompting a tuft of feathers to rise up into the air.

It's deeply satisfying. I take another deep breath and slam the racket back down onto the bed; this time a sound roars out of me that I didn't think I was capable of emitting, and the pressure in my chest releases. I start pounding the crap out of the pillows for all of the things I've "agreed to." All the injustices I've experienced, then for all the injustices females everywhere: living in fear, abandonment, not being heard, ridicule, rape. For "agreeing" to seek male validation, believing that I needed to be perfect for my father so he would love me, and for the illusion that Aidan would take care of me, for believing the illusion that *anyone* but me can take care of me at all, and finally for betraying myself. Exhausted, I slide the pillows aside with my forearm and flop down on the bed.

"Sweet Pea?" James peeks his head in to find me laying face down with a poof of feathers floating around my head—like something out of an *I Love Lucy* episode. "How we *dooo-ing?*" he asks softly.

I look up to meet James' curious gaze and burst out laughing, thinking of how ridiculous this scene would look to anyone else but us, which causes James to burst into laughter too.

"Pretty amazing, isn't it?"

"Who knew?" I stammer, laughing so hard that I snort a feather up into my nose, which just makes me laugh harder.

"This is key," he says, trying to regain his composure. "When we suppress anger, we eventually explode and take our rage out on others, but if we allow the energy of anger to flow through us, the vibration cuts through the densities of our old pictures like Liquid Drain-o running through a matrix of clogged pipes."

"Ahhhhh..." I exhale deeply.

In the afternoon of day four, Disco and I camp out on the couch while James fixes a snack of Asian pears dusted with fresh cinnamon. My eyelids grow very heavy, but I fight to stay awake. Sleep has never come that easily to me, and napping is almost unheard of, but this sensation is so delicious I succumb.

The next thing I know, I'm looking down on my arms, but when I try to move them, I can't. I start to panic that I'm paralyzed and jolt myself awake, relieved to discover that my arms work just fine. I lay in stunned silence for a few minutes until I relay to James what just happened.

"You just went out of body consciously, Sweet Pea!"

"Well," he corrects himself, "you just *hovered* above your body for a couple moments, but you were out and you were conscious! Most people think they're dying when they go out and look down to see their body laying there lifeless."

Still dazed I announce, "I want to do it again!"

"I bet you do!" he says, laughing. Next thing I know you're going to be telling me that you're flying through walls.

Day six, just as we're finishing a meditation to rev creative passion called "The White Studio", an entirely new melody and lyrics instantly materialize in my mind. I pick up my guitar and write a new song in less than eight minutes. I feel high as high can be from this effortless creation.

"What so many people get tripped up on is in looking to somebody else to do it for them. They want Mommy and Daddy, or a partner, a material object, or even a vacation to make them feel alive, when a never-ending surplus of joy exists when we tap into the unique magic that's inherent in all of us," he explains as I stand there grinning like a kid who just won the biggest prize at the fair.

On day seven, I come down with the flu. Of course, James laughs at this diagnosis and assures me that this is no flu. In fact, not only is this to be expected, but it's actuality what I want to happen.

"Remember, as we go about our daily lives, we accumulate energy, including energy from people and places, that isn't even us. If we don't ground the energy out with mediation or exercise, the body will eventually become overloaded and go into an energy release, which most people know as a common cold or flu. Right now we are dramatically altering your frequency, so all the energy that you've been carrying around with you that no longer matches your vibration needs to detox out of you."

Surrounded by tissues, feeling like I've been trampled by a stampede of pregnant elephants, I try and remind myself this is, indeed, a good thing. James stays by my side morning, noon, and night, exchanging hot compresses on my face like he did back in my sister's apartment, which feels like a few lifetimes ago, and serving me mugs of hot sage and honey tea and steaming bowls of vegetable soup. For the first three days, all I do is sleep, and when I wake to drink my meals, James rubs my feet with coconut oil and entertains me with the adventures of Clarice, the animated heroine of the novel he's writing. By day eleven, I'm well enough to hoist myself up on the healing table so James can help accelerate this energy release and finally, once and for all, rid me of the lingering discomfort in my root chakra, otherwise known as a transient yeast infection.

"I want you to go back through the movie reel of your life to when you were a little girl," he directs me. What was the energy like in your house?"

I fall back in time to age four, right before my parents split. Their faces are contorted with anger, sadness, and frustration.

"Conflict."

"So at a young age you equated love and intimacy as a good thing... or a not so good thing?"

"I don't know. Maybe unconsciously as a not so good a thing?"

"I'm seeing this is a big piece of the puzzle with this recurring irritation in your first energy center. You wanted so badly for the family to be harmonious and cohesive that you were illusion healing up a storm and sucked this conflict right inside of your physical form."

"But why in that place? Why not in my heart or my sinuses or lower back?"

He's quiet for some time, and I can tell he's reading my pictures. "Well, what happens if you put the energy there?"

"I live in misery," I say dramatically.

"And what else happens?" He prompts me to go deeper.

"At times, when it's been really bad, it's difficult to connect intimately."

"Exactly," he confirms. "As a little girl you registered that intimacy is dangerous. It leads to conflict. So you stored this energy in your first energy center as a sort of protection."

Tears slide out of the corner of my eyes and onto the table, and a big cat-like yawn escapes with this recognition of truth.

"You are safe to ground this out of you now."

Like water draining out of a tub, I see dark inky black leave my yoni through a matrix of thick roots that spiral down through the many layers of dense dark soil and into that fiery fireball that is powering the planet.

I have no idea how long I'm doing this for, until James finally says, "Wow. That was powerful."

∾

In the days that follow, I'm amazed that this low-grade irritation I've learned to live with for decades seems to have vanished. The relief is as immediate as my Ayahuasca ceremony bladder infection. I'm anxious that it's just a reprieve and it will be back like before, but as the months pass, I'm cautiously optimistic that the infection is finally healed once and for all.

During this same time, some unusual things begin to unfold. It starts with an email from my friend Jenny, who's been eating her way through Italy during the seventh month of her pregnancy. I'm immediately ravenous for la dolce vita of Italy—the flavors, the pace, the countryside.

I begin scouring the internet for some possible way to get there. I squander a few too many afternoons trying to piece together some viable itinerary, but with almost no vacation time or budget left, I eventually just get dressed up in my best Italian chic outfit—an oversized sweater with black cigarette pants and matching ballet flats—and post up at Little Dom's with my laptop, where I proceed to eat pasta and drink decaf, lattes, pretending to be on a writing sabbatical. It's so pleasurable and I get so much accomplished that I return every Sunday for three weeks until finally, I have to abandon my writing to get focused on my day job. Bright and early Monday morning, I fly out to Dallas for my regional sales meeting.

Trying my best to muster up some enthusiasm as we all gather in an overly air-conditioned hotel ballroom, I do a double take, as my name is displayed up on the leader board beside rank #1. Seeing as I've been in Peru, on a walkabout with James, and burning my afternoons trying to find any possible way to get to Italy, the last thing I was expecting was to move up thirty-one ranks since last quarter. My manager and colleagues congregate around me with congratulations and demands what I'm doing that's so impactful.

I've achieved number-one status with my company before, but only after putting in long hours and implementing carefully crafted strategies.

Is this what James means when he says when your vibration is high, your creations are effortless?

Then, a few weeks after the meeting, I get an unnerving email from my boss' boss, Phil, on a Friday afternoon at four-thirty, requesting a call with me first thing Monday morning.

Why on Earth does he want to talk to me? I just saw him in Dallas. He couldn't know I've been burning afternoons combing the internet for a way to visit Italy, could he?

Maybe he can. After all, Phil is a no B.S. kinda guy. When he looks at me, it's like his steely gaze is peering into my soul, reading my every emotion. So when I get on the phone with him at eight o'clock Monday morning, the last thing I'm expecting him to say is, "Emily, you've been selected to go to Italy."

ITALY?! Am I being punked?

"The VPs have been asked by Global to pick three specialists to travel to Rome for the European launch of Nuleva, and based on your recent performance and tenure with the company, you're an obvious choice."

What the heck? Maybe this guy really can read my mind?

I'm literally speechless, which I suppose he interprets as hesitation because he continues on as if he needs to sell me, "For international flights, home office approves business class travel, and you don't need to go to all of the sessions, but they do want you to share any 'best practices' that you may have."

Despite the hubbub surrounding the pharmaceutical industry, I've never known my company to host a meeting anywhere more exotic than a Sheraton in Orlando, so this really is something.

Something I created?

When I share the news with James, he's swings into his best Trucker James twang, "I told you, you ain't seen nothin' yet."

Being that the work commitment is just four days, I sink deeper into the folds of my writing fantasy and book a quaint bed and breakfast in a picturesque town in southern Umbria. Walker declines my invitation to join, blaming an important meeting, but I think he's secretly supporting my desire to have a writing sabbatical.

~

After a few eventful days in Rome getting acquainted with my European counterparts, attending lavish parties that my U.S. colleagues couldn't even dream of, and inventing "best practices" (something tells me that raising my vibration as a result of my Ayahuasca ceremony and my seven-day walkabout isn't *exactly* the type of scalable practice my company is looking for), I take the train thirty minutes north to Orvieto. My charming, moss-covered residence is set just below the walled city, overlooking an expanse of fuzzy hills, colored vibrant green from the winter rains.

I fall into a routine, rising early each morning to do a short meditation before heading down to the living room where the other guests have gathered around an inviting fire with warm cups of espresso or herbal tea. Serafina, the gregarious owner who speaks in heavily accented English, has lots of questions about what brings a tourist like me to Orvieto by myself in the off season. The others only speak Italian, so we do our best with smiles and gestures.

After a hearty breakfast of toasted oats and fruit, I climb the misty, switchback, cobblestone streets to the interior of the city walls. I sit in a welcoming café where I can write without too many distractions.

Relishing the solitude, I bang away on my laptop for hours, only pausing to gorge on linguine ala tartufo, velvety mozzarella, and tart arugula salads. With my vegan days nothing but a not-so-distant memory, I indulge in one creamy latte after the next, glad I packed elastic-waisted pants.

Day and after day, I return to my little corner of the café as the servers greet me with effusive *Buongiornos!* Within a week, I've churned out four chapters.

I'm not even fazed by the questioning looks I get from the other patrons and the inquiries from the curious *cameriei* who, in their broken English, ask, "Why a young, pretty donna come to Orvieto—un città romantica—all alone?"

But what could be more romantic than being so content with yourself that a weeklong sabbatical alone with your passion is the most dreamy thing ever?

31.

"We are the water, the sacred cup
It's in our hands that all life grows
It's in your dance, it's in your hands
It's in your love we rise above
It's in your song I hear my soul
So rise up, my sisters, rise up
Let us lift each other up"

—Ajeet Kaur

"What?"

"Whaaaat?" James asks right back with a glimmer in his eyes.

"Why are you looking at me like that?"

"I'm just looking," he says innocently, swirling a mound of honey into his mug.

Although we talk on the phone frequently, this is the first time I've seen James since my walkabout.

"Uh huh."

"There's just so much more joy in your eyes," he marvels. "And it's emanating from your heart."

Joy! That's what this is! I've had a lot of fun and plenty of excitement in my life, but I'm not sure I've really known joy before.

"Ten years ago, when we had our first session, I saw this woman inside you!"

"You saw it all way back then?"

"When I read a person, I see so many things, and not all of them always manifest. But I saw all of this: your immense creative levels, that true essence in your body that the physical plane is now validating. When you were running more masculine energy, you wanted to hang with the boys, be a boy, compete like a boy, and your primary interest was athletics." He stops. "Is this true?"

I nod.

"But your original spirit is so much gentler, so passionate about art."

"James," I ask nervously, "do you have the same concerns about Walker that you had initially?"

He takes a deep breath. "He's come a long way," he says. "He's doing so much spiritual work. He's so loving to you. But his spirit-to-body connection..." He hesitates. "It's weak, Sweet Pea, and that makes it easier for other energy beings to come through him. It can also be hard for some people to be truly authentic, and..." He hesitates again.

I suddenly feel overcome with a strange gripping sensation in my heart. I realize it's fear.

"I still see he has this urge inside of him to run." James looks at me.

"Oh, is that all?" I say more sarcastically than I intended. I can't imagine Walker ever running away. Walker seems so happy, so consistent and stable.

"Don't despair," James says quietly. "It isn't about you." He shakes his head. "It's something from another life. He has this notion that he wants to run away, to escape, but it may never manifest in this lifetime, it's only that the possibility exists."

I can feel my brow furrow.

"But that's Walker's life," James says sternly. "Not yours."

"But Walker and I are sharing our lives together," I argue.

"A relationship is just a way for you to better understand yourself. As long as you trust yourself and your path, it doesn't really matter what happens; it's all working out for your benefit."

Even though he's not in an official reading space, his eyes scan something before him. "And you, Sweet Pea, are coming into your destiny," he announces with a soft certainty.

"I am?" Excitement rises in my chest. "What does that mean?" I sip my tea, searching his eyes.

"Oh, how about being full of zest for life, writing, painting, playing guitar, creating original songs, healing your own body, and loving unconditionally, instead of poisoning your body and spirit in dreary drug and alcohol-fueled relationships, totally unaware of any of the magic of your creative genius?"

"Well, when you put it like that..." I laugh.

"Destiny is when you use all of your spiritual impetus, allowing for your optimal creative genius to manifest on the planet."

I nod slowly.

"You are beginning to know who you are."

I think of how much I know about myself since that fateful day when I was alone in my sister's house, having what felt like a nervous breakdown, and called James in a last-ditch effort to save myself. What has transpired since feels like one crazy, beautiful, long dream. But this is actually my life.

"You are a spiritual archetype," James says.

"Okaaaay... but isn't everyone an archetype to some extent?"

"Yes, the archetype encompasses every persona in some way: the mother, father, brother, warrior, creator, monk, and so on." He stops briefly to crush more sage into the teakettle. "But there's one key element separating a spiritual archetype from a planetary one, and the difference is vast."

I close my eyes for a moment. "Because of consciousness?"

James smiles, happily surprised. "Yes! Some people come onto the planet and have worked through enough of their agreements from past lifetimes that they are able to assimilate unique spiritual information and can start vibrating with a much greater purpose. This is often referred to as enlightenment, but essentially these people are spiritual archetypes."

"I have a greater purpose..." I murmur.

No wonder I got so depressed, when years ago, I accepted Aidan's perspective, rejecting the idea of having a purpose at all.

"With each new lifetime we have the possibility of descending into tragedy, reaching our destiny, or creating somewhere in between. You have immense spiritual will, but it's not always easy to separate from agendas enough to seek assistance and heal. And now..." He grins at me. "You did it!"

"For so long, I knew deep down I was going against something inside of me, but I didn't know what it was or how to explain it to anyone... even myself. I think that's why I wanted to escape with drugs and alcohol," I tell James. "Because it was the best way to silence that voice inside of me that told me something was so wrong with how I was living my life."

He smiles understandingly. "Spiritual archetypes rarely know who they are. They don't fly down onto the planet in a pink clamshell, fully realized. Most of the time, they journey deep into their tragedy so they can gain real understanding and compassion for others. They want to heal, and that ultimately leads to truth."

"How do you know if someone is a spiritual archetype?" I ask curiously.

"Their vibration."

"You saw all this back in Mill Valley?"

"I didn't see it all in Mill Valley. I just knew you were a very bright spirit," he admits. "At your sister's apartment, I saw a green healing vibration for the first time. And despite how devastated you were, when I saw that vibration, I knew there were infinite possibilities open to you." He pauses, then elaborates. "There are different kinds of spiritual archetypes, and we can fit into all of them or some of them or one of them at any one time. Healers heal others from pain and sorrow—the emerald-green healer you already know about. Messengers bring forth information forgotten from the past, as well as present-time information that's been covered over by illusion, and even some bring information from the future. These individuals are dedicated to healing and seeking truth despite how unpopular or challenging it may be."

Disco wanders into the kitchen and rubs up against James' leg. He begins pulling Disco's fur along his spine, and Disco nestles deeper into him, clearly loving it.

"Custodians," he continues, "collect objects and ephemera as documentation of life on the planet. Librarians are keepers of information from the past to present. Garden Keepers protect the natural world. Navigators gather spiritual information from the planetary frequencies and astral dimensions, which they then assimilate into the physical plane. Creators are the true passion players of creative expression and meaning, who foster understanding of the authentic depth of what being human means." He ticks them off, as if he's running through the ingredients for his favorite dessert. "Advocates validate others in gaining an alternate vision of their understanding of self beyond hierarchical repression, and Seers can assist others with their psychic abilities."

It seems like James fits into every single category.

"People who are living in their spiritual archetypes are not necessarily publicly visible. They may be just quietly vibrating as archetypes, assisting the planet," he continues.

That's James, preferring life under the radar.

"Do you know which one you are?" A smile curls on the corners of his mouth.

"From what you've told me about the emerald-green energy, and healing my ankle and a nearly lifelong infection, it seems like I might be a healer."

James raises his eyebrows in amusement. "You are a true healer. Even if you never met me, eventually you'd come into a much greater understanding of those powers. It's not surprising to me that you embarked on a career in pharmaceuticals. Often archetypes have to journey into the full spectrum of the dichotomy in order to fully understand who they really are." Then, in a provocative tone, "What about messenger?"

"Well, aside from a few friends, I haven't shared what I've been up to with too many others because I learned early on that truth isn't exactly... I stop, searching for the right words.

"Popular?"

"Yeah. But I am writing my story, so I suppose one day I could be considered a messenger."

"Remember, there's no time or space. These are merely human constructs that really limit our perceptions of so many things. You can have a frequency within you that has yet to manifest on the physical plane. Does the word 'Azure' mean anything to you?"

Azure sounds like azul, which means blue in Spanish.

"Does it have anything to do with the sky?"

He beams, like I just confirmed something for him. "The Azures encompass all that exists between the blue sky and the oceans of this planet."

I stare at him.

"When someone vibrates as each of the spiritual archetypes, they become an Azure."

I mull his explanation over for a moment. "Why would spiritual archetypes be limited to just blue skies and oceans of this planet? Those boundaries seem more appropriate for the planetary archetypes."

"The Azure's role is to unlock this planet—the blue planet—from unconsciousness."

Just as he says this, I let out a long, catlike yawn, then another and another and another. I count sixteen yawns before I finally object.

"But—"

"But it's just so sad that I git no val-i-dation?" He grins obviously satisfied.

I giggle. I know by now that yawns are sure signs that something very real is being revealed, but an Azure?

"But I don't read like you do."

"Yet. Throughout your epic, you've been gathering pieces to the puzzle. As you evolve, you'll collect more. You've been able to read perfectly in many lifetimes and will regain this ability again. Your frequency for many of the archetypes is already strong, while others you are still growing into. But since there is no time or space, I see this for you, even if it isn't all realized in this lifetime."

James is so certain of himself. *How does he know what he does?*

Reading my thoughts, he says, "Deep meditation is where all of the universal truths live. I didn't see everything instantly, but after years and years of looking and confirming over and over again, I found these answers," he says, his eyes glowing a soft hazel. "When you go very deep into your mediations, you will see all of this very clearly for yourself."

"But... I mean... how am I..." I try to recall the various archetypes. "A librarian?"

"Librarians are keepers of information from the past to present," he repeats. "Would you say that the dominant information that you were raised with had much truth to it?"

"What? Competition's not a positive thing?" I tease. "Large amounts of money only come from men, and when our bodies break down, naturally we need to ingest chemicals to make us well again?"

"You grew up believing in many things that weren't true and, in fact, caused you great pain. But you gathered additional information and were able to separate from the programming and heal; now you've amassed a compendium of information that can in turn assist others. Librarian," he affirms.

"I see."

"Navigators gather spiritual information from the astral dimensions. Do you not have conscious astrals?"

"Well, I haven't really gone out of body consciously, unless you count the incident where I thought I was paralyzed!" I laugh.

"Um, thank you very much. That counts!"

"And I suppose I have set astral directives that have helped me access information."

"You unlocked your epic continuum and recovered your creativity on the astral! If that's not navigation, I don't know what is!" For once I don't think he's being overly enthusiastic.

"And now you are truly a creator," his voice drops a few notches in seriousness. You've been willing to shed so much of your competitive skin and let go of the 'perfection performance' to try new things and create with unabashed passion. What makes someone a spiritual archetype is the willingness to lay yourself bare and reveal yourself authentically through your creations. It's this vulnerability that makes it possible for others to recognize the truth inside of themselves."

Contentment wraps around me as I reflect on the comfort and excitement my creative passions have delivered, neutralizing that constant need to consume.

"As your ability to love yourself continues to grow, your creativity will increase beyond what you can even comprehend right now." He's quiet for a moment.

"It's so clear to me now that judgment really is the killer of creativity," I say.

He nods. "And it's also the killer of clairvoyance."

"Really?"

"Yep, and although the energy from others' judgments can impact us, it's usually our judgments that stop us in our tracks.

Just like you give yourself permission to create, you can also give yourself permission to access your full clairvoyance—which is different from just seeing psychically. Clairvoyance is accessing spiritual information via deep meditation."

I know he's right. There's a part of me that's still scared of what I'll see, just as I was terrified about what I'd see in the Ayahuasca ceremony.

"As you let go more and more of your judgments about good, bad, scary, ugly, right, and wrong, you'll get more neutral and come into a whole new way of being that includes clairvoyance."

He makes it sound so easy!

"How do you feel?" he asks.

"I do feel like a dramatically different person than when you came to see me that day in my sister's apartment."

"Yes," he confirms quietly. "You've ditched the script and rewritten the story of your life."

My heart tingles as gratitude swells inside me, knowing that calling in James and letting his teachings in, I was able to lead myself away from a life of despair. "You say I'm a spiritual arche-type, with the possibility of being an Azure, but... I just still feel like such a beginner."

"Good. It's good to feel like a beginner. The cosmic joke is you actually do have a great deal of information, but anyone who amasses any real information knows it's still very little in the whole scheme of what there is to know. Being a beginner is great power, and I hope, at age 182, you still consider yourself a beginner."

"Ha! Living to 182? Now that would be interesting."

James pulls the stool out next to mine and takes a seat before he goes on, "When we look at the condition of the planet, it's easy to see that people are struggling with daily life because of this idea that they need more to be enough."

I flash back to my revelation in the Amazon about how all the destruction on the planet are branches of the same tree called not enough.

"That old belief system of not having enough has gotten us so far away from understanding who we really are, as purely spiritual beings. Without this understanding it's very hard to find lasting happiness."

You can say that again.

"If your computer system wasn't working and was wreaking havoc over all of your creations, you wouldn't stand for it; you'd want a new system that works," he says neutrally. "But for centuries, we've gotten used to this programming of pain, competition, illness, and destruction, thinking how we live will bring us shiny external things that are supposed to make us enough. This programming has blinded us to our true brilliance that is spirit."

An image comes to me of a succession of gorgeous, muscled mares, bridled and saddled, who have been blinded by a "master" behind them with the reins. What they don't know is that in their periphery is an endless sun-kissed meadow with the most delicious grass, giant hardwoods to shade in, and a babbling brook that will never run dry.

No wonder people believe they aren't enough and "it's" never enough.

"To get back to our true spiritual nature, we have to learn to live in the heart. Living in the heart is the only way to find genuine joy and passion for life."

I think about how that isn't even an option in most people's minds.

What is it going to take before our civilization is ready to embrace a new understanding of who we are and what we are capable of?

"What are you thinking, Sweet Pea?" James asks.

"I have a purpose," I declare calmly.

"Oh, you have a purpose all right," he says with a chuckle. "Your purpose is to change the planet."

Ya know... no big deal.

I stare at his face intently, and he stares back at me.

Finally, I break the silence, "I know you've said a gazillion times that it's a complete illusion to think you can change anyone else, but I also know that when women are able to let go of fear and how to transcend the programming, that's when the feminine can rise. Enough will become a vaporous concept that dissolves in the face of knowing who we truly are."

"Exactamundo, Sweet Pea." James chuckles; his eyes sparkle with pride. I know he is thinking of all we've been through together, all the fear I've been able to let go of, and all that's arrived in its place. "Then we will be at the beginning of an entirely new Earth."

I smile back. "I suppose this is just the beginning."

PREVIEW OF
BOOK 2

A YEAR LATER...

Intentions are no joke, *apparently.* The minute you declare your desire in earnest, the cosmic puppeteers manipulate the energetic strings of reality to align you with that intention. What I didn't know, when I set my intention that December day, was that intentions can also unapologetically desecrate everything you've come to count on and dream about just like a violent twister might destroy an unsuspecting Midwestern town.

If I'd known, I'm not sure I would've had the courage to have set such a bold intention.

That afternoon, the sun was flooding through the west-ward-facing windows of my art studio, warming up an otherwise chilly day and leaving a single streak of light across a painting I hadn't touched in three weeks.

"Sweet Pea, you seem a little low on the go. You gonna tell me what's going on?" James's question is laden with faux exasperation.

"Nothing's wrong." I shrug apathetically. "It's just—for like six years, I felt like my spiritual growth was like this..." I shoot my hand in the air and then dip it dramatically. "It's like I hit a plateau."

James' eyeballs speed-read the space by my head. He responds matter-of-factly, "You need to unfreeze your heart."

"Oh jeeeeze, haven't I done that already?" *A gazillion sessions, a helluva lot of permission, a huge dose of creative passion, a healed body, a loving husband, and, let's face it, the greatest dog on Earth.*

"This much has melted," James forms a circle with his index finger and thumb.

"When you thaw out the rest, you aren't even going to rec-ognize yourself."

Do I not want to recognize myself?

But I know a 75 percent frozen heart isn't optimal.

Imagine what a fully melted heart is capable of.

"I'd like one unfrozen heart, please." As if ordering a tuna salad on rye.

"Now we're talkin'."

I lean against the studio doorway and cross my arms. "How *exactly* does one go about defrosting a heart?"

James is leaning against the opposite door jamb; in a very blasé way he says, "Consciousness." He winks at me. "There's nothing like it." Then he tilts his head, and his glasses slide down his straight Greek nose. Very seriously he asks, "Are you willing to lose everything to get it?"

His question stalls me in my tracks. I want to grow up to be like James, thriving in his seventh decade with hands that heal and information that isn't in books, but lose everything? As in Walker and Disco? My friends and family? My income and my peaceful, art-filled sanctuary of a home? My health? *Everything?*

I won't be able to remember later what caused me to agree. The disquieting signs of apathy creeping back into my life? An imprint in my spiritual DNA? James's sparkling brown eyes? And the fact that he is the happiest, most giving, gratitude-filled, creative-genius clairvoyant I could ever hope to meet? Consciousness seems to be where it's at.

"I do," I announce in a gritty voice that sounds more gunslinger than a thirty-four-year-old girl from Silver Lake. "I want consciousness." I am surprised by how certain I sound.

"Wull, put on your seat belt, Sweet Pea," Trucker James tells me. "Things are about to get *real* interesting."

The way he says it makes me feel like I just announced I am running for president, and my personal weaknesses will be magnified, my character tested, my will challenged beyond anything I can comprehend. The truth? I have no flipping idea how big this could really get.

~

Later that night, lying in bed, listening to Walker's even breath, I can't settle the unnerving feeling that I really have set something massive into motion. An interview I saw once with Eckhart Tolle pops into my mind. He spoke of how it wasn't until he was homeless with nothing and contemplating suicide on a park bench, that he'd stepped into consciousness.

I imagine myself homeless, sitting on a park bench in New York City. Weird, because if I were homeless, I would definitely go to Miami. Then Disco appears in my vision, and let's just say, he isn't amused.

As if to affirm this, I see Disco in the light of the half moon, standing up briefly, circling a few times, and then plopping down with a big sigh, as if barely tolerating the cushy dog pillow and goose feather comforter he's forced to sleep on.

It's only then that I realize I'm practically holding my breath while chewing the skin of my pinky fingernail. I look over at Walker, peacefully sleeping beside me.

Shit. Am I willing to lose everything for consciousness?